The Book of
Bible
NAMES

D0974510

The Book of
Bible
NAMES

Pamela L. McQuade

BARBOUR
PUBLISHING

© 2011 by Barbour Publishing, Inc.

Editorial assistance by Jennifer Hahn

ISBN 978-1-61626-210-5

All rights reserved. No part of this publication may be reproduced or transmitted for commercial purposes, except for brief quotations in printed reviews, without written permission of the publisher.

Churches and other noncommercial interests may reproduce portions of this book without the express written permission of Barbour Publishing, provided that the text does not exceed 500 words and that the text is not material quoted from another publisher. When reproducing text from this book, include the following credit line: "From *The Book of Bible Names*, published by Barbour Publishing, Inc. Used by permission."

All scripture quotations are taken from the King James Version of the Bible.

Published by Barbour Publishing, Inc., P.O. Box 719, Uhrichsville, Ohio 44683 www.barbourbooks.com

Our mission is to publish and distribute inspirational products offering exceptional value and biblical encouragement to the masses.

 Member of the
Evangelical Christian
Publishers Association

Printed in the United States of America.

Welcome to
The Book of Bible Names

Here's a quick Bible reference, a fun trivia resource, even a baby names book—*The Book of Bible Names*, featuring more than 2,000 entries.

For every person named in the King James Version of scripture—2,026 names covering nearly 3,400 individuals—you'll find relevant information, including

- the number of men and/or women by that name
- the number of times that name is mentioned
- a brief biography for the most prominent individuals
- related scripture references (one for every person by that name)
- name meanings, if from the Hebrew or Greek

It's a fascinating glimpse into the people of scripture, from Aaron to Zurishaddai.

AARON
(Meaning uncertain)
1 MAN/350 REFERENCES
Older brother of Moses and first priest
of Israel.
EXODUS 4:14

ABAGTHA
1 MAN/1 REFERENCE
ESTHER 1:10

ABDA
(Work)
2 MEN/2 REFERENCES
1 KINGS 4:6; NEHEMIAH 11:17

ABDEEL
(Serving God)
1 MAN/1 REFERENCE
JEREMIAH 36:26

ABDI
(Serviceable)
2 MEN/3 REFERENCES
1 CHRONICLES 6:44; EZRA 10:26

ABDIEL
(Servant of God)
1 MAN/1 REFERENCE
1 CHRONICLES 5:15

ABDON
(Servitude)
4 MEN/6 REFERENCES
Most notably, twelfth judge of Israel.
JUDGES 12:13; 1 CHRONICLES 8:23;
    1 CHRONICLES 8:30;
    2 CHRONICLES 34:20

ABED-NEGO
1 MAN/15 REFERENCES
Babylonian name for Azariah, one of
Daniel's companions in exile.
DANIEL 1:7

ABEL
(Emptiness or vanity)
1 MAN/12 REFERENCES
Second son of Adam and Eve, murdered
by his jealous brother, Cain.
GENESIS 4:2

ABI
(Fatherly)
1 WOMAN/1 REFERENCE
Mother of Judah's good king Hezekiah.
2 KINGS 18:2

ABIA
(Worshipper of God)
2 MEN/4 REFERENCES
Notably, a grandson of Solomon and
king of Judah. Also called Abijah.
1 CHRONICLES 3:10; LUKE 1:5

ABIAH
(Worshipper of God)
2 MEN/1 WOMAN/4 REFERENCES
Notably, second son of the prophet
Samuel.
1 SAMUEL 8:2; 1 CHRONICLES 2:24;
    1 CHRONICLES 7:8

ABI-ALBON
(Father of strength)
1 MAN/1 REFERENCE
A "mighty man" of King David.
2 SAMUEL 23:31

ABIASAPH
(Gatherer)
1 MAN/1 REFERENCE
EXODUS 6:24

ABIATHAR
(Father of abundance)
1 MAN/31 REFERENCES
Priest and trusted counselor of King
David.
1 SAMUEL 22:20

ABIDA
(Knowing)
1 MAN/1 REFERENCE
1 CHRONICLES 1:33

ABIDAH
(Knowing)
1 MAN/1 REFERENCE
GENESIS 25:4

ABIDAN
(*Judge*)
1 MAN/5 REFERENCES
NUMBERS 1:11

ABIEL
(*Possessor of God*)
2 MEN/3 REFERENCES
1 SAMUEL 9:1; 1 CHRONICLES 11:32

ABIEZER
(*Helpful*)
2 MEN/7 REFERENCES
JOSHUA 17:2; 2 SAMUEL 23:27

ABIGAIL
(*Source of joy*)
2 WOMEN/17 REFERENCES
Notably, widow of Nabal and wife of
    King David.
1 SAMUEL 25:3; 2 SAMUEL 17:25

ABIHAIL
(*Possessor of might*)
3 MEN/2 WOMEN/6 REFERENCES
NUMBERS 3:35; 1 CHRONICLES 2:29;
    1 CHRONICLES 5:14;
    2 CHRONICLES 11:18;
    ESTHER 2:15

ABIHU
(*Worshipper of God*)
1 MAN/12 REFERENCES
EXODUS 6:23

ABIHUD
(*Possessor of renown*)
1 MAN/1 REFERENCE
1 CHRONICLES 8:3

ABIJAH
(*Worshipper of God*)
5 MEN/1 WOMAN/20 REFERENCES
Most notably, a son of King Rehoboam
    of Judah and successor to the
    throne. Also known as Abia.
1 KINGS 14:1; 1 CHRONICLES 24:10;
    2 CHRONICLES 11:20; 2 CHRONICLES
    29:1; NEHEMIAH 10:7; NEHEMIAH 12:4

ABIJAM
(*Seaman*)
1 MAN/5 REFERENCES
An evil king of Judah.
1 KINGS 14:31

ABIMAEL
(*Father of Mael*)
1 MAN/2 REFERENCES
GENESIS 10:28

ABIMELECH
(*Father of the king*)
3 MEN/66 REFERENCES
Philistine king who took Abraham's
    wife, Sarah, as concubine after
    Abraham called her his sister. Also a
    son of Gideon who killed all but one
    of his brothers and was made king.
GENESIS 20:2; JUDGES 8:31;
    1 CHRONICLES 18:16

ABINADAB
(*Liberal* or *generous*)
4 MEN/13 REFERENCES
A son (also known as Ishui) of Israel's
    king Saul, who died with Saul in
    battle on Mount Gilboa. Also a
    brother of King David.
1 SAMUEL 7:1; 1 SAMUEL 16:8;
    1 SAMUEL 31:2; 1 KINGS 4:11

ABINOAM
(*Gracious*)
1 MAN/4 REFERENCES
JUDGES 4:6

ABIRAM
(*Lofty*)
2 MEN/11 REFERENCES
Notably, a man who conspired against
    Moses and was swallowed by the
    earth.
NUMBERS 16:1; 1 KINGS 16:34

ABISHAG

(*Blundering*)

1 WOMAN/5 REFERENCES

Beautiful young woman called to serve the dying King David by lying with him to keep him warm.

1 KINGS 1:3

ABISHAI

(*Generous*)

1 MAN/25 REFERENCES

Brother of David's commander, Joab. Became a military leader himself.

1 SAMUEL 26:6

ABISHALOM

(*Friendly*)

1 MAN/2 REFERENCES

1 KINGS 15:2

ABISHUA

(*Prosperous*)

2 MEN/5 REFERENCES

1 CHRONICLES 6:4; 1 CHRONICLES 8:4

ABISHUR

(*Mason*)

1 MAN/2 REFERENCES

1 CHRONICLES 2:28

ABITAL

(*Fresh*)

1 WOMAN/2 REFERENCES

A wife of King David.

2 SAMUEL 3:4

ABITUB

(*Good*)

1 MAN/1 REFERENCE

1 CHRONICLES 8:11

ABIUD

(*My father is majesty*)

1 MAN/2 REFERENCES

MATTHEW 1:13

ABNER

(*Enlightening*)

1 MAN/63 REFERENCES

Uncle of King Saul of Israel and captain of his army. Later supported David's kingship.

1 SAMUEL 14:50

ABRAHAM

(*Father of a multitude*)

1 MAN/250 REFERENCES

New name for Abram, whom God called out of Ur of the Chaldees and into the Promised Land. The name was a symbol of the covenant between God and Abraham, to build a nation through Abraham and his wife, Sarai (renamed Sarah).

GENESIS 17:5

ABRAM

(*High father*)

1 MAN/58 REFERENCES

A man from Ur of the Chaldees, married to Sarai (renamed Sarah). God called him to the Promised Land and promised to bless him. When Abram was ninety years old, God made a covenant with him and changed his name to Abraham.

GENESIS 11:26

ABSALOM

(*Friendly*)

1 MAN/102 REFERENCES

King David's son by his wife Maacah.

2 SAMUEL 3:3

ACHAICUS

1 MAN/1 REFERENCE

Corinthian Christian who visited the apostle Paul in Ephesus.

1 CORINTHIANS 16:17

ACHAN

(*Troublesome*)

1 MAN/6 REFERENCES

Israelite who ignored Joshua's command that nothing in Jericho should live or be taken from the city.

JOSHUA 7:1

ACHAR
(*Troublesome*)
1 MAN/1 REFERENCE
Variant spelling of Achan, "the troubler of Israel."
1 CHRONICLES 2:7

ACHAZ
1 MAN/2 REFERENCES
Same as Ahaz.
MATTHEW 1:9

ACHBOR
3 MEN/7 REFERENCES
GENESIS 36:38; 2 KINGS 22:12; JEREMIAH 26:22

ACHIM
1 MAN/2 REFERENCES
MATTHEW 1:14

ACHISH
2 MEN/21 REFERENCES
Notably, Philistine king of Gath.
1 SAMUEL 21:10; 1 KINGS 2:39

ACHSA
(*Anklet*)
1 WOMAN/1 REFERENCE
Same as Achsah.
1 CHRONICLES 2:49

ACHSAH
(*Anklet*)
1 WOMAN/4 REFERENCES
Caleb's daughter, whom he promised in marriage to the man who could capture the city of Kirjathsepher. Same as Achsa.
JOSHUA 15:16

ADAH
(*Ornament*)
2 WOMEN/8 REFERENCES
Wife of Lamech, the first man in scripture to have two wives. Also, a wife of Esau. Same as Bashemath.
GENESIS 4:19; GENESIS 36:2

ADAIAH
(*God has adorned*)
9 MEN/9 REFERENCES
2 KINGS 22:1; 1 CHRONICLES 6:41; 1 CHRONICLES 8:21; 1 CHRONICLES 9:12; 2 CHRONICLES 23:1; EZRA 10:29; EZRA 10:39; NEHEMIAH 11:5; NEHEMIAH 11:12

ADALIA
1 MAN/1 REFERENCE
ESTHER 9:8

ADAM
(*Ruddy*)
1 MAN/30 REFERENCES
The first man, created by God to have dominion over the earth. His first act was to name the animals; then God created Adam's wife, Eve.
GENESIS 2:19

ADBEEL
(*Disciplined of God*)
1 MAN/2 REFERENCES
GENESIS 25:13

ADDAR
(*Ample*)
1 MAN/1 REFERENCE
1 CHRONICLES 8:3

ADDI
1 MAN/1 REFERENCE
LUKE 3:28

ADER
(*An arrangement*)
1 MAN/1 REFERENCE
1 CHRONICLES 8:15

ADIEL
(*Ornament of God*)
3 MEN/3 REFERENCES
1 CHRONICLES 4:36; 1 CHRONICLES 9:12; 1 CHRONICLES 27:25

ADIN
(*Voluptuous*)
3 MEN/4 REFERENCES
EZRA 2:15; NEHEMIAH 10:16; EZRA 8:6

ADINA
(*Effeminacy*)
1 MAN/1 REFERENCE
One of King David's valiant warriors.
1 CHRONICLES 11:42

ADINO
(*Slender*)
1 MAN/1 REFERENCE
A "mighty man" of King David.
2 SAMUEL 23:8

ADLAI
1 MAN/1 REFERENCE
1 CHRONICLES 27:29

ADMATHA
1 MAN/1 REFERENCE
One of seven Persian princes serving
   under King Ahasuerus.
ESTHER 1:14

ADNA
(*Pleasure*)
2 MEN/2 REFERENCES
EZRA 10:30; NEHEMIAH 12:15

ADNAH
(*Pleasure*)
2 MEN/2 REFERENCES
Notably, captain in David's army.
1 CHRONICLES 12:20; 2 CHRONICLES 17:14

ADONI-BEZEK
(*Lord of Bezek*)
1 MAN/3 REFERENCES
Ruler of a Canaanite city who ran
   from the army of Judah during its
   cleansing of the Promised Land.
JUDGES 1:5

ADONIJAH
(*Worshipper of God*)
3 MEN/26 REFERENCES
Most notably, son of King David
   who attempted to take the throne,
   though David had promised it to
   Solomon.
2 SAMUEL 3:4; 2 CHRONICLES 17:8;
   NEHEMIAH 10:16

ADONIKAM
(*High*)
1 MAN/3 REFERENCES
EZRA 2:13

ADONIRAM
(*Lord of height*)
1 MAN/2 REFERENCES
King Solomon's official over forced
   labor for building the temple.
1 KINGS 4:6

ADONI-ZEDEC
(*Lord of justice*)
1 MAN/2 REFERENCES
Pagan king of Jerusalem during Joshua's
   conquest of the Promised Land.
JOSHUA 10:1

ADORAM
(*Lord of height*)
2 MEN/2 REFERENCES
Notably, King David's official over
   forced labor.
2 SAMUEL 20:24; 1 KINGS 12:18

ADRAMMELECH
(*Splendor of the king*)
1 MAN/2 REFERENCES
Son of the Assyrian king Sennacherib,
   who, with his brother Sharezer,
   killed his father with a sword.
2 KINGS 19:37

ADRIEL
(*Flock of God*)
Man who married Saul's daughter
   Merab, who had been promised to
   David.
2 SAMUEL 18:19

AENEAS

1 MAN/2 REFERENCES

Lame man of Lydda healed by the apostle Peter.

ACTS 9:33

AGABUS

(*Locust*)

1 MAN/2 REFERENCES

Early Christian prophet from Jerusalem.

ACTS 11:28

AGAG

(*Flame*)

2 MEN/8 REFERENCES

Notably, king mentioned by Balaam in his prophecy concerning God's blessing on Israel. Also, king of the Amalekites whom King Saul of Israel spared in defiance of God's command.

NUMBERS 24:7; 1 SAMUEL 15:8

AGAR

1 WOMAN/2 REFERENCES

Greek form of the name *Hagar*, used in the New Testament.

GALATIANS 4:24

AGEE

1 MAN/1 REFERENCE

2 SAMUEL 23:11

AGRIPPA

(*Wild horse tamer*)

1 MAN/12 REFERENCES

Herod Agrippa II, great-grandson of Herod the Great. Same as Herod.

ACTS 25:13

AGUR

(*Gathered*)

1 MAN/1 REFERENCE

Little-known biblical writer who penned the thirtieth chapter of Proverbs.

PROVERBS 30:1

AHAB

(*Friend of his father*)

2 MEN/94 REFERENCES

Notably, an evil king of Israel who humbled himself before God.

1 KINGS 16:28; JEREMIAH 29:21

AHARAH

(*After his brother*)

1 MAN/1 REFERENCE

1 CHRONICLES 8:1

AHARHEL

(*Safe*)

1 MAN/1 REFERENCE

1 CHRONICLES 4:8

AHASAI

(*Seizer*)

1 MAN/1 REFERENCE

NEHEMIAH 11:13

AHASBAI

1 MAN/1 REFERENCE

2 SAMUEL 23:34

AHASUERUS

3 MEN/31 REFERENCES

Most notably, Persian king who reigned over an empire that ran from India to Ethiopia and replaced his queen Vashti with Esther, whom he was unaware was a Jew. Also, king of Media and the father of Darius the Mede.

EZRA 4:6; DANIEL 9:1; ESTHER 1:1

AHAZ

(*Possessor*)

2 MEN/42 REFERENCES

Notably, king of Judah who became deeply involved in paganism.

2 KINGS 15:38; 1 CHRONICLES 8:35

AHAZIAH

(*God has seized*)

2 MEN/37 REFERENCES

Notably, king of Israel and the son of Ahab, who walked in the pagan ways of his parents. Also, king of Judah.

1 KINGS 22:40; 2 KINGS 8:24

AHBAN
(*Possessor of understanding*)
1 MAN/1 REFERENCE
1 CHRONICLES 2:29

AHER
(*Hinder*)
1 MAN/1 REFERENCE
1 CHRONICLES 7:12

AHI
(*Brotherly*)
2 MEN/2 REFERENCES
1 CHRONICLES 5:15; 1 CHRONICLES 7:34

AHIAH
(*Worshipper of God*)
3 MEN/4 REFERENCES
Most notably, priest who was with
    King Saul at Gibeah when Jonathan
    and his armor bearer conquered the
    Philistines.
1 SAMUEL 14:3; 1 KINGS 4:3;
    1 CHRONICLES 8:7

AHIAM
(*Uncle*)
1 MAN/2 REFERENCES
One of King David's valiant warriors.
2 SAMUEL 23:33

AHIAN
(*Brotherly*)
1 MAN/1 REFERENCE
1 CHRONICLES 7:19

AHIEZER
(*Brother of help*)
2 MEN/6 REFERENCES
Notably, man of the tribe of Dan who
    helped Aaron number the Israelites,
    serving as captain of his tribe. Also,
    "mighty man" of David.
NUMBERS 1:12; 1 CHRONICLES 12:3

AHIHUD
(*Possessor of renown, mysterious*)
2 MEN/2 REFERENCES
Notably, prince of the tribe of Asher
    when the Israelites entered the
    Promised Land.
NUMBERS 34:27; 1 CHRONICLES 8:7

AHIJAH
(*Worshipper of God*)
6 MEN/20 REFERENCES
Most notably, prophet who prophesied
    the division of Israel into the coun-
    tries of Israel and Judah.
1 KINGS 11:29; 1 KINGS 15:27;
    1 CHRONICLES 2:25; 1 CHRONICLES
    11:36; 1 CHRONICLES 26:20;
    NEHEMIAH 10:26

AHIKAM
(*High*)
1 MAN/20 REFERENCES
Man sent to consult Huldah the
    prophetess after King Josiah redis-
    covered the book of the law
    and supported Jeremiah,
    protecting him from death.
2 KINGS 22:12

AHILUD
(*Brother of one born*)
1 MAN/5 REFERENCES
2 SAMUEL 8:16

AHIMAAZ
(*Brother of anger*)
3 MEN/15 REFERENCES
1 SAMUEL 14:50; 2 SAMUEL 15:27;
    1 KINGS 4:15

AHIMAN
(*Gift*)
2 MEN/4 REFERENCES
Notably, one of the gigantic children of
    Anak who was killed after Joshua's
    death, as Judah battled against the
    Canaanites.
NUMBERS 13:22; 1 CHRONICLES 9:17

AHIMELECH
(*Brother of the king*)
2 MEN/16 REFERENCES
Notably, priest of Nob who gave David
    the hallowed bread to feed his men
    when David was fleeing from Saul.
1 SAMUEL 21:1; 1 SAMUEL 26:6

AHIMOTH
(*Brother of death*)
1 MAN/1 REFERENCE
1 CHRONICLES 6:25

AHINADAB
(*Brother of liberality*)
1 MAN/1 REFERENCE
One of King Solomon's twelve officials over provisions.
1 KINGS 4:14

AHINOAM
(*Brother of pleasantness*)
2 WOMEN/7 REFERENCES
Notably, wife of Saul, Israel's first king.
1 SAMUEL 14:50; 1 SAMUEL 25:43

AHIO
(*Brotherly*)
3 MEN/6 REFERENCES
Most notably, son of Abinadab who went before the ark of the covenant then transported it into Jerusalem.
2 SAMUEL 6:3; 1 CHRONICLES 8:14;
    1 CHRONICLES 8:31

AHIRA
(*Brother of wrong*)
1 MAN/5 REFERENCES
Prince of the tribe of Napthali, after the Exodus.
NUMBERS 1:15

AHIRAM
(*High*)
1 MAN/1 REFERENCE
NUMBERS 26:38

AHISAMACH
(*Brother of support*)
1 MAN/3 REFERENCES
EXODUS 31:6

AHISHAHAR
(*Brother of the dawn*)
1 MAN/1 REFERENCE
1 CHRONICLES 7:10

AHISHAR
(*Brother of the singer*)
1 MAN/1 REFERENCE
King Solomon's official over his household.
1 KINGS 4:6

AHITHOPHEL
(*Brother of folly*)
1 MAN/20 REFERENCES
King David's counselor who conspired with David's son Absalom to overthrow the throne.
2 SAMUEL 15:12

AHITUB
(*Brother of goodness*)
4 MEN/15 REFERENCES
1 SAMUEL 14:3; 2 SAMUEL 8:17;
    1 CHRONICLES 6:11; 1 CHRONICLES 9:11

AHLAI
(*Wishful*)
1 MAN/1 WOMAN/2 REFERENCES
1 CHRONICLES 2:31; 1 CHRONICLES 11:41

AHOAH
(*Brotherly*)
1 MAN/1 REFERENCE
1 CHRONICLES 8:4

AHOLIAB
(*Tent of his father*)
1 MAN/5 REFERENCES
Engraver and embroiderer given special ability by God to work on the tabernacle, "a cunning workman."
EXODUS 31:6

AHOLIBAMAH
(*Tent of the height*)
1 MAN/1 WOMAN/8 REFERENCES
GENESIS 36:2; GENESIS 36:41

AHUMAI
(*Neighbor of water*)
1 MAN/1 REFERENCE
1 CHRONICLES 4:2

AHUZAM
(*Seizure*)
1 MAN/1 REFERENCE
1 CHRONICLES 4:6

AHUZZATH
(*Possession*)
1 MAN/1 REFERENCE
GENESIS 26:26

AIAH
(*Hawk*)
2 MEN/5 REFERENCES
1 CHRONICLES 1:40; 2 SAMUEL 3:7

AJAH
(*Hawk*)
1 MAN/1 REFERENCE
GENESIS 36:24

AKAN
(*Tortuous*)
1 MAN/1 REFERENCE
Same as Jaakan and Jakan.
GENESIS 36:27

AKKUB
(*Insidious*)
5 MEN/8 REFERENCES
1 CHRONICLES 3:24; 1 CHRONICLES 9:17;
    EZRA 2:42; EZRA 2:45; NEHEMIAH 8:7

ALAMETH
(*A covering*)
1 MAN/1 REFERENCE
1 CHRONICLES 7:8

ALEMETH
(*A covering*)
1 MAN/2 REFERENCES
1 CHRONICLES 8:36

ALEXANDER
(*Man-defender*)
4 MEN/6 REFERENCES
MARK 15:21; ACTS 4:6; ACTS 19:33;
    1 TIMOTHY 1:20

ALIAH
(*Perverseness*)
1 MAN/1 REFERENCE
Same as Alvah.
1 CHRONICLES 1:51

ALIAN
(*Lofty*)
1 MAN/1 REFERENCE
Same as Alvan.
1 CHRONICLES 1:40

ALLON
(*Oak*)
1 MAN/1 REFERENCE
1 CHRONICLES 4:37

ALMODAD
1 MAN/2 REFERENCES
GENESIS 10:26

ALPHAEUS
2 MEN/5 REFERENCES
Notably, father of one of two apostles
    named James.
MATTHEW 10:3; MARK 2:14

ALVAH
(*Perverseness*)
1 MAN/1 REFERENCE
"Duke of Edom." Same as Aliah.
GENESIS 36:40

ALVAN
(*Lofty*)
1 MAN/1 REFERENCE
GENESIS 36:23

AMAL
(*Worry*)
1 MAN/1 REFERENCE
1 CHRONICLES 7:35

AMALEK
1 MAN/3 REFERENCES
GENESIS 36:12

AMARIAH
(*God has promised*)
9 MEN/16 REFERENCES
1 CHRONICLES 6:7; 1 CHRONICLES 6:11;
1 CHRONICLES 23:19; 2 CHRONICLES
19:11; 2 CHRONICLES 31:15; EZRA
10:42; NEHEMIAH 10:3; NEHEMIAH
11:4; ZEPHANIAH 1:1

AMASA
(*Burden*)
2 MEN/16 REFERENCES
Notably, King David's nephew who
   became Absalom's commander during
   Absalom's rebellion against his father.
2 SAMUEL 17:25; 2 CHRONICLES 28:12

AMASAI
(*Burdensome*)
3 MEN/5 REFERENCES
Most notably, chief captain in David's
   army. Also, Levite who blew a trumpet before the ark of the covenant
   when David brought it to Jerusalem.
1 CHRONICLES 6:25; 1 CHRONICLES 12:18;
   1 CHRONICLES 15:24

AMASHAI
(*Burdensome*)
1 MAN/1 REFERENCE
Jewish exile from the tribe of Levi who
   resettled Jerusalem.
NEHEMIAH 11:13

AMASIAH
(*God has loaded*)
1 MAN/1 REFERENCE
Warrior who raised 200,000 brave men
   for King Jehoshaphat.
2 CHRONICLES 17:16

AMAZIAH
(*Strength of God*)
4 MEN/40 REFERENCES
Most notably, son and successor of
   King Joash of Judah.
2 KINGS 12:21; 1 CHRONICLES 4:34;
   1 CHRONICLES 6:45; AMOS 7:10

AMI
(*Skilled*)
1 MAN/1 REFERENCE
EZRA 2:57

AMINADAB
(*People of liberality*)
1 MAN/3 REFERENCES
MATTHEW 1:4

AMITTAI
(*Truthful*)
1 MAN/2 REFERENCES
Father of the prophet Jonah,
   who preached in Nineveh.
2 KINGS 14:25

AMMIEL
(*People of God*)
4 MEN/6 REFERENCES
Most notably, one of twelve spies sent
   by Moses to Canaan. Also, man who
   housed Saul's crippled son, Mephibosheth, after the king's death.
NUMBERS 13:12; 2 SAMUEL 9:4;
   1 CHRONICLES 3:5; 1 CHRONICLES 26:5

AMMIHUD
(*People of splendor*)
5 MEN/10 REFERENCES
NUMBERS 1:10; NUMBERS 34:20;
   NUMBERS 34:28; 2 SAMUEL 13:37;
   1 CHRONICLES 9:4

AMMINADAB
(*People of liberality*)
4 MEN/13 REFERENCES
EXODUS 6:23; NUMBERS 1:7;
   1 CHRONICLES 6:22;
   1 CHRONICLES 15:10

AMMISHADDAI
(*People of the Almighty*)
1 MAN/5 REFERENCES
NUMBERS 1:12

AMMIZABAD
(*People of endowment*)
1 MAN/1 REFERENCE
Army officer of King David.
1 CHRONICLES 27:6

AMNON
(*Faithful*)
2 MEN/28 REFERENCES
Notably, David's firstborn son. He fell
in love with his half sister Tamar
and raped her. Tamar's full brother,
Absalom, eventually had him killed.
2 SAMUEL 3:2; 1 CHRONICLES 4:20

AMOK
(*Deep*)
1 MAN/2 REFERENCES
Exiled priest who returned to Judah
under Zerubbabel.
NEHEMIAH 12:7

AMON
(*Skilled*)
3 MEN/19 REFERENCES
1 KINGS 22:26; 2 KINGS 21:18;
NEHEMIAH 7:59

AMOS
(*Burdensome*)
2 MEN/8 REFERENCES
Notably, Judean prophet during the
reigns of King Uzziah of Judah and
King Jeroboam of Israel.
AMOS 1:1; LUKE 3:25

AMOZ
(*Strong*)
1 MAN/13 REFERENCES
Father of the prophet Isaiah.
2 KINGS 19:2

AMPLIAS
(*Enlarged*)
1 MAN/1 REFERENCE
ROMANS 16:8

AMRAM
(*High people*)
3 MEN/14 REFERENCES
Most notably, father of Moses,
Aaron, and Miriam.
EXODUS 6:18; EZRA 10:34;
1 CHRONICLES 1:41

AMRAPHEL
1 MAN/2 REFERENCES
King of Shinar in the days of Abram.
GENESIS 14:1

AMZI
(*Strong*)
2 MEN/2 REFERENCES
1 CHRONICLES 6:46; NEHEMIAH 11:12

ANAH
(*Answer*)
2 MEN/1 WOMAN /12 REFERENCES
GENESIS 36:2; GENESIS 36:20;
GENESIS 36:24

ANAIAH
(*God has answered*)
2 MEN/2 REFERENCES
Notably, priest who assisted Ezra in
reading the book of the law to the
people of Jerusalem.
NEHEMIAH 8:4; NEHEMIAH 10:22

ANAK
(*Strangling*)
1 MAN/9 REFERENCES
Founder of a tribe in Hebron. His gigantic sons lived there when Joshua's
spies searched the land.
NUMBERS 13:22

ANAN
(*Cloud*)
1 MAN/1 REFERENCE
Jewish leader who renewed the
covenant under Nehemiah.
NEHEMIAH 10:26

ANANI
(*Cloudy*)
1 MAN/1 REFERENCE
1 CHRONICLES 3:24

ANANIAH
(*God has covered*)
1 MAN/1 REFERENCE
NEHEMIAH 3:23

ANANIAS

(*God has favored*)

3 MEN/11 REFERENCES

Most notably, Christian who lied to the
   apostle Peter, saying that he and his
   wife, Sapphira, had donated the full
   price of a land sale to the church.
   He died for his sin.

ACTS 5:1; ACTS 9:10; ACTS 23:2

ANATH

(*Answer*)

1 MAN/2 REFERENCES

JUDGES 3:31

ANATHOTH

(*Answers*)

2 MEN/2 REFERENCES

1 CHRONICLES 7:8; NEHEMIAH 10:19

ANDREW

(*Manly*)

1 MAN/13 REFERENCES

Brother of Peter and one of Jesus'
   disciples and apostles.

MATTHEW 4:18

ANDRONICUS

(*Man of victory*)

1 MAN/1 REFERENCE

Roman Christian who spent time in
   jail with the apostle Paul and who
   may have been related to Paul.

ROMANS 16:7

ANER

(*Boy*)

1 MAN/2 REFERENCES

GENESIS 14:13

ANIAM

(*Groaning of the people*)

1 MAN/1 REFERENCE

1 CHRONICLES 7:19

ANNA

(*Favored*)

1 WOMAN/1 REFERENCE

Widowed prophetess who lived in the
   temple and recognized Jesus as the
   Messiah when He was first brought
   to the temple.

LUKE 2:36

ANNAS

(*God has favored*)

1 MAN/4 REFERENCES

High priest during Jesus' ministry.

LUKE 3:2

ANTIPAS

(*Instead of father*)

1 MAN/1 REFERENCE

Christian martyr commended by Jesus.

REVELATION 2:13

ANTOTHIJAH

(*Answers of God*)

1 MAN/1 REFERENCE

1 CHRONICLES 8:24

ANUB

(*Borne*)

1 MAN/1 REFERENCE

1 CHRONICLES 4:8

APELLES

1 MAN/1 REFERENCE

ROMANS 16:10

APHIAH

(*Breeze*)

1 MAN/1 REFERENCE

1 SAMUEL 9:1

APHSES

(*Sever*)

One of twenty-four priests in David's
   time who was chosen by lot to serve
   in the tabernacle.

1 CHRONICLES 24:15

APOLLOS
(*The sun*)
1 MAN/10 REFERENCES
Jewish preacher from Alexandria.
ACTS 18:24

APPAIM
(*Two nostrils*)
1 MAN/2 REFERENCES
1 CHRONICLES 2:30

APPHIA
1 WOMAN/1 REFERENCE
Christian woman of Colosse.
PHILEMON 1:2

AQUILA
(*Eagle*)
1 MAN/6 REFERENCES
Tentmaker, married to Priscilla.
Together this couple helped
Paul's ministry.
ACTS 18:2

ARA
(*Lion*)
1 MAN/1 REFERENCE
1 CHRONICLES 7:38

ARAD
(*Fugitive*)
2 MEN/3 REFERENCES
Notably, Canaanite king who fought
the Israelites as they entered the
Promised Land.
NUMBERS 21:1; 1 CHRONICLES 8:15

ARAH
(*Wayfaring*)
3 MEN/4 REFERENCES
1 CHRONICLES 7:39; EZRA 2:5;
NEHEMIAH 6:18

ARAM
(*The highland*)
3 MEN/8 REFERENCES
GENESIS 10:22; GENESIS 22:21;
1 CHRONICLES 7:34

ARAN
(*Shrill*)
1 MAN/2 REFERENCE
GENESIS 36:28

ARAUNAH
(*Strong*)
1 MAN/9 REFERENCES
Jebusite who sold his threshing floor to
King David so the king could build
an altar and make a sacrifice there.
Same as Ornan.
2 SAMUEL 24:16

ARBA
(*Four*)
1 MAN/3 REFERENCES
JOSHUA 15:13

ARCHELAUS
(*People-ruling*)
1 MAN/1 REFERENCE
MATTHEW 2:22

ARCHIPPUS
(*Horse-ruler*)
1 MAN/2 REFERENCES
COLOSSIANS 4:17

ARD
(*Fugitive*)
2 MEN/3 REFERENCES
GENESIS 46:21; NUMBERS 26:40

ARDON
(*Roaming*)
1 CHRONICLES 2:18

ARELI
(*Heroic*)
1 MAN/2 REFERENCES
GENESIS 46:16

ARETAS
1 MAN/1 REFERENCE
Arabian king who ruled over Syria.
2 CORINTHIANS 11:32

ARGOB
(*Stony*)
1 MAN/1 REFERENCE
Israelite official assassinated along with
 King Pekahiah.
2 KINGS 15:25

ARIDAI
1 MAN/1 REFERENCE
ESTHER 9:9

ARIDATHA
1 MAN/1 REFERENCE
ESTHER 9:8

ARIEH
(*Lion*)
1 MAN/1 REFERENCE
Israelite official assassinated along with
 King Pekahiah.
2 KINGS 15:25

ARIEL
(*Lion of God*)
1 MAN/1 REFERENCE
Jewish exile charged with finding
 Levites and temple servants to
 travel to Jerusalem with Ezra.
EZRA 8:16

ARIOCH
2 MEN/7 REFERENCES
Notably, king of Ellasar in the days of
 Abram. Also, captain of King Nebuchadnezzar's guard, who took Daniel to the king when the wise men
 could not interpret his dream.
GENESIS 14:1; DANIEL 2:14

ARISAI
1 MAN/1 REFERENCE
ESTHER 9:9

ARISTARCHUS
(*Best ruling*)
1 MAN/5 REFERENCES
One of Paul's companions who accompanied him on various travels,
 including his trip to Rome.
ACTS 19:29

ARISTOBULUS
(*Best counseling*)
1 MAN/1 REFERENCE
ROMANS 16:10

ARMONI
(*Palatial*)
1 MAN/1 REFERENCE
Son of King Saul.
2 SAMUEL 21:8

ARNAN
(*Noisy*)
1 MAN/1 REFERENCE
1 CHRONICLES 3:21

AROD
(*Fugitive*)
1 MAN/1 REFERENCE
NUMBERS 26:17

ARPHAXAD
1 MAN/10 REFERENCES
GENESIS 10:22

ARTAXERXES
3 MEN/15 REFERENCES
Most notably, Persian king who
 received letters objecting to the
 rebuilding of Jerusalem from those
 who opposed the Jews. Also called
 Longimanus.
EZRA 4:7; EZRA 6:14; EZRA 7:1

ARTEMAS
(*Gift of Artemis*)
1 MAN/1 REFERENCE
TITUS 3:12

ARZA
(*Earthiness*)
1 MAN/1 REFERENCE
Palace steward of Israel's king Elah.
1 KINGS 16:9

ASA
2 MEN/60 REFERENCES
Notably, king of Judah who reigned
 forty-one years and removed many
 idols from Judah.
1 KINGS 15:8; 1 CHRONICLES 9:16

ASAHEL
(*God has made*)
4 MEN/18 REFERENCES
Most notably, brother of Joab, who
was David's army commander. Also,
Levite sent by King Jehoshaphat to
teach the law of the Lord throughout the nation of Judah.
2 SAMUEL 2:18; 2 CHRONICLES 17:8;
2 CHRONICLES 31:13; EZRA 10:15

ASAHIAH
(*God has made*)
1 MAN/2 REFERENCES
Servant of King Josiah who was part of
a delegation sent to the prophetess
Huldah after the "book of the law"
was discovered in the temple. Same
as Asaiah.
2 KINGS 22:12

ASAIAH
(*God has made*)
5 MEN/6 REFERENCES
Same as Asahiah.
1 CHRONICLES 4:36; 1 CHRONICLES 6:30;
1 CHRONICLES 9:5; 1 CHRONICLES 15:6;
2 CHRONICLES 34:20

ASAPH
(*Collector*)
5 MEN/45 REFERENCES
2 KINGS 18:18; 1 CHRONICLES 6:39;
1 CHRONICLES 9:15;
1 CHRONICLES 26:1;
NEHEMIAH 2:8

ASAREEL
(*Right of God*)
1 MAN/1 REFERENCE
1 CHRONICLES 4:16

ASARELAH
(*Right toward God*)
1 MAN/1 REFERENCE
1 CHRONICLES 25:2

ASENATH
1 WOMAN/3 REFERENCES
Daughter of an Egyptian priest,
she was given as a wife to Joseph
by the pharaoh.
GENESIS 41:45

ASER
(*Happy*)
1 MAN/2 REFERENCES
Greek form of the Hebrew name
Asher; one of twelve tribes of Israel.
LUKE 2:36

ASHBEA
(*Adjurer*)
1 MAN/1 REFERENCE
1 CHRONICLES 4:21

ASHBEL
(*Flowing*)
1 MAN/3 REFERENCES
GENESIS 46:21

ASHCHENAZ
1 MAN/1 REFERENCE
Same as Ashkenaz.
1 CHRONICLES 1:6

ASHER
(*Happy*)
1 MAN/9 REFERENCES
GENESIS 30:13

ASHKENAZ
1 MAN/1 REFERENCE
GENESIS 10:3

ASHPENAZ
1 MAN/1 REFERENCE
Chief eunuch of the Babylonian king
Nebuchadnezzar.
DANIEL 1:3

ASHRIEL
(*Right of God*)
1 MAN/1 REFERENCE
1 CHRONICLES 7:14

ASHUR
(*Successful*)
1 MAN/2 REFERENCES
1 CHRONICLES 2:24

ASHVATH
(*Bright*)
1 MAN/1 REFERENCE
1 CHRONICLES 7:33

ASIEL
(*Made of God*)
1 MAN/1 REFERENCE
1 CHRONICLES 4:35

ASNAH
1 MAN/1 REFERENCE
EZRA 2:50

ASNAPPER
1 MAN/1 REFERENCE
An Assyrian king who resettled
    Samaria with other people,
    after the Israelites were captured.
EZRA 4:10

ASPATHA
1 MAN/1 REFERENCE
ESTHER 9:7

ASRIEL
(*Right of God*)
1 MAN/2 REFERENCES
NUMBERS 26:31

ASSHUR
(*Successful*)
2 MEN/3 REFERENCES
GENESIS 10:11; GENESIS 10:22

ASSIR
(*Prisoner*)
3 MEN/5 REFERENCES
EXODUS 6:24; 1 CHRONICLES 6:23;
    1 CHRONICLES 3:17

ASYNCRITUS
(*Incomparable*)
1 MAN/1 REFERENCE
ROMANS 16:14

ATARAH
(*Crown*)
1 WOMAN/1 REFERENCE
1 CHRONICLES 2:26

ATER
(*Maimed*)
3 MEN/5 REFERENCES
EZRA 2:16; EZRA 2:42; NEHEMIAH 10:17

ATHAIAH
(*God has helped*)
1 MAN/1 REFERENCE
NEHEMIAH 11:4

ATHALIAH
(*God has constrained*)
2 MEN/1 WOMAN/17 REFERENCES
Notably, wife of Jehoram and mother
    of Ahaziah, two kings of Judah.
2 KINGS 8:26; 1 CHRONICLES 8:26;
    EZRA 8:7

ATHLAI
(*Constricted*)
1 MAN/1 REFERENCE
EZRA 10:28

ATTAI
(*Timely*)
3 MEN/4 REFERENCES
1 CHRONICLES 2:35; 1 CHRONICLES 12:11;
    2 CHRONICLES 11:20

AUGUSTUS
(*August*)
1 MAN/4 REFERENCES
Roman emperor who called for the
    census that brought Mary and
    Joseph to Bethlehem and still ruled
    when Paul appealed to Caesar dur-
    ing his imprisonment in Jerusalem.
    Also called Caesar Augustus.
LUKE 2:1

AZALIAH
(*God has reserved*)
1 MAN/2 REFERENCES
2 KINGS 22:3

AZANIAH

(*Heard by God*)

1 MAN/1 REFERENCE

Levite who renewed the covenant
under Nehemiah.

NEHEMIAH 10:9

AZARAEL

(*God has helped*)

1 MAN/1 REFERENCE

Priest who helped to dedicate the
rebuilt walls of Jerusalem by
playing a musical instrument.

NEHEMIAH 12:36

AZAREEL

(*God has helped*)

5 MEN/5 REFERENCES

Most notably, a "mighty man" who supported the future king David during
his conflict with Saul. Also, leader
of the tribe of Dan in the days of
King David.

1 CHRONICLES 12:6; 1 CHRONICLES 25:18;
1 CHRONICLES 27:22; EZRA 10:41;
NEHEMIAH 11:13

AZARIAH

(*God has helped*)

28 MEN/49 REFERENCES

Most notably, officer in Solomon's
army. Also, king of Judah who was
obedient to God but did not remove the idolatrous altars from the
high places. Same as Uzziah. Also,
prophet who encouraged King Asa
of Judah to follow the Lord. Also,
chief priest during the reign of King
Hezekiah of Judah. Also, man who
repaired Jerusalem's walls under
Nehemiah. Also, Hebrew name for
Abed-nego, one of Daniel's companions in exile.

1 KINGS 4:2; 1 KINGS 4:5; 2 KINGS 14:21;
1 CHRONICLES 2:8; 1 CHRONICLES 2:38;
1 CHRONICLES 6:9; 1 CHRONICLES 6:10;
1 CHRONICLES 6:13; 1 CHRONICLES
6:36; 2 CHRONICLES 15:1;
2 CHRONICLES 21:2; 2 CHRONICLES
21:2; 2 CHRONICLES 22:6;
2 CHRONICLES 23:1; 2 CHRONICLES
23:1; 2 CHRONICLES 26:17;
2 CHRONICLES 28:12; 2 CHRONICLES
29:12; 2 CHRONICLES 29:12;
2 CHRONICLES 31:10; EZRA 7:3;
NEHEMIAH 3:23; NEHEMIAH 7:7;
NEHEMIAH 8:7; NEHEMIAH 10:2;
NEHEMIAH 12:33; JEREMIAH 43:2;
DANIEL 1:6

AZAZ

(*Strong*)

1 MAN/1 REFERENCE

1 CHRONICLES 5:8

AZAZIAH

(*God has strengthened*)

3 MEN/3 REFERENCES

Most notably, Levite musician who
performed in celebration when
King David brought the ark of
the covenant to Jerusalem.

1 CHRONICLES 15:21; 1 CHRONICLES
27:20; 2 CHRONICLES 31:13

AZBUK

(*Stern depopulator*)

1 MAN/1 REFERENCE

NEHEMIAH 3:16

AZEL

(*Noble*)

1 MAN/6 REFERENCES

1 CHRONICLES 8:37

AZGAD

(*Stern troop*)

3 MEN/4 REFERENCES

EZRA 2:12; EZRA 8:12; NEHEMIAH 10:15

AZIEL

(*Strengthened of God*)

1 MAN/1 REFERENCE

Levite musician who performed in celebration when King David brought
the ark of the covenant to Jerusalem.
Same as Jaaziel.

1 CHRONICLES 15:20

AZIZA
(*Strengthfulness*)
1 MAN/1 REFERENCE
EZRA 10:27

AZMAVETH
(*Strong one of death*)
4 MEN/6 REFERENCES
Most notably, one of King David's
valiant warriors.
2 SAMUEL 23:31; 1 CHRONICLES 8:36;
    1 CHRONICLES 12:3;
    1 CHRONICLES 27:25

AZOR
(*Helpful*)
1 MAN/2 REFERENCES
MATTHEW 1:13

AZRIEL
(*Help of God*)
3 MEN/3 REFERENCES
Most notably, one of the "mighty men
of valour, famous men" who led the
half tribe of Manasseh.
1 CHRONICLES 5:24; 1 CHRONICLES 27:19;
    JEREMIAH 36:26

AZRIKAM
(*Help of an enemy*)
4 MEN/6 REFERENCES
1 CHRONICLES 3:23; 1 CHRONICLES 8:38;
    1 CHRONICLES 9:14; 2 CHRONICLES 28:7

AZUBAH
(*Desertion*)
2 WOMEN/4 REFERENCES
1 KINGS 22:42; 1 CHRONICLES 2:18

AZUR
(*Helpful*)
2 MEN/2 REFERENCES
JEREMIAH 28:1; EZEKIEL 11:1

AZZAN
(*Strong one*)
1 MAN/1 REFERENCE
NUMBERS 34:26

AZZUR
(*Helpful*)
1 MAN/1 REFERENCE
Jewish leader who renewed the
covenant under Nehemiah.
NEHEMIAH 10:17

—B—

BAAL
(*Master*)
2 MEN/3 REFERENCES
1 CHRONICLES 5:5; 1 CHRONICLES 8:30

BAAL-HANAN
(*Possessor of grace*)
2 MEN/5 REFERENCES
Notably, king of Edom. Also, Gederite
who had charge of King David's
olive and sycamore trees.
GENESIS 36:38; 1 CHRONICLES 27:28

BAALIS
(*In exultation*)
1 MAN/1 REFERENCE
Ammonite king who sent an assassin
against Gedaliah, the Babylonian-
appointed governor of Judah.
JEREMIAH 40:14

BAANA
(*In affliction*)
2 MEN/2 REFERENCES
One of King Solomon's twelve officials
over provisions.
1 KINGS 4:12; NEHEMIAH 3:4

BAANAH
(*In affliction*)
4 MEN/10 REFERENCES
Most notably, leader of one of the raiding bands of Saul's son. Also, one of
King Solomon's twelve officials over
provisions.
2 SAMUEL 4:22; 2 SAMUEL 22:39;
    1 KINGS 4:16; EZRA 2:2

BAARA
(*Brutish*)
1 WOMAN/1 REFERENCE
1 CHRONICLES 8:8

BAASEIAH
(*In the work of God*)
1 MAN/1 REFERENCE
1 CHRONICLES 6:40

BAASHA
(*Offensiveness*)
1 MAN/28 REFERENCES
Idolatrous king of Israel.
1 KINGS 15:16

BAKBAKKAR
(*Searcher*)
1 MAN/1 REFERENCE
1 CHRONICLES 9:15

BAKBUK
(*Bottle*)
1 MAN/2 REFERENCES
EZRA 2:51

BAKBUKIAH
1 MAN/3 REFERENCES
(*Emptying of God*)
NEHEMIAH 11:17

BALAAM
(*Foreigner*)
1 MAN/63 REFERENCES
Mesopotamian prophet, sent for by
    Balak, king of Moab, to curse the
    Israelites. His donkey spoke to him
    when the angel of the Lord barred
    the donkey's way.
NUMBERS 22:5

BALAC
(*Waster*)
1 MAN/1 REFERENCE
Greek form of the name *Balak*;
    a king of Moab.
REVELATION 2:14

BALADAN
(*Bel is his lord*)
1 MAN/2 REFERENCES
2 KINGS 20:12

BALAK
(*Waster*)
1 MAN/43 REFERENCES
King of Moab who sent for the
    Mesopotamian prophet Balaam
    to curse the Israelites.
NUMBERS 22:2

BANI
(*Built*)
10 MEN/15 REFERENCES
Most notably, a "mighty man" of King
    David.
2 SAMUEL 23:36; 1 CHRONICLES 6:46;
    1 CHRONICLES 9:4; EZRA 2:10; EZRA
    10:34; EZRA 10:38; NEHEMIAH 3:17;
    NEHEMIAH 9:4; NEHEMIAH 10:14;
    NEHEMIAH 11:22

BARABBAS
(*Son of Abba*)
1 MAN/11 REFERENCES
Prison inmate when Jesus came to trial.
    When given the choice by Pilate of
    which of the two should be released,
    the people chose Barabbas.
MATTHEW 27:16

BARACHEL
(*God has blessed*)
1 MAN/2 REFERENCES
JOB 32:2

BARACHIAS
(*Blessing of God*)
1 MAN/1 REFERENCE
MATTHEW 23:35

BARAK
(*Lightning*)
1 MAN/14 REFERENCES
Judge Deborah's battle captain who
    refused to enter battle without her
    support.
JUDGES 4:6

BARIAH
(*Fugitive*)
1 MAN/1 REFERENCE
1 CHRONICLES 3:22

BAR-JESUS
(*Son of Jesus*)
1 MAN/1 REFERENCE
Jewish sorcerer, also called Elymas.
ACTS 13:6

BARJONA
(*Son of Jonas*)
1 MAN/1 REFERENCE
Another name for the apostle Peter,
    used by Jesus Christ.
MATTHEW 16:17

BARKOS
1 MAN/2 REFERENCES
EZRA 2:53

BARNABAS
(*Son of prophecy*)
1 MAN/29 REFERENCES
Introduced Saul to the apostles and
    spoke up for him. Also traveled on
    missionary journeys with Paul and
    Mark. Same as Joses.
ACTS 4:36

BARSABAS
(*Son of Sabas*)
2 MEN/2 REFERENCES
Notably, also called Joseph Justus,
    potential apostolic replacement for
    Judas Iscariot who lost by lot to the
    other candidate, Matthias. Same as
    Joseph and Justus.
ACTS 1:23; ACTS 15:22

BARTHOLOMEW
(*Son of Tolmai*)
1 MAN/4 REFERENCES
One of Jesus' disciples. Probably the
    same as Nathanael.
MATTHEW 10:3

BARTIMAEUS
(*Son of Timaeus*)
1 MAN/1 REFERENCE
Blind beggar of Jericho who shouted
    for Jesus' attention and Jesus healed
    him.
MARK 10:46

BARUCH
(*Blessed*)
3 MEN/26 REFERENCES
Most notably, rebuilder of the walls of
    Jerusalem and a priest who renewed
    the covenant under Nehemiah.
    Also, scribe who wrote down all the
    words the prophet Jeremiah received
    from God.
NEHEMIAH 3:20; NEHEMIAH 11:5;
    JEREMIAH 32:12

BARZILLAI
(*Iron-hearted*)
2 MEN/12 REFERENCES
Notably, elderly man who brought food
    and supplies to King David and his
    soldiers.
2 SAMUEL 17:27; 2 SAMUEL 21:8

BASHEMATH
(*Fragrance*)
2 WOMEN/6 REFERENCES
Notably, Hittite wife of Esau. Same
    as Adah. Also possibly the same as
    Bashemath.
GENESIS 26:34; GENESIS 36:3

BASMATH
(*Fragrance*)
1 WOMAN/1 REFERENCE
1 KINGS 4:15

BATH-SHEBA
(*Daughter of an oath*)
1 WOMAN/11 REFERENCES
Wife of the warrior Uriah the Hittite.
    King David committed adultery
    with her, and she became pregnant
    then married him when Uriah died.
2 SAMUEL 11:3

BATH-SHUA
(*Daughter of wealth*)
1 WOMAN/1 REFERENCE
Form of the name *Bath-sheba*; a wife of
    King David.
1 CHRONICLES 3:5

BAVAI

1 MAN/1 REFERENCE

Man who repaired Jerusalem's walls
under Nehemiah.

NEHEMIAH 3:18

BAZLITH

(*Peeling*)

1 MAN/1 REFERENCE

NEHEMIAH 7:54

BAZLUTH

(*Peeling*)

1 MAN/1 REFERENCE

Same as Bazlith.

EZRA 2:52

BEALIAH

(*God is master*)

1 MAN/1 REFERENCE

"Mighty man" who supported the
future king David during his
conflict with Saul.

1 CHRONICLES 12:5

BEBAI

3 MEN/6 REFERENCES

EZRA 2:11; EZRA 8:11; NEHEMIAH 10:15

BECHER

(*Young camel*)

2 MEN/5 REFERENCES

GENESIS 46:21; NUMBERS 26:35

BECHORATH

(*Firstborn*)

1 MAN/1 REFERENCE

1 SAMUEL 9:1

BEDAD

(*Solitary*)

1 MAN/2 REFERENCES

GENESIS 36:35

BEDAN

(*Servile*)

2 MEN/2 REFERENCES

Notably, judge of Israel who delivered
the nation from its enemies.

1 SAMUEL 12:11; 1 CHRONICLES 7:17

BEDEIAH

(*Servant of Jehovah*)

1 MAN/1 REFERENCE

EZRA 10:35

BEELIADA

(*Baal has known*)

Son of King David, born in Jerusalem.

1 CHRONICLES 14:7

BEERA

(*A well*)

1 MAN/1 REFERENCE

1 CHRONICLES 7:37

BEERAH

(*A well*)

1 MAN/1 REFERENCE

1 CHRONICLES 5:6

BEERI

(*Fountained*)

1 MEN/2 REFERENCES

GENESIS 26:34; HOSEA 1:1

BELA

(*A gulp*)

3 MEN/11 REFERENCES

Most notably, king of Edom.

GENESIS 36:32; NUMBERS 26:38;
1 CHRONICLES 5:8

BELAH

(*A gulp*)

1 MAN/1 REFERENCE

Form of the name *Bela*; a son of
Benjamin.

GENESIS 46:21

BELSHAZZAR

1 MAN/8 REFERENCES

Babylonian king who saw handwriting
on the wall and sought to have it
interpreted. When his own sooth-
sayers could not do so, the prophet
Daniel read it to him.

DANIEL 5:1

BELTESHAZZAR

1 MAN/10 REFERENCES

Babylonian name given to the exiled
Israelite Daniel upon entering King
Nebuchadnezzar's service.

DANIEL 1:7

BEN
(*Son*)

1 MAN/1 REFERENCE

Levite musician who performed in celebration when King David brought
the ark of the covenant to Jerusalem.

1 CHRONICLES 15:18

BENAIAH
(*God has built*)

12 MEN/42 REFERENCES

Most notably, one of David's three
mighty men and a commander in
King David's army.

2 SAMUEL 8:18; 2 SAMUEL 23:30;
    1 CHRONICLES 4:36; 1 CHRONICLES
    15:18; 1 CHRONICLES 27:34;
    2 CHRONICLES 20:14; 2 CHRONICLES
    31:13; EZRA 10:25; EZRA 10:30;
    EZRA 10:35; EZRA 10:43; EZEKIEL 11:1

BENAMMI
(*Son of my people*)

1 MAN/1 REFERENCE

GENESIS 19:38

BEN-HADAD
(*Son of Hadad*)

3 MEN/26 REFERENCES

Most notably, king of Syria who supported Asa, king of Judah, against
Israel.

1 KINGS 15:18; 1 KINGS 20:1; 2 KINGS 13:3

BEN-HAIL
(*Son of might*)

1 MAN/1 REFERENCE

Prince of Judah sent by King
Jehoshaphat to teach the law of
the Lord throughout the nation.

2 CHRONICLES 17:7

BEN-HANAN
(*Son of Chanan*)

1 MAN/1 REFERENCE

1 CHRONICLES 4:20

BENINU
(*Our son*)

1 MAN/1 REFERENCE

NEHEMIAH 10:13

BENJAMIN
(*Son of the right hand*)

5 MEN/20 REFERENCES

Most notably, Jacob's youngest son and
the only full brother of Joseph.

GENESIS 35:18; 1 CHRONICLES 7:10;
    EZRA 10:32; NEHEMIAH 3:23;
    NEHEMIAH 12:34

BENO
(*Son*)

1 MAN/2 REFERENCES

1 CHRONICLES 24:26

BEN-ONI
(*Son of my sorrow*)

1 MAN/1 REFERENCE

Name given by Rachel to her second
son as she was dying in childbirth.
The boy's father, Jacob, called him
Benjamin.

GENESIS 35:18

BEN-ZOHETH
(*Son of Zocheth*)

1 MAN/1 REFERENCE

1 CHRONICLES 4:20

BEOR
(*A lamp*)

2 MEN/10 REFERENCES

Same as Bosor.

GENESIS 36:32; NUMBERS 22:5

BERA

1 MAN/1 REFERENCE

King of Sodom in the days of Abram.

GENESIS 14:2

BERACHAH

(*Benediction*)

1 MAN/1 REFERENCE

"Mighty man" who supported the future king David during his conflict with Saul.

1 CHRONICLES 12:3

BERACHIAH

(*Blessing of God*)

1 MAN/1 REFERENCE

Same as Berechiah.

1 CHRONICLES 6:39

BERAIAH

(*God has created*)

1 MAN/1 REFERENCE

1 CHRONICLES 8:21

BERECHIAH

(*Blessing of God*)

7 MEN/10 REFERENCES

1 CHRONICLES 3:20; 1 CHRONICLES 9:16;
1 CHRONICLES 15:17; 1 CHRONICLES
15:23; 2 CHRONICLES 28:12;
NEHEMIAH 3:4; ZECHARIAH 1:1

BERED

(*Hail*)

1 MAN/1 REFERENCE

1 CHRONICLES 7:20

BERI

(*Fountained*)

1 MAN/1 REFERENCE

1 CHRONICLES 7:36

BERIAH

(*In trouble*)

4 MEN/11 REFERENCES

GENESIS 46:17; 1 CHRONICLES 7:23;
1 CHRONICLES 8:13;
1 CHRONICLES 23:10

BERNICE

(*Victorious*)

1 WOMAN/3 REFERENCES

Daughter of Herod Agrippa and sister of Agrippa II.

ACTS 25:13

BERODACH-BALADAN

1 MAN/1 REFERENCE

Babylonian king who sent wishes for recovery to Judah's ill king Hezekiah.

2 KINGS 20:12

BESAI

(*Domineering*)

1 MAN/2 REFERENCES

EZRA 2:49

BESODEIAH

(*In the counsel of Jehovah*)

1 MAN/1 REFERENCE

NEHEMIAH 3:6

BETHLEHEM

(*Native of Bethlehem*)

1 MAN/3 REFERENCES

1 CHRONICLES 2:51

BETH-RAPHA

(*House of the giant*)

1 MAN/1 REFERENCE

1 CHRONICLES 4:12

BETHUEL

(*Destroyed of God*)

1 MAN/9 REFERENCES

GENESIS 22:22

BETH-ZUR

(*House of the rock*)

1 MAN/1 REFERENCE

1 CHRONICLES 2:45

BEZAI

(*Domineering*)

2 MEN/3 REFERENCES

EZRA 2:17; NEHEMIAH 10:18

BEZALEEL

(*In the shadow of God*)

2 MEN, 9 REFERENCES

Notably, craftsman given special ability by God to work on the tabernacle.

EXODUS 31:2; EZRA 10:30

BEZER
(*Inaccessible*)
1 MAN/1 REFERENCE
1 CHRONICLES 7:37

BICHRI
(*Youthful*)
1 MAN/8 REFERENCES
2 SAMUEL 20:1

BIDKAR
(*Assassin*)
1 MAN/1 REFERENCE
Army captain serving Israel's king Jehu.
2 KINGS 9:25

BIGTHA
1 MAN/1 REFERENCE
Eunuch serving the Persian king
Ahasuerus in Esther's time.
ESTHER 1:10

BIGTHAN
1 MAN/1 REFERENCE
One of two palace doorkeepers
who conspired to kill their king,
Ahasuerus of Persia. The plot was
uncovered by Mordecai, and both
doorkeepers were hanged. Same as
Bigthana.
ESTHER 2:21

BIGTHANA
1 MAN/1 REFERENCE
One of two palace doorkeepers who
conspired to kill their king, Ahasuerus of Persia, but was hanged when
the plot was discovered. Same as
Bigthan.
ESTHER 6:2

BIGVAI
4 MEN/6 REFERENCES
EZRA 2:2; EZRA 2:14; EZRA 8:14;
    NEHEMIAH 10:16

BILDAD
1 MAN/5 REFERENCES
One of three friends of Job who
mourned Job's losses for a week then
accused him of wrongdoing.
JOB 2:11

BILGAH
(*Stopping*)
2 MEN/3 REFERENCES
Notably, one of twenty-four priests in
David's time who was chosen by lot
to serve in the tabernacle.
1 CHRONICLES 24:14; NEHEMIAH 12:5

BILGAI
(*Stoppable*)
1 MAN/1 REFERENCE
Priest who renewed the covenant under
Nehemiah.
NEHEMIAH 10:8

BILHAH
(*Timid*)
1 WOMAN/10 REFERENCES
Rachel's handmaid, whom she gave
to Jacob to bear children for her.
Bilhah had two sons, Dan and
Naphtali.
GENESIS 29:29

BILHAN
(*Timid*)
2 MEN/4 REFERENCES
GENESIS 36:27; 1 CHRONICLES 7:10

BILSHAN
1 MAN/2 REFERENCES
EZRA 2:2

BIMHAL
(*With pruning*)
1 MAN/1 REFERENCE
1 CHRONICLES 7:33

BINEA
1 MAN/2 REFERENCES
1 CHRONICLES 8:37

BINNUI
(*Built up*)
6 MEN/7 REFERENCES
EZRA 8:33; EZRA 10:30; EZRA 10:38;
  NEHEMIAH 3:24; NEHEMIAH 7:15;
  NEHEMIAH 12:8

BIRSHA
(*With wickedness*)
1 MAN/1 REFERENCE
King of Sodom in the days of Abram.
GENESIS 14:2

BIRZAVITH
(*Holes*)
1 MAN/1 REFERENCE
1 CHRONICLES 7:31

BISHLAM
1 MAN/1 REFERENCE
Man who tried to stop the rebuilding
  of Jerusalem's walls.
EZRA 4:7

BITHIAH
(*Daughter of God*)
1 WOMAN/1 REFERENCE
1 CHRONICLES 4:18

BIZTHA
1 MAN/1 REFERENCE
Eunuch serving the Persian king Ahasuerus in Esther's time.
ESTHER 1:10

BLASTUS
(*To germinate*)
1 MAN/1 REFERENCE
Eunuch serving Herod Agrippa I.
ACTS 12:20

BOANERGES
(*Sons of commotion*)
2 MEN/1 REFERENCE
Nickname given to the disciples James
  and John, the sons of Zebedee, by
  Jesus.
MARK 3:17

BOAZ
1 MAN/22 REFERENCES
Relative of Naomi who acted as
  kinsman-redeemer for her and her
  daughter-in-law Ruth, marrying
  Ruth and having a son with her.
  Same as Booz.
RUTH 2:1

BOCHERU
(*Firstborn*)
1 MAN/2 REFERENCES
1 CHRONICLES 8:38

BOOZ
1 MAN/3 REFERENCES
Greek form of the name *Boaz*;
  hero of the story of Ruth.
MATTHEW 1:5

BOSOR
(*A lamp*)
1 MAN/1 REFERENCE
Same as Beor.
2 PETER 2:15

BUKKI
(*Wasteful*)
2 MEN/5 REFERENCES
1 CHRONICLES 6:5; NUMBERS 34:22

BUKKIAH
(*Wasting of God*)
1 MAN/2 REFERENCES
1 CHRONICLES 25:4

BUNAH
(*Discretion*)
1 MAN/1 REFERENCE
1 CHRONICLES 2:25

BUNNI
(*Built*)
3 MEN/3 REFERENCES
Most notably, one of a group of Levites
  who led a revival among the Israel-
  ites in the time of Nehemiah.
NEHEMIAH 9:4; NEHEMIAH 10:15;
  NEHEMIAH 11:15

BUZ
(*Disrespect*)
2 MEN/2 REFERENCES
GENESIS 22:21; 1 CHRONICLES 5:14

BUZI
(*Disrespect*)
1 MAN/1 REFERENCE
EZEKIEL 1:3

—C—

CAIAPHAS
(*The dell*)
1 MAN/9 REFERENCES
Jewish high priest who judged Jesus at
His trial.
MATTHEW 26:3

CAIN
(*Lance*)
1 MAN/19 REFERENCES
Adam and Eve's first son who became
jealous of his brother Abel and
killed him when God refused Cain's
unrighteous offering but accepted
Abel's offering.
GENESIS 4:1

CAINAN
(*Fixed*)
1 MAN/7 REFERENCES
GENESIS 5:9

CALCOL
(*Sustenance*)
1 MAN/1 REFERENCE
1 CHRONICLES 2:6

CALEB
(*Forcible*)
3 MEN/36 REFERENCES
Most notably, sent by Moses to spy out
Canaan before the Israelites entered
the Promised Land. Of the twelve,
only he and Joshua entered the
Promised Land.
NUMBERS 13:6; 1 CHRONICLES 2:18;
1 CHRONICLES 2:50

CANAAN
(*Humiliated*)
1 MAN/9 REFERENCES
GENESIS 9:18

CANDACE
1 WOMAN/1 REFERENCE
Queen of Ethiopia whose treasurer was
converted to Christianity by Philip
the evangelist.
ACTS 8:27

CARCAS
1 MAN/1 REFERENCE
Eunuch serving the Persian king
Ahasuerus in Esther's time.
ESTHER 1:10

CAREAH
(*Bald*)
1 MAN/1 REFERENCE
2 KINGS 25:23

CARMI
(*Gardener*)
2 MEN/8 REFERENCES
JOSHUA 7:1; GENESIS 46:9

CARPUS
(*Fruit*)
1 MAN/1 REFERENCE
2 TIMOTHY 4:13

CARSHENA
1 MAN/1 REFERENCE
One of seven Persian princes serving
under King Ahasuerus.
ESTHER 1:14

CEPHAS
(*The rock*)
1 MAN/6 REFERENCES
Name Jesus gave the apostle Peter.
It is used most often in the book
of 1 Corinthians.
JOHN 1:42

CHALCOL
(*Sustenance*)

1 MAN/1 REFERENCE

Wise man mentioned in comparison to
    Solomon's wisdom.

1 KINGS 4:31

CHEDORLAOMER

1 MAN/5 REFERENCES

King of Elam in the days of Abram.

GENESIS 14:1

CHELAL
(*Complete*)

1 MAN/1 REFERENCE

EZRA 10:30

CHELLUH
(*Completed*)

1 MAN/1 REFERENCE

EZRA 10:35

CHELUB
(*Basket*)

2 MEN/2 REFERENCES

1 CHRONICLES 4:11; 1 CHRONICLES 27:26

CHELUBAI
(*Forcible*)

1 MAN/1 REFERENCE

Same as Caleb.

1 CHRONICLES 2:9

CHENAANAH
(*Humiliated*)

2 MEN/5 REFERENCES

Notably, false prophet who told King
    Ahab to fight against Ramoth-
    gilead.

1 KINGS 22:11; 1 CHRONICLES 7:10

CHENANI
(*Planted*)

1 MAN/1 REFERENCE

One of a group of Levites who led a
    revival among the Israelites in the
    time of Nehemiah.

NEHEMIAH 9:4

CHENANIAH
(*God has planted*)

2 MEN/3 REFERENCES

Notably, Levite musician, "the master
    of the song," who led singers in cel-
    ebration when King David brought
    the ark of the covenant to Jerusalem.

1 CHRONICLES 15:22; 1 CHRONICLES 26:29

CHERAN

1 MAN/2 REFERENCES

GENESIS 36:26

CHERUB

2 MEN/3 REFERENCES

EZRA 2:59

CHESED

1 MAN/1 REFERENCE

GENESIS 22:22

CHILEAB
(*Restraint of his father*)

1 MAN/1 REFERENCE

2 SAMUEL 3:3

CHILION
(*Pining*)

1 MAN/3 REFERENCES

RUTH 1:2

CHIMHAM
(*Pining*)

1 MAN/4 REFERENCES

2 SAMUEL 19:37

CHISLON
(*Hopeful*)

1 MAN/1 REFERENCE

NUMBERS 34:21

CHLOE
(*Green*)

1 WOMAN/1 REFERENCE

Corinthian Christian and acquaintance
    of Paul.

1 CORINTHIANS 1:11

CHUSHAN-RISHATHAIM

(*Cushan of double wickedness*)

1 MAN/4 REFERENCES

Mesopotamian king into whose hands
God gave the disobedient Israelites.

JUDGES 3:8

CHUZA

1 MAN/1 REFERENCE

King Herod's household manager
whose wife, Joanna, financially
supported the ministry of Jesus.

LUKE 8:3

CIS

(*A bow*)

1 MAN/1 REFERENCE

Same as Kish.

ACTS 13:21

CLAUDIA

1 WOMAN/1 REFERENCE

2 TIMOTHY 4:21

CLAUDIUS

2 MEN/3 REFERENCES

Most notably, Roman emperor who
ruled when a famine affected the
empire.

ACTS 11:28; ACTS 23:26

CLEMENT

(*Merciful*)

1 MAN/1 REFERENCE

PHILIPPIANS 4:3

CLEOPAS

(*Renowned father*)

1 MAN/1 REFERENCE

Christian who met Jesus on the road to
Emmaus.

LUKE 24:18

CLEOPHAS

1 MAN/1 REFERENCE

JOHN 19:25

COL-HOZEH

(*Every seer*)

1 MAN/2 REFERENCES

NEHEMIAH 3:15

CONANIAH

(*God has sustained*)

1 MAN/1 REFERENCE

Levite (worship leader) who distributed
sacrificial animals for the Passover
celebration under King Josiah.

2 CHRONICLES 35:9

CONIAH

(*God will establish*)

1 MAN/3 REFERENCES

An alternative name for Judah's king
Jehoiachin. Same as Jeconiah.

JEREMIAH 22:24

CONONIAH

(*God has sustained*)

1 MAN/2 REFERENCES

Levite (worship leader) in charge of
tithes and offerings during King
Hezekiah's reign.

2 CHRONICLES 31:12

CORE

(*Ice*)

1 MAN/1 REFERENCE

Greek form of the name *Korah*; a man
who led a rebellion against Moses.

JUDE 1:11

CORNELIUS

1 MAN/10 REFERENCES

God-fearing centurion of the Italian
band.

ACTS 10:1

COSAM

(*Divination*)

1 MAN/1 REFERENCE

LUKE 3:28

COZ

(*Thorn*)

1 MAN/1 REFERENCE

1 CHRONICLES 4:8

COZBI

(*False*)

1 WOMAN/2 REFERENCES

NUMBERS 25:15

CRESCENS

(*Growing*)

1 MAN/1 REFERENCE

Coworker of Paul who left the apostle in Rome before preaching in Galatia.

2 TIMOTHY 4:10

CRISPUS

(*Crisp*)

1 MAN/2 REFERENCES

Head of the Corinthian synagogue who, along with his household, believed in Jesus and was baptized by Paul.

ACTS 18:8

CUSH

2 MEN/7 REFERENCES

GENESIS 10:6; PSALM 7 (TITLE)

CUSHAN

1 MAN/1 REFERENCE

Mesopotamian king into whose hands God gave the disobedient Israelites. Same as Chushan-rishathaim.

HABAKKUK 3:7

CUSHI

(*A Cushite*)

3 MEN/10 REFERENCES

Most notably, messenger who brought David the news that his son Absalom was dead.

2 SAMUEL 18:21; JEREMIAH 36:14; ZEPHANIAH 1:1

CYRENIUS

1 MAN/1 REFERENCE

Roman governor of Syria at the time when Jesus was born.

LUKE 2:2

CYRUS

1 MAN/23 REFERENCES

King of Persia who commanded that the temple in Jerusalem be rebuilt.

2 CHRONICLES 36:22

—D—

DALAIAH

(*God has delivered*)

1 MAN/1 REFERENCE

1 CHRONICLES 3:24

DALPHON

(*Dripping*)

1 MAN/1 REFERENCE

ESTHER 9:7

DAMARIS

(*Gentle*)

1 WOMAN/1 REFERENCE

ACTS 17:34

DAN

(*Judge*)

1 MAN/10 REFERENCES

GENESIS 30:6

DANIEL

(*Judge of God*)

3 MEN/83 REFERENCES

Most notably, Old Testament major prophet who, as a child, was taken into exile in Babylon. Was condemned to the lions' den for praying to God, but God kept him safe. Also, son of David, born to his wife Abigail.

1 CHRONICLES 3:1; EZRA 8:2; EZEKIEL 14:14

DARA

(*Pearl of knowledge*)

1 MAN/1 REFERENCE

1 CHRONICLES 2:6

DARDA

(*Pearl of knowledge*)

1 MAN/1 REFERENCE

Wise man whose wisdom is compared to Solomon's.

1 KINGS 4:31

DARIUS

3 MEN/25 REFERENCES

Most notably, king of Persia. Also, Darius the Mede, king of Persia, during Daniel's lifetime.

EZRA 4:5; NEHEMIAH 12:22; DANIEL 5:31

DARKON
1 MAN/2 REFERENCES
EZRA 2:56

DATHAN
1 MAN/10 REFERENCES
Conspirer against Moses. Because of his disobedience, the ground broke open at Dathan's feet and swallowed him, his family, and his possessions.
NUMBERS 16:1

DAVID
(*Loving*)
1 MAN/1139 REFERENCES
Popular king of Israel. As a young shepherd and musician, he was anointed king by the prophet Samuel. He defeated the Philistine giant Goliath, then defeated the Philistines and brought the ark of the covenant to Jerusalem. He fell into sin with Bathsheba and killed her husband, Uriah. He repented, and scripture refers to David as a man after God's own heart.
RUTH 4:17

DEBIR
(*Shrine*)
1 MAN/1 REFERENCE
Pagan king of Eglon during Joshua's conquest of the Promised Land.
JOSHUA 10:3

DEBORAH
(*Bee*)
2 WOMEN/10 REFERENCES
Notably, nurse who accompanied Rebekah when she married Isaac. Also, Israel's only female judge and prophetess, who held court under a palm tree.
GENESIS 35:8; JUDGES 4:4

DEDAN
2 MEN/5 REFERENCES
GENESIS 10:7; GENESIS 25:3

DEKAR
(*Stab*)
1 MAN/1 REFERENCE
1 KINGS 4:9

DELAIAH
(*God has delivered*)
4 MEN/6 REFERENCES
Most notably, one of twenty-four priests in David's time who was chosen by lot to serve in the tabernacle.
1 CHRONICLES 24:18; EZRA 2:60; NEHEMIAH 6:10; JEREMIAH 36:12

DELILAH
(*Languishing*)
1 WOMAN/6 REFERENCES
Woman Samson fell in love with who was bribed by the Philistines to discover the source of his strength. When she shared his secret, his hair was shaved, and the Philistines could then overpower him.
JUDGES 16:4

DEMAS
1 MAN/3 REFERENCES
Christian worker who was with Paul at Corinth, leaving when he was attracted by worldly things.
COLOSSIANS 4:14

DEMETRIUS
2 MEN/3 REFERENCES
Notably, silversmith of Ephesus who opposed Paul and his teachings because they tended to destroy his business of making pagan shrines.
ACTS 19:24; 3 JOHN 1:12

DEUEL
(*Known of God*)
1 MAN/4 REFERENCES
NUMBERS 1:14

DIBLAIM
(*Two cakes*)
1 MAN/1 REFERENCE
HOSEA 1:3

DIBRI
(*Wordy*)
1 MAN/1 REFERENCE
LEVITICUS 24:11

DIDYMUS
(*Twin*)
1 MAN/3 REFERENCES
Alternate name for Thomas, one of the
   twelve disciples of Jesus.
JOHN 11:16

DIKLAH
1 MAN/2 REFERENCES
GENESIS 10:27

DINAH
(*Justice*)
1 MAN/8 REFERENCES
GENESIS 30:21

DIONYSIUS
(*Reveler*)
1 MAN/1 REFERENCE
Man of Athens converted under the
   ministry of the apostle Paul.
ACTS 17:34

DIOTREPHES
(*Jove-nourished*)
1 MAN/1 REFERENCE
Arrogant church member condemned
   by the apostle John.
3 JOHN 1:9

DISHAN
(*Antelope*)
1 MAN/5 REFERENCES
GENESIS 36:21

DISHON
(*Antelope*)
2 MEN/7 REFERENCES
GENESIS 36:21; GENESIS 36:25

DODAI
(*Sick*)
1 MAN/1 REFERENCE
Commander in King David's army.
1 CHRONICLES 27:4

DODAVAH
(*Love of God*)
1 MAN/1 REFERENCE
2 CHRONICLES 20:37

DODO
(*Loving*)
3 MEN/5 REFERENCES
JUDGES 10:1; 2 SAMUEL 23:9;
   2 SAMUEL 23:24

DOEG
(*Anxious*)
1 MAN/6 REFERENCES
King Saul's chief herdsman.
1 SAMUEL 21:7

DORCAS
(*Gazelle*)
1 WOMAN/2 REFERENCES
Christian of Joppa who did many good
   works. When she died, her friends
   called Peter, who raised her back to
   life. Same as Tabitha.
ACTS 9:36

DRUSILLA
1 WOMAN/1 REFERENCE
Wife of Felix, the Roman governor of
   Judea in Paul's time.
ACTS 24:24

DUMAH
(*Silence*)
1 MAN/2 REFERENCES
GENESIS 25:14

—E—

EBAL
(*Bare*)
2 MEN/3 REFERENCES
GENESIS 36:23; 1 CHRONICLES 1:22

EBED
(*Servant*)
2 MEN/6 REFERENCES
JUDGES 9:26; EZRA 8:6

EBED-MELECH
(*Servant of a king*)
1 MAN/6 REFERENCES
Ethiopian eunuch who rescued Jeremiah from a dungeon by reporting his situation to King Zedekiah.
JEREMIAH 38:7

EBIASAPH
(*Gatherer*)
1 MAN/3 REFERENCES
1 CHRONICLES 6:23

EDEN
(*Pleasure*)
2 MEN/2 REFERENCES
Notably, Levite who cleansed the Jerusalem temple during the revival of King Hezekiah's day. Also, priest in the time of King Hezekiah who helped to distribute the people's freewill offerings to his fellow priests.
2 CHRONICLES 29:12; 2 CHRONICLES 31:15

EDER
(*Arrangement*)
1 MAN/2 REFERENCES
1 CHRONICLES 23:23

EDOM
(*Red*)
1 MAN/3 REFERENCES
Name given to Esau when he sold his birthright to his brother, Jacob, for a meal.
GENESIS 25:30

EGLAH
(*Calf*)
1 WOMAN/2 REFERENCES
2 SAMUEL 3:5

EGLON
(*Calflike*)
1 MAN/5 REFERENCES
King of Moab who attacked Israel.
JUDGES 3:12

EHI
(*Brotherly*)
1 MAN/1 REFERENCE
GENESIS 46:21

EHUD
(*United*)
2 MEN/10 REFERENCES
Second judge of Israel who subdued the oppressing Moabites. Noted as being a left-handed man.
JUDGES 3:15; 1 CHRONICLES 7:10

EKER
(*A transplanted person*)
1 MAN/1 REFERENCE
1 CHRONICLES 2:27

ELADAH
(*God has decked*)
1 MAN/1 REFERENCE
1 CHRONICLES 7:20

ELAH
(*Oak*)
6 MEN/14 REFERENCES
GENESIS 36:41; 1 KINGS 4:18; 1 KINGS 16:6; 2 KINGS 15:30; 1 CHRONICLES 4:15; 1 CHRONICLES 9:8

ELAM
(*Distant*)
9 MEN/13 REFERENCES
GENESIS 10:22; 1 CHRONICLES 8:24; 1 CHRONICLES 26:3; EZRA 2:7; EZRA 2:31; EZRA 8:7; EZRA 10:2; NEHEMIAH 10:14; NEHEMIAH 12:42

ELASAH
(*God has made*)
2 MEN/2 REFERENCES
EZRA 10:22; JEREMIAH 29:3

ELDAAH
(*God of knowledge*)
1 MAN/2 REFERENCES
GENESIS 25:4

ELDAD

(*God has loved*)

1 MAN/2 REFERENCES

NUMBERS 11:26

ELEAD

(*God has testified*)

1 MAN/1 REFERENCE

1 CHRONICLES 7:21

ELEASAH

(*God has made*)

2 MEN/4 REFERENCES

1 CHRONICLES 2:39; 1 CHRONICLES 8:37

ELEAZAR

(*God is helper*)

8 MEN/74 REFERENCES

Most notably, chief over the Levites, overseeing temple worship. Became high priest after Aaron's death.

EXODUS 6:23; 1 SAMUEL 7:1; 2 SAMUEL 23:9; 1 CHRONICLES 23:21; EZRA 8:33; EZRA 10:25; NEHEMIAH 12:42; MATTHEW 1:15

ELHANAN

(*God is gracious*)

2 MEN/4 REFERENCES

Killed Goliath's brother.

2 SAMUEL 21:19; 2 SAMUEL 23:24

ELI

(*Lofty*)

1 MAN/33 REFERENCES

High priest in Shiloh who rebuked Hannah for being drunk as she prayed for God to give her a child. Samuel was born, and she brought him to Eli, dedicating him to God. Eli acted as Samuel's foster father and trained him in the priesthood.

1 SAMUEL 1:3

ELIAB

(*God of his father*)

6 MEN/21 REFERENCES

Most notably, prince of Zebulun, assisting Moses in taking the census of his tribe.

NUMBERS 1:9; NUMBERS 16:1; 1 SAMUEL 16:6; 1 CHRONICLES 6:27; 1 CHRONICLES 12:9; 1 CHRONICLES 15:18

ELIADA

(*God is knowing*)

2 MEN/3 REFERENCES

2 SAMUEL 5:16; 2 CHRONICLES 17:17

ELIADAH

(*God is knowing*)

1 MAN/1 REFERENCE

1 KINGS 11:23

ELIAH

(*God of Jehovah*)

1 MAN/2 REFERENCES

1 CHRONICLES 8:27

ELIAHBA

(*God will hide*)

1 MAN/2 REFERENCES

2 SAMUEL 23:32

ELIAKIM

(*God of raising*)

4 MEN/15 REFERENCES

Most notably, palace administrator for King Hezekiah of Judah.

2 KINGS 18:18; 2 KINGS 23:34; NEHEMIAH 12:41; MATTHEW 1:13

ELIAM

(*God of the people*)

2 MEN/2 REFERENCES

2 SAMUEL 11:3; 2 SAMUEL 23:34

ELIAS

(*God of Jehovah*)

1 MAN/30 REFERENCES

Greek form of the name *Elijah*.

MATTHEW 11:14

ELIASAPH

(*God is gatherer*)

2 MEN/6 REFERENCES

Notably, prince of Gad who helped
Moses take a census of his tribe.

NUMBERS 1:14; NUMBERS 3:24

ELIASHIB

(*God will restore*)

7 MEN/17 REFERENCES

1 CHRONICLES 3:24; 1 CHRONICLES 24:12;
Ezra 10:6; Ezra 10:24; Ezra 10:27;
Ezra 10:36; Nehemiah 3:1

ELIATHATH

(*God of his consent*)

1 MAN/2 REFERENCES

1 CHRONICLES 25:4

ELIDAD

(*God of his love*)

1 MAN/1 REFERENCE

Prince of the tribe of Benjamin when
the Israelites entered the Promised
Land.

NUMBERS 34:21

ELIEL

(*God of his God*)

10 MEN/10 REFERENCES

Most notably, one of the "mighty men
of valour, famous men" leading the
half tribe of Manasseh.

1 CHRONICLES 5:24; 1 CHRONICLES 6:34;
1 CHRONICLES 8:20; 1 CHRONICLES
8:22; 1 CHRONICLES 11:46;
1 CHRONICLES 11:47; 1 CHRONICLES
12:11; 1 CHRONICLES 15:9;
1 CHRONICLES 15:11;
2 CHRONICLES 31:13

ELIENAI

(*Toward Jehovah are my eyes*)

1 MAN/1 REFERENCE

1 CHRONICLES 8:20

ELIEZER

(*God of help*)

10 MEN/15 REFERENCES

Most notably, steward of Abraham's
house and Abraham's presumed heir
before the miraculous birth of Isaac.

GENESIS 15:2; EXODUS 18:4;
1 CHRONICLES 15:24; 1 CHRONICLES
27:16; 2 CHRONICLES 20:37; Ezra 8:16;
Ezra 10:18; Ezra 10:23; Ezra 10:31;
LUKE 3:29

ELIHOENAI

(*Toward Jehovah are my eyes*)

1 MAN/1 REFERENCE

Ezra 8:4

ELIHOREPH

(*God of autumn*)

1 MAN/1 REFERENCE

Scribe serving Israel's king Solomon.

1 KINGS 4:3

ELIHU

(*God of him*)

5 MEN/11 REFERENCES

Most notably, young man who became
a mediator in the discussion between Job and his comforters. Also,
a warrior who defected to David at
Ziglag and became an army
commander.

1 SAMUEL 1:1; 1 CHRONICLES 12:20;
1 CHRONICLES 26:7; 1 CHRONICLES
27:18; JOB 32:2

ELIJAH

(*God of Jehovah*)

2 MEN/69 REFERENCES

Most notably, a major prophet. His
prophecy that no rain would fall
in Israel except at his command
angered wicked King Ahab. At
Mount Carmel, he had a showdown
with the priests of Baal that proved
the Lord was God. Later Elijah
went up into heaven in a whirlwind.
Same as Elias.

1 KINGS 17:1; Ezra 10:21

ELIKA
(*God of rejection*)
1 MAN/1 REFERENCE
2 SAMUEL 23:25

ELIMELECH
(*God of the king*)
1 MAN/6 REFERENCES
Naomi's husband.
RUTH 1:2

ELIOENAI
(*Toward Jehovah are my eyes*)
7 MEN/8 REFERENCES
1 CHRONICLES 3:23; 1 CHRONICLES 4:36;
1 CHRONICLES 7:8; 1 CHRONICLES 26:3;
EZRA 10:22; EZRA 10:27;
NEHEMIAH 12:41

ELIPHAL
(*God of judgment*)
1 MAN/1 REFERENCE
One of King David's valiant warriors.
1 CHRONICLES 11:35

ELIPHALET
(*God of deliverance*)
1 MAN/2 REFERENCES
2 SAMUEL 5:16

ELIPHAZ
(*God of gold*)
2 MEN/15 REFERENCES
Most notably, one of three friends of
Job who mourned his losses for a
week then accused him of wrong-
doing.
GENESIS 36:4; JOB 2:11

ELIPHELEH
(*God of his distinction*)
1 MAN/2 REFERENCES
Levite musician who performed in celebration when King David brought
the ark of the covenant to Jerusalem.
1 CHRONICLES 15:18

ELIPHELET
(*God of deliverance*)
6 MEN/6 REFERENCES
Most notably, one of King David's
"mighty men."
2 SAMUEL 23:34; 1 CHRONICLES 3:6;
1 CHRONICLES 3:8; 1 CHRONICLES 8:39;
EZRA 8:13; EZRA 10:33

ELISABETH
(*God of the oath*)
1 WOMAN/9 REFERENCES
Wife of Zacharias, cousin of Jesus'
mother, Mary, and mother of John
the Baptist.
LUKE 1:5

ELISEUS
(*God of supplication*)
1 MAN/1 REFERENCE
Greek form of the Old Testament
name *Elisha*.
LUKE 4:27

ELISHA
(*God of supplication*)
1 MAN/58 REFERENCES
Elijah's successor and disciple, Elisha
saw Elijah carried up to heaven in
a whirlwind of fire and received a
double portion of his spirit. Elisha
then took the role of prophet.
1 KINGS 19:16

ELISHAH
1 MAN/3 REFERENCES
GENESIS 10:4

ELISHAMA
(*God of hearing*)
7 MEN/17 REFERENCES
NUMBERS 1:10; 2 SAMUEL 5:16; JEREMIAH
41:1; 1 CHRONICLES 2:41;
2 CHRONICLES 17:8; 2 KINGS 25:25;
JEREMIAH 36:12

ELISHAPHAT
(*God of judgment*)
1 MAN/1 REFERENCE
Commander who entered into a
   covenant with the priest Jehoiada,
   young King Joash's protector.
2 CHRONICLES 23:1

ELISHEBA
(*God of the oath*)
1 WOMAN/1 REFERENCE
EXODUS 6:23

ELISHUA
(*God of supplication*)
1 MAN/2 REFERENCES
Same as Elishama.
2 SAMUEL 5:15

ELIUD
(*God of majesty*)
1 MAN/2 REFERENCES
MATTHEW 1:14

ELIZAPHAN
(*God of treasure*)
2 MEN/3 REFERENCES
Notably, prince of the tribe of Zebulun
   when the Israelites entered the
   Promised Land. Same as Elzaphan.
NUMBERS 3:30; NUMBERS 34:25

ELIZUR
(*God of the rock*)
1 MAN/5 REFERENCES
Prince of Reuben who helped Moses
   take a census of his tribe and led the
   tribe out of Sinai.
NUMBERS 1:5

ELKANAH
(*God has obtained*)
8 MEN/20 REFERENCES
Most notably, father of the prophet
   Samuel. Also, "mighty man" of King
   David.
EXODUS 6:24; 1 SAMUEL 1:1;
   1 CHRONICLES 6:25; 1 CHRONICLES
   6:26; 1 CHRONICLES 9:16;
   1 CHRONICLES 12:6; 1 CHRONICLES
   15:23; 2 CHRONICLES 28:7

ELMODAM
1 MAN/1 REFERENCE
LUKE 3:28

ELNAAM
(*God is his delight*)
1 MAN/1 REFERENCE
1 CHRONICLES 11:46

ELNATHAN
(*God is the giver*)
4 MEN/7 REFERENCES
2 KINGS 24:8; EZRA 8:16; EZRA 8:16;
   EZRA 8:16

ELON
(*Oak grove*)
3 MEN/6 REFERENCES
Most notably, eleventh judge of Israel
   who led the nation for ten years.
GENESIS 26:34; GENESIS 46:14;
   JUDGES 12:11

ELPAAL
(*God act*)
1 MAN/3 REFERENCES
1 CHRONICLES 8:11

ELPALET
(*Meaning*)
1 MAN/1 REFERENCE
1 CHRONICLES 14:5

ELUZAI
(*God is defensive*)
1 MAN/1 REFERENCE
"Mighty man" who supported the
   future king David during his
   conflict with Saul.
1 CHRONICLES 12:5

ELYMAS
1 MAN/1 REFERENCE
Jewish sorcerer miraculously blinded
   for opposing the apostle Paul's
   preaching of the gospel. Same as
   Bar-jesus.
ACTS 13:8

ELZABAD
(*God has bestowed*)
2 MEN/2 REFERENCES
Notably, one of several warriors from
the tribe of Gad who left Saul to
join David during his conflict with
the king.
1 CHRONICLES 12:12; 1 CHRONICLES 26:7

ELZAPHAN
(*God of treasure*)
1 MAN/2 REFERENCES
Same as Elizaphan.
EXODUS 6:22

EMMANUEL
(*God with us*)
1 MAN/1 REFERENCE
Prophetic name for Jesus, given by
the angel of the Lord to Joseph,
husband of Mary.
MATTHEW 1:23

EMMOR
(*Ass*)
1 MAN/1 REFERENCE
Prince of Shechem whose sons sold
Abraham a tomb.
ACTS 7:16

ENAN
(*Having eyes*)
1 MAN/5 REFERENCES
NUMBERS 1:15

ENOCH
(*Initiated*)
2 MEN/11 REFERENCES
Notably, Cain's eldest son, after whom
he named a city. Also, descendant of
Seth, son of Adam. He was imme-
diately translated into eternity. Same
as Henoch.
GENESIS 4:17; GENESIS 5:18

ENOS
(*Mortal*)
1 MAN/7 REFERENCES
Same as Enosh.
GENESIS 4:26

ENOSH
(*Mortal*)
1 MAN/1 REFERENCE
Another form of the name *Enos*;
son of Seth.
1 CHRONICLES 1:1

EPAENETUS
(*Praised*)
1 MAN/1 REFERENCE
Christian acquaintance of the apostle
Paul in Rome and the first Christian
convert from Achaia.
ROMANS 16:5

EPAPHRAS
(*Devoted*)
1 MAN/3 REFERENCES
Native of Colossae and fellow servant,
with Paul, to the Colossian church.
COLOSSIANS 1:7

EPAPHRODITUS
(*Devoted*)
1 MAN/2 REFERENCES
Fellow laborer with Paul whom
the apostle sent to the church at
Philippi.
PHILIPPIANS 2:25

EPHAH
(*Obscurity*)
2 MEN/1 WOMAN/5 REFERENCES
GENESIS 25:4; 1 CHRONICLES 2:46;
1 CHRONICLES 2:47

EPHAI
(*Birdlike*)
1 MAN/1 REFERENCE
JEREMIAH 40:8

EPHER
(*Gazelle*)
3 MEN/4 REFERENCES
Most notably, one of the "mighty men
of valour, famous men" leading the
half tribe of Manasseh.
GENESIS 25:4; 1 CHRONICLES 4:17;
1 CHRONICLES 5:24

EPHLAL
(*Judge*)
1 MAN/2 REFERENCES
1 CHRONICLES 2:37

EPHOD
(*Girdle*)
1 MAN/1 REFERENCE
NUMBERS 34:23

EPHRAIM
(*Double fruit*)
1 MAN/11 REFERENCES
Joseph and his wife Asenath's second
son, adopted and blessed by Jacob.
GENESIS 41:52

EPHRATAH
(*Fruitfulness*)
1 WOMAN/2 REFERENCES
Same as Ephrath.
1 CHRONICLES 2:50

EPHRATH
(*Fruitfulness*)
1 WOMAN/1 REFERENCE
Alternative form of the name *Ephratah*.
1 CHRONICLES 2:19

EPHRON
(*Fawnlike*)
1 MAN/12 REFERENCES
Hittite from whom Abraham bought
the cave of Machpelah, where he
buried Sarah.
GENESIS 23:8

ER
(*Watchful*)
3 MEN/11 REFERENCES
Most notably, Judah's firstborn son,
who was wicked.
GENESIS 38:3; 1 CHRONICLES 4:21;
LUKE 3:28

ERAN
(*Watchful*)
1 MAN/1 REFERENCE
NUMBERS 26:36

ERASTUS
(*Beloved*)
2 MEN/3 REFERENCES
Notably, companion of Timothy on a
mission to Macedonia.
ACTS 19:22; ROMANS 16:23

ERI
(*Watchful*)
1 MAN/2 REFERENCES
GENESIS 46:16

ESAIAS
(*God has saved*)
1 MAN/21 REFERENCES
Greek form of the name *Isaiah*,
used in the New Testament.
MATTHEW 3:3

ESAR-HADDON
1 MAN/3 REFERENCES
Son of Sennacherib who inherited the
throne of Assyria.
2 KINGS 19:37

ESAU
(*Rough*)
1 MAN/82 REFERENCES
Son of Isaac and Rebekah and twin
brother of Jacob, a good hunter and
the favorite of his father, but he sold
his birthright to Jacob for some
lentil stew.
GENESIS 25:25

ESH-BAAL
(*Man of Baal*)
1 MAN/2 REFERENCES
1 CHRONICLES 8:33

ESHBAN
(*Vigorous*)
1 MAN/2 REFERENCES
GENESIS 36:26

ESHCOL
(*Bunch of grapes*)
1 MAN/2 REFERENCES
GENESIS 14:13

ESHEK
(*Oppression*)
1 MAN/1 REFERENCE
1 CHRONICLES 8:39

ESHTEMOA
(*Obedience*)
1 MAN/2 REFERENCES
1 CHRONICLES 4:17

ESHTON
(*Restful*)
1 MAN/2 REFERENCES
1 CHRONICLES 4:11

ESLI
(*Toward Jehovah are my eyes*)
1 MAN/1 REFERENCE
LUKE 3:25

ESROM
(*Courtyard*)
1 MAN/3 REFERENCES
MATTHEW 1:3

ESTHER
1 WOMAN/56 REFERENCES
Jewish wife of Persian King Ahasuerus,
    whose counselor, Haman, plotted
    to kill the Jewish people. Esther's
    cousin Mordecai, who had raised
    her, convinced the new queen to
    confront her husband. She told the
    king of Haman's plan and her people
    were saved. Same as Hadassah.
ESTHER 2:7

ETAM
(*Hawk-ground*)
1 MAN/1 REFERENCE
1 CHRONICLES 4:3

ETHAN
(*Permanent*)
4 MEN/8 REFERENCES
Notably, wise man who wrote Psalm 89.
1 KINGS 4:31; 1 CHRONICLES 2:6;
    1 CHRONICLES 6:42; 1 CHRONICLES 6:44

ETHBAAL
(*With Baal*)
1 MAN/1 REFERENCE
1 KINGS 16:31

ETHNAN
(*Gift*)
1 MAN/1 REFERENCE
1 CHRONICLES 4:7

ETHNI
(*Munificence*)
1 MAN/1 REFERENCE
1 CHRONICLES 6:41

EUBULUS
(*Good-willer*)
1 MAN/1 REFERENCE
2 TIMOTHY 4:21

EUNICE
(*Victorious*)
1 WOMAN/1 REFERENCE
The Jewish mother of the apostle Paul's
    protégé Timothy.
2 TIMOTHY 1:5

EUODIAS
(*Fine traveling*)
1 WOMAN/1 REFERENCE
Christian woman of Philippi who
    had conflict with another church
    member, Syntyche.
PHILIPPIANS 4:2

EUTYCHUS
(*Fortunate*)
1 MAN/1 REFERENCE
Young man of Troas who drifted off
    to sleep during a late-night sermon
    of the apostle Paul. He fell from
    his window seat three floors to his
    death. Paul brought him back to life.
ACTS 20:9

EVE
(*Life-giver*)
1 WOMAN/4 REFERENCES
Adam's wife, "the mother of all living."
Tempted by the serpent, Eve ate the
fruit of the tree of the knowledge of
good and evil and offered it to her
husband, who also ate. For her part
in the sin, Eve would suffer greatly
during childbirth, desire her husband, and be ruled over by him.
GENESIS 3:20

EVI
(*Desirous*)
1 MAN/2 REFERENCES
Midianite king killed by the Israelites
at God's command.
NUMBERS 31:8

EVIL-MERODACH
(*Soldier of Merodak*)
1 MAN/2 REFERENCES
Successor to Babylonian king
Nebuchadnezzar.
2 KINGS 25:27

EZAR
(*Treasure*)
1 MAN/1 REFERENCE
1 CHRONICLES 1:38

EZBAI
(*Hyssoplike*)
1 MAN/1 REFERENCE
1 CHRONICLES 11:37

EZBON
2 MEN/2 REFERENCES
GENESIS 46:16; 1 CHRONICLES 7:7

EZEKIAS
(*Strengthened of God*)
1 MAN/2 REFERENCES
Greek form of the name *Hezekiah*,
used in the New Testament.
MATTHEW 1:9

EZEKIEL
(*God will strengthen*)
1 MAN/2 REFERENCES
Priest taken into exile when Nebuchadnezzar, king of Babylon, carried
off most of Jerusalem. Probably best
known for his prophetic vision of
the dry bones that came to life.
EZEKIEL 1:3

EZER
(*Treasure, help*)
6 MEN/9 REFERENCES
GENESIS 36:21; 1 CHRONICLES 4:4;
    1 CHRONICLES 7:21; 1 CHRONICLES
    12:9; NEHEMIAH 3:19; NEHEMIAH 12:42

EZRA
(*Aid*)
3 MEN/26 REFERENCES
Most notably, Israelite scribe and
teacher of the law who returned
from the Babylonian Exile along
with some priests, Levites, temple
servants, and other Israelites.
1 CHRONICLES 4:17; EZRA 7:1;
    NEHEMIAH 12:1

EZRI
(*Helpful*)
1 MAN/1 REFERENCE
Superintendent of agriculture who
served under King David.
1 CHRONICLES 27:26

—F—

FELIX
(*Happy*)
1 MAN/9 REFERENCES
Governor of Judea before whom Paul
appeared after the Roman guard
rescued him from his appearance at
the Jewish council.
ACTS 23:24

FESTUS
(*Festal*)
1 MAN/13 REFERENCES
Governor of Judea who replaced Felix.
Also called Porcius Festus.
ACTS 24:27

FORTUNATUS
(*Fortunate*)
1 MAN/1 REFERENCE
Corinthian Christian who visited the
apostle Paul in Ephesus.
1 CORINTHIANS 16:17

—G—

GAAL
(*Loathing*)
1 MAN/9 REFERENCES
JUDGES 9:26

GABBAI
(*Collective*)
1 MAN/1 REFERENCE
NEHEMIAH 11:8

GAD
(*Attack*)
2 MEN/19 REFERENCES
Notably, son of Jacob and Leah's
handmaid Zilpah.
GENESIS 30:11; 1 SAMUEL 22:5

GADDI
(*Fortunate*)
1 MAN/1 REFERENCE
NUMBERS 13:11

GADDIEL
(*Fortune of God*)
1 MAN/1 REFERENCE
NUMBERS 13:10

GADI
(*Fortunate*)
1 MAN/2 REFERENCES
2 KINGS 15:14

GAHAM
(*Flame*)
1 MAN/1 REFERENCE
GENESIS 22:24

GAHAR
(*Lurker*)
1 MAN/2 REFERENCES
EZRA 2:47

GAIUS
4 MEN/5 REFERENCES
Most notably, Corinthian Christian
who hosted the apostle Paul when
he wrote the letter to the Romans.
Also, the "wellbeloved" of John,
addressee of John's third letter.
ACTS 19:29; ACTS 20:4; ROMANS 16:23;
3 JOHN 1:1

GALAL
(*Great*)
2 MEN/3 REFERENCS
1 CHRONICLES 9:15; 1 CHRONICLES 9:16

GALLIO
1 MAN/3 REFERENCES
Deputy (proconsul) of Achaia who refused to hear the case when the Jews
accused Paul of breaking the law.
ACTS 18:12

GAMALIEL
(*Reward of God*)
2 MEN/7 REFERENCES
Notably, leader of the tribe of
Manasseh under Moses during the
Exodus.
NUMBERS 1:10; ACTS 5:34

GAMUL
(*Rewarded*)
1 MAN/1 REFERENCE
1 CHRONICLES 24:17

GAREB
(*Scabby*)
1 MAN/2 REFERENCES
One of King David's valiant warriors.
2 SAMUEL 23:38

GASHMU
(*A shower*)
1 MAN/1 REFERENCE
NEHEMIAH 6:6

GATAM
1 MAN/3 REFERENCES
GENESIS 36:11

GAZEZ
(*Shearer*)
2 MEN/2 REFERENCES
1 CHRONICLES 2:46; 1 CHRONICLES 2:46

GAZZAM
(*Devourer*)
1 MAN/2 REFERENCES
EZRA 2:48

GEBER
(*Warrior*)
2 MEN/2 REFERENCES
1 KINGS 4:13; 1 KINGS 4:19

GEDALIAH
(*God has become great*)
5 MEN/32 REFERENCES
Most notably, ruler appointed by
Nebuchadnezzar over the remnant
of Jews left behind in Judah at the
time of the Babylonian Exile.
2 KINGS 25:22; 1 CHRONICLES 25:3; EZRA
10:18; ZEPHANIAH 1:1; JEREMIAH 38:1

GEDEON
(*Warrior*)
1 MAN/1 REFERENCE
Greek form of the name *Gideon*,
used in the New Testament.
HEBREWS 11:32

GEDOR
(*Enclosure*)
2 MEN/4 REFERENCES
More notably, leader of the tribe of
Benjamin who lived in Jerusalem.
1 CHRONICLES 8:31; 1 CHRONICLES 4:4

GEHAZI
(*Valley of a visionary*)
1 MAN/12 REFERENCES
Prophet Elisha's servant.
2 KINGS 4:12

GEMALLI
(*Camel driver*)
1 MAN/1 REFERENCE
NUMBERS 13:12

GEMARIAH
(*God has perfected*)
2 MEN/5 REFERENCES
Notably, scribe and prince of Judah
in whose room Baruch read the
prophecies of Jeremiah.
JEREMIAH 36:10; JEREMIAH 29:3

GENUBATH
(*Theft*)
1 MAN/2 REFERENCES
1 KINGS 11:20

GERA
(*Grain*)
4 MEN/9 REFERENCES
GENESIS 46:21; JUDGES 3:15; 2 SAMUEL
16:5; 1 CHRONICLES 8:3

GERSHOM
(*Refugee*)
4 MEN/14 REFERENCES
EXODUS 2:22; JUDGES 18:30;
1 CHRONICLES 6:16; EZRA 8:2

GERSHON
(*Refugee*)
1 MAN/18 REFERENCES
Same as Gershom.
GENESIS 46:11

GESHAM
(*Lumpish*)
1 MAN/1 REFERENCE
1 CHRONICLES 2:47

GESHEM
(*A shower*)
1 MAN/3 REFERENCES
Arabian who opposed Nehemiah's
rebuilding of the walls of Jerusalem.
NEHEMIAH 2:19

GETHER
1 MAN/2 REFERENCES
GENESIS 10:23

GEUEL
(*Majesty of God*)
1 MAN/1 REFERENCE
NUMBERS 13:15

GIBBAR
(*Warrior*)
1 MAN/1 REFERENCE
EZRA 2:20

GIBEA
(*A hill*)
1 MAN/1 REFERENCE
1 CHRONICLES 2:49

GIDDALTI
(*I have made great*)
1 MAN/2 REFERENCES
1 CHRONICLES 25:4

GIDDEL
(*Stout*)
2 MEN/4 REFERENCES
EZRA 2:47; EZRA 2:56

GIDEON
(*Warrior*)
1 MAN/39 REFERENCES
Fifth judge of Israel who sought proof
of God's will by placing a fleece on
the ground and asking God to make
either the fleece or the ground wet;
God answered his request. Same
as Gedeon, Jerubbaal, and
Jerubbesheth.
JUDGES 6:11

GIDEONI
(*Warlike*)
1 MAN/5 REFERENCES
NUMBERS 1:11

GILALAI
(*Dungy*)
1 MAN/1 REFERENCE
Priest who helped to dedicate the rebuilt walls of Jerusalem by playing a
musical instrument.
NEHEMIAH 12:36

GILEAD
(*Heap of testimony*)
3 MEN/13 REFENCES
NUMBERS 26:29; JUDGES 11:1;
   1 CHRONICLES 5:14

GINATH
1 MAN/2 REFERENCES
1 KINGS 16:21

GINNETHO
(*Gardener*)
1 MAN/1 REFERENCE
NEHEMIAH 12:4

GINNETHON
(*Gardener*)
1 MAN/2 REFERENCES
NEHEMIAH 10:6

GISPA
1 MAN/1 REFERENCE
NEHEMIAH 11:21

GOG
2 MEN/11 REFERENCES
Notably, prince of Magog, a place
   perhaps in Scythia, against whom
   Ezekiel prophesied.
1 CHRONICLES 5:4; EZEKIEL 38:2

GOLIATH
(*Exile*)
1 MAN/6 REFERENCES
Nine-foot-nine-inch-tall Philistine
   champion who challenged any
   Israelite to a fight; the losing
   nation would become the winner's
   servants. David fought Goliath with
   a slingshot and killed him and then
   cut off his head.
1 SAMUEL 17:4

GOMER
(*Completion*)
1 MAN/1 WOMAN/5 REFERENCES
Notably, the unfaithful wife of the
   prophet Hosea who represented the
   unfaithfulness of God's people.
GENESIS 10:2; HOSEA 1:3

GUNI
(*Protected*)
2 MEN/4 REFERENCES
GENESIS 46:24; 1 CHRONICLES 5:15

HAAHASHTARI
(*Courier*)
1 MAN/1 REFERENCE
1 CHRONICLES 4:6

HABAIAH
(*God has hidden*)
1 MAN/2 REFERENCES
EZRA 2:6

HABAKKUK
(*Embrace*)
1 MAN/2 REFERENCES
Old Testament minor prophet who
served during the reign of King
Josiah of Judah.
HABAKKUK 1:1

HABAZINIAH
1 MAN/1 REFERENCE
JEREMIAH 35:3

HACHALIAH
(*Darkness of God*)
1 MAN/2 REFERENCES
NEHEMIAH 1:1

HACHMONI
(*Skillful*)
1 MAN/1 REFERENCE
1 CHRONICLES 27:32

HADAD
4 MEN/14 REFERENCES
Most notably, king of Edom.
GENESIS 36:35; 1 KINGS 11:14;
    1 CHRONICLES 1:30; 1 CHRONICLES 1:51

HADADEZER
(*Hadad is his help*)
1 MAN/9 REFERENCES
Syrian king of Zobah whose troops
David defeated along with the
Syrians of Damascus who supported
Hadadezer. Same as Hadarezer.
2 SAMUEL 8:3

HADAR
(*Magnificence*)
2 MEN/2 REFERENCES
GENESIS 25:15; GENESIS 36:39

HADAREZER
(*Hadad is his help*)
1 MAN/12 REFERENCES
Same as Hadadezer.
2 SAMUEL 10:16

HADASSAH
(*Myrtle*)
1 WOMAN/1 REFERENCE
Alternative name for Esther, the Jew-
ish woman who became queen of
Persia and saved her people from
destruction.
ESTHER 2:7

HADLAI
(*Idle*)
1 MAN/1 REFERENCE
2 CHRONICLES 28:12

HADORAM
3 MEN/4 REFERENCES
GENESIS 10:27; 1 CHRONICLES 18:10;
    2 CHRONICLES 10:18

HAGAB
(*Locust*)
1 MAN/1 REFERENCE
Same as Hagaba and Hagabah.
EZRA 2:46

HAGABA
(*Locust*)
1 MAN/1 REFERENCE
Same as Hagab and Hagabah.
NEHEMIAH 7:48

HAGABAH
(*Locust*)
1 MAN/1 REFERENCE
Same as Hagab and Hagaba.
EZRA 2:45

HAGAR
1 WOMAN/12 REFERENCES
Sarai's Egyptian maid who became a
surrogate wife to Abram so he and
Sarai could have a child.
GENESIS 16:1

HAGGAI
(*Festive*)
1 MAN/11 REFERENCES
Prophet of Judah who wrote the book that bears his name.
EZRA 5:1

HAGGERI
1 MAN/1 REFERENCE
1 CHRONICLES 11:38

HAGGI
(*Festive*)
1 MAN/2 REFERENCES
GENESIS 46:16

HAGGIAH
(*Festival of God*)
1 MAN/1 REFERENCE
1 CHRONICLES 6:30

HAGGITH
(*Festive*)
1 WOMAN/5 REFERENCES
One of several wives of King David and mother of David's son Adonijah.
2 SAMUEL 3:4

HAKKATAN
(*Small*)
1 MAN/1 REFERENCE
EZRA 8:12

HAKKOZ
(*Thorn*)
1 MAN/1 REFERENCE
One of twenty-four priests in David's time who was chosen by lot to serve in the tabernacle.
1 CHRONICLES 24:10

HAKUPHA
(*Crooked*)
1 MAN/2 REFERENCES
EZRA 2:51

HALLOHESH
(*Enchanter*)
1 MAN/1 REFERENCE
Same as Halohesh.
NEHEMIAH 10:24

HALOHESH
(*Enchanter*)
1 MAN/1 REFERENCE
Same as Hallohesh.
NEHEMIAH 3:12

HAM
(*Hot*)
1 MAN/12 REFERENCES
Youngest of Noah's three sons.
GENESIS 5:32

HAMAN
1 MAN/53 REFERENCES
King Ahasuerus's wicked counselor who plotted to eradicate the Jews from the Persian kingdom. Ahasuerus, angry at the deceit of his counselor, had him hanged on the gallows that Haman had erected to destroy Mordecai.
ESTHER 3:1

HAMMEDATHA
1 MAN/5 REFERENCES
ESTHER 3:1

HAMMELECH
(*King*)
1 MAN/2 REFERENCES
JEREMIAH 36:26

HAMMOLEKETH
(*Queen*)
1 WOMAN/1 REFERENCE
1 CHRONICLES 7:18

HAMOR
(*Ass*)
1 MAN/13 REFERENCES
GENESIS 33:19

HAMUEL
(*Anger of God*)
1 MAN/1 REFERENCE
1 CHRONICLES 4:26

HAMUL
(*Pitied*)
1 MAN/3 REFERENCES
GENESIS 46:12

HAMUTAL
(*Father-in-law of dew*)
1 WOMAN/3 REFERENCES
2 KINGS 23:31

HANAMEEL
(*God has favored*)
1 MAN/4 REFERENCES
JEREMIAH 32:7

HANAN
(*Favor*)
9 MEN/12 REFERENCES
1 CHRONICLES 8:23; 1 CHRONICLES 8:38;
1 CHRONICLES 11:43; EZRA 2:46;
NEHEMIAH 8:7; NEHEMIAH 10:10;
NEHEMIAH 10:22; NEHEMIAH 10:26;
JEREMIAH 35:4

HANANI
(*Gracious*)
6 MEN/11 REFERENCES
1 CHRONICLES 25:4; 2 CHRONICLES 16:7;
1 KINGS 16:1; EZRA 10:20; NEHEMIAH
1:2; NEHEMIAH 12:36

HANANIAH
(*God has favored*)
14 MEN/29 REFERENCES
Most notably, Hebrew name of
Daniel's friend, better known as
Shadrach.
1 CHRONICLES 3:19; 1 CHRONICLES 8:24;
1 CHRONICLES 25:4; 1 CHRONICLES
26:11; EZRA 10:28; NEHEMIAH 3:8;
NEHEMIAH 3:30; NEHEMIAH 7:2;
NEHEMIAH 10:23; NEHEMIAH 12:41;
JEREMIAH 28:1; JEREMIAH 36:12;
JEREMIAH 37:13; DANIEL 1:6

HANIEL
(*Favor of God*)
1 MAN/1 REFERENCE
1 CHRONICLES 7:39

HANNAH
(*Favored*)
1 WOMAN/13 REFERENCES
Wife of Elkanah who could not bear
a child and went to the temple to
pray, promising God that if He
gave her a child, she would give
the boy to Him for his whole life. She
conceived, bore Samuel, and fulfilled
her pledge.
1 SAMUEL 1:2

HANNIEL
(*Favor of God*)
1 MAN/1 REFERENCE
Prince of the tribe of Manasseh when
the Israelites entered the Promised
Land.
NUMBERS 34:23

HANOCH
(*Initiated, favor of God*)
2 MEN/5 REFERENCES
Same as Henoch.
GENESIS 25:4; GENESIS 46:9

HANUN
(*Favored*)
3 MEN/11 REFERENCES
Most notably, Ammonite king.
2 SAMUEL 10:1; NEHEMIAH 3:30;
NEHEMIAH 3:13

HARAN
(*Rest, mountaineer, parched*)
3 MEN/9 REFERENCES
Most notably, brother of Abram and
father of Lot. Also, head Levite who
was part of King David's religious-
leadership reorganization.
GENESIS 11:26; 1 CHRONICLES 2:46;
1 CHRONICLES 23:9

HARBONA
1 MAN/1 REFERENCE
Eunuch serving the Persian king Aha-
suerus in Esther's time. Same as
Harbonah.
ESTHER 1:10

HARBONAH

1 MAN/1 REFERENCE

Same as Harbona.

ESTHER 7:9

HAREPH

(*Reproachful*)

1 MAN/1 REFERENCE

1 CHRONICLES 2:51

HARHAIAH

(*Fearing God*)

1 MAN/1 REFERENCE

NEHEMIAH 3:8

HARHAS

(*Shining*)

1 MAN/1 REFERENCE

Same as Hasrah.

2 KINGS 22:14

HARHUR

(*Inflammation*)

1 MAN/2 REFERENCES

EZRA 2:51

HARIM

(*Snub-nosed*)

5 MEN/11 REFERENCES

Most notably, one of twenty-four priests
   in David's time who was chosen by
   lot to serve in the tabernacle.

1 CHRONICLES 24:8; EZRA 2:32; EZRA
   10:31; NEHEMIAH 10:5;
   NEHEMIAH 10:27

HARIPH

(*Autumnal*)

2 MEN/2 REFERENCES

NEHEMIAH 7:24; NEHEMIAH 10:19

HARNEPHER

1 MAN/1 REFERENCE

1 CHRONICLES 7:36

HAROEH

(*Prophet*)

1 MAN/1 REFERENCE

1 CHRONICLES 2:52

HARSHA

(*Magician*)

1 MAN/2 REFERENCES

EZRA 2:52

HARUM

(*High*)

1 MAN/1 REFERENCE

1 CHRONICLES 4:8

HARUMAPH

(*Snub-nosed*)

1 MAN/1 REFERENCE

NEHEMIAH 3:10

HARUZ

(*Earnest*)

1 MAN/1 REFERENCE

2 KINGS 21:19

HASADIAH

(*God has favored*)

1 MAN/1 REFERENCE

1 CHRONICLES 3:20

HASENUAH

(*Pointed*)

1 MAN/1 REFERENCE

1 CHRONICLES 9:7

HASHABIAH

(*God has regarded*)

14 MEN/15 REFERENCES

Most notably, leader of the tribe of
   Levi in the days of King David.
   Also, priest trusted by Ezra to carry
   money and temple vessels to Israel.

1 CHRONICLES 6:45; 1 CHRONICLES 9:14;
   1 CHRONICLES 25:3; 1 CHRONICLES
   26:30; 1 CHRONICLES 27:17;
   2 CHRONICLES 35:9; EZRA 8:19;
   EZRA 8:24; NEHEMIAH 3:17;
   NEHEMIAH 10:11; NEHEMIAH 11:15;
   NEHEMIAH 11:22; NEHEMIAH 12:21;
   NEHEMIAH 12:24

HASHABNAH

(*Inventiveness*)

1 MAN/1 REFERENCE

NEHEMIAH 10:25

HASHABNIAH
(*Thought of God*)
2 MAN/2 REFERENCES
NEHEMIAH 3:10; NEHEMIAH 9:5

HASHBADANA
(*Considerate judge*)
1 MAN/1 REFERENCE
Priest who assisted Ezra in reading
  the book of the law to the people
  of Jerusalem.
NEHEMIAH 8:4

HASHEM
(*Wealthy*)
1 MAN/1 REFERENCE
1 CHRONICLES 11:34

HASHUB
(*Intelligent*)
4 MEN/4 REFERENCES
NEHEMIAH 3:11; NEHEMIAH 3:23;
  NEHEMIAH 10:23; NEHEMIAH 11:15

HASHUBAH
(*Estimation*)
1 MAN/1 REFERENCE
1 CHRONICLES 3:20

HASHUM
(*Enriched*)
3 MEN/5 REFERENCES
Priest who assisted Ezra in reading
  the book of the law to the people
  of Jerusalem.
EZRA 2:19; NEHEMIAH 8:4;
  NEHEMIAH 10:18

HASHUPHA
(*Nakedness*)
1 MAN/1 REFERENCE
NEHEMIAH 7:46

HASRAH
(*Want*)
1 MAN/1 REFERENCE
Grandfather of Shallum, husband of
  the prophetess Huldah in the days
  of King Josiah. Same as Harhas.
2 CHRONICLES 34:22

HASSENAAH
(*Thorny*)
1 MAN/1 REFERENCE
NEHEMIAH 3:3

HASSHUB
(*Intelligent*)
1 MAN/1 REFERENCE
1 CHRONICLES 9:14

HASUPHA
(*Nakedness*)
1 MAN/1 REFERENCE
EZRA 2:43

HATACH
1 MAN/4 REFERENCES
One of King Ahasuerus's eunuchs who
  attended Queen Esther. He acted as
  a messenger between her and Mordecai when Mordecai discovered
  Haman's plot.
ESTHER 4:5

HATHATH
(*Dismay*)
1 MAN/1 REFERENCE
1 CHRONICLES 4:13

HATIPHA
(*Robber*)
1 MAN/2 REFERENCES
EZRA 2:54

HATITA
(*Explorer*)
1 MAN/2 REFERENCES
EZRA 2:42

HATTIL
(*Fluctuating*)
1 MAN/2 REFERENCES
EZRA 2:57

HATTUSH
5 MEN/5 REFERENCES
1 CHRONICLES 3:22; EZRA 8:2;
  NEHEMIAH 3:10; NEHEMIAH 10:4;
  NEHEMIAH 12:12

HAVILAH
(*Circular*)
2 MEN/4 REFERENCES
GENESIS 10:7; GENESIS 10:29

HAZAEL
(*God has seen*)
1 MAN/23 REFERENCES
King of Syria anointed to his position
by Elijah.
1 KINGS 19:15

HAZAIAH
(*God has seen*)
1 MAN/1 REFERENCE
NEHEMIAH 11:5

HAZARMAVETH
(*Village of death*)
1 MAN/2 REFERENCES
GENESIS 10:26

HAZELELPONI
(*Shade-facing*)
1 MAN/1 REFERENCE
1 CHRONICLES 4:3

HAZIEL
(*Seen of God*)
1 MAN/1 REFERENCE
Chief Levite who was part of King
David's religious-leadership
reorganization.
1 CHRONICLES 23:9

HAZO
(*Seer*)
1 MAN/1 REFERENCE
Abraham's brother.
GENESIS 22:22

HEBER
(*Community, across*)
6 MEN/14 REFERENCES
Heber the Kenite, husband of Jael,
the woman who killed the Canaanite commander Sisera.
GENESIS 46:17; JUDGES 4:11;
    1 CHRONICLES 4:18; 1 CHRONICLES
    5:13; 1 CHRONICLES 8:17;
    1 CHRONICLES 8:22

HEBRON
(*Association*)
2 MEN/10 REFERENCES
EXODUS 6:18; 1 CHRONICLES 2:42

HEGAI
1 MAN/3 REFERENCES
Keeper of the harem for King Ahasuerus of Persia. He treated Esther
preferentially, and she took his ad-
vice on what to take when she went
to the king. Same as Hege.
ESTHER 2:8

HEGE
1 MAN/1 REFERENCE
Alternative name for Hegai, servant of
the Persian king Ahasuerus.
ESTHER 2:3

HELAH
(*Rust*)
1 WOMAN/2 REFERENCES
Wife of Ashur, descendant of Abraham
through Jacob's son Judah.
1 CHRONICLES 4:5

HELDAI
(*Worldliness*)
2 MEN/2 REFERENCES
Notably, commander in King David's
army overseeing twenty-four thousand men in the twelfth month of
each year. Also, same as Helem.
1 CHRONICLES 27:15; ZECHARIAH 6:10

HELEB
(*Fatness*)
1 MAN/1 REFERENCE
One of King David's valiant warriors.
Same as Heled.
2 SAMUEL 23:29

HELED
(*To glide*)
1 MAN/1 REFERENCE
One of King David's valiant warriors.
Same as Heleb.
1 CHRONICLES 11:30

HELEK
(*Portion*)
1 MAN/2 REFERENCES
NUMBERS 26:30

HELEM
(*Dream*)
2 MEN/2 REFERENCES
Same as Heldai.
1 CHRONICLES 7:35; ZECHARIAH 6:14

HELEZ
(*Strength*)
2 MEN/5 REFERENCES
Commander in King David's army overseeing twenty-four thousand men in the seventh month of each year.
2 SAMUEL 23:26; 1 CHRONICLES 2:39

HELI
(*Lofty*)
1 MAN/1 REFERENCE
Father of Jesus' earthly father, Joseph.
LUKE 3:23

HELKAI
(*Apportioned*)
1 MAN/1 REFERENCE
NEHEMIAH 12:15

HELON
(*Strong*)
1 MAN/5 REFERENCES
Helped Moses take a census of his tribe.
NUMBERS 1:9

HEMAM
(*Raging*)
1 MAN/1 REFERENCE
GENESIS 36:22

HEMAN
(*Faithful*)
2 MEN/16 REFERENCES
Notably, wise man mentioned in comparison to Solomon's wisdom. Also, one of the key musicians serving in the Jerusalem temple.
1 KINGS 4:31; 1 CHRONICLES 6:33

HEMATH
(*Walled*)
1 MAN/1 REFERENCE
1 CHRONICLES 2:55

HEMDAN
(*Pleasant*)
1 MAN/1 REFERENCE
GENESIS 36:26

HEN
(*Grace*)
1 MAN/1 REFERENCE
Son of Zephaniah who received a memorial crown in the temple.
ZECHARIAH 6:14

HENADAD
(*Favor of Hadad*)
1 MAN/4 REFERENCES
EZRA 3:9

HENOCH
(*Initiated*)
2 MEN/2 REFERENCES
Notably, same as Enoch. Also, same as Hanoch.
1 CHRONICLES 1:3; 1 CHRONICLES 1:33

HEPHER
(*Shame*)
3 MEN/7 REFERENCES
Most notably, one of King David's valiant warriors.
NUMBERS 26:32; 1 CHRONICLES 4:6; 1 CHRONICLES 11:36

HEPHZIBAH
(*My delight is in her*)
1 WOMAN/1 REFERENCE
Wife of Judah's good king Hezekiah and mother of the evil king Manasseh.
2 KINGS 21:1

HERESH
(*Magical craft*)
1 MAN/1 REFERENCE
1 CHRONICLES 9:15

HERMAS
(*To utter*)
1 MAN/1 REFERENCE
Christian acquaintance of the apostle
Paul, greeted in Paul's letter to the
Romans.
ROMANS 16:14

HERMES
(*To utter*)
1 MAN/1 REFERENCE
Christian acquaintance of the apostle
Paul, greeted in Paul's letter to the
Romans.
ROMANS 16:14

HERMOGENES
(*Born of Hermes*)
1 MAN/1 REFERENCE
Asian Christian who turned away from
Paul.
2 TIMOTHY 1:15

HEROD
(*Heroic*)
4 MEN/44 REFERENCES
Most notably, known as Herod the
Great, evil king of Judea. When
the wise men from the East appeared, looking for the king of the
Jews, Herod feared for his throne
and killed all the male toddlers and
infants in Bethlehem. But Joseph and
his family escaped into Egypt and
returned upon Herod's death. Also,
Herod Antipas, son of Herod the
Great, tetrarch of Galilee and Perea.
He promised to grant any request
to his stepdaughter and sorrow-
fully fulfilled her request—John the
Baptist's head on a plate. Hearing of
Jesus' miracles, he believed John had
returned from the dead. When Pilate
learned that Jesus was from Galilee,
he passed him on to Herod to judge.
Herod mocked Him and dressed
Him in fine clothing. Also, grandson
of Herod the Great who ruled over
the tetrarchy of Philip and Lysanias,
Herod Agrippa I had the apostle
James killed and arrested and also
imprisoned Peter. Also, son of Herod
Agrippa I, Herod Agrippa II. Heard
Paul's case with his sister, Bernice,
with whom he had an incestuous
relationship. Same as Agrippa.
MATTHEW 2:1; MATTHEW 14:1; ACTS
12:1; ACTS 25:13

HERODIAS
(*Heroic*)
1 WOMAN/6 REFERENCES
Granddaughter of Herod the Great
whose second marriage was opposed by John the Baptist. When
Herodias's daughter asked what she
should request from Herod Antipas,
she pushed her to ask for John the
Baptist's head on a plate.
MATTHEW 14:3

HERODION
(*Heroic*)
1 MAN/1 REFERENCE
Relative of the apostle Paul.
ROMANS 16:11

HESED
(*Favor*)
1 MAN/1 REFERENCE
1 KINGS 4:10

HETH
(*Terror*)
1 MAN/14 REFERENCES
GENESIS 10:15

HEZEKI
(*Strong*)
1 MAN/1 REFERENCE
1 CHRONICLES 8:17

HEZEKIAH
(*Strengthened of God*)
3 MEN/128 REFERENCES
Most notably, king of Judah, son of
Ahaz, who did right in God's eyes,
removing pagan worship from the
kingdom and keeping God's commandments. Same as Ezekias.
2 KINGS 16:20; 1 CHRONICLES 3:23;
EZRA 2:16

HEZION
(*Vision*)
1 MAN/1 REFERENCE
1 KINGS 15:18

HEZIR
(*Protected*)
2 MEN/2 REFERENCES
Notably, one of twenty-four priests in
    David's time who was chosen by lot
    to serve in the tabernacle.
1 CHRONICLES 24:15; NEHEMIAH 10:20

HEZRAI
(*Enclosure*)
1 MAN/1 REFERENCE
One of King David's valiant warriors.
    Same as Hezro.
2 SAMUEL 23:35

HEZRO
(*Enclosure*)
1 MAN/1 REFERENCE
One of King David's valiant warriors.
    Same as Hezrai.
1 CHRONICLES 11:37

HEZRON
(*Courtyard*)
2 MEN/16 REFERENCES
GENESIS 46:9; GENESIS 46:12

HIDDAI
1 MAN/1 REFERENCE
One of King David's warriors known
    as the "mighty men."
2 SAMUEL 23:30

HIEL
(*Living of God*)
1 MAN/1 REFERENCE
Rebuilder of Jericho.
1 KINGS 16:34

HILKIAH
(*Portion of God*)
6 MEN/34 REFERENCES
Most notably, high priest during the
    reign of King Josiah of Judah. Also,
    father of the prophet Jeremiah. Also,
    priest and father of Eliakim. Also,
    priest who assisted Ezra in reading
    the book of the law to the people of
    Jerusalem.
2 KINGS 18:18; 2 KINGS 22:4;
    1 CHRONICLES 6:45; 1 CHRONICLES
    26:11; NEHEMIAH 8:4; JEREMIAH 1:1

HILLEL
(*Praising*)
1 MAN/2 REFERENCES
Father of Israel's twelfth judge, Abdon.
JUDGES 12:13

HIRAH
(*Splendor*)
1 MAN/2 REFERENCES
GENESIS 38:1

HIRAM
(*Milk*)
2 MEN/23 REFERENCES
Notably, king of Tyre who provided
    cedar trees and workmen for
    building the temple in Israel.
2 SAMUEL 5:11; 1 KINGS 7:13

HIZKIAH
(*Strengthened of God*)
1 MAN/1 REFERENCE
ZEPHANIAH 1:1

HIZKIJAH
(*Strengthened of God*)
1 MAN/1 REFERENCE
NEHEMIAH 10:17

HOBAB
(*Cherished*)
1 MAN/2 REFERENCES
Father-in-law of Moses. Same as
    Jethro.
NUMBERS 10:29

HOD
(*How?*)
1 MAN/1 REFERENCE
1 CHRONICLES 7:37

HODAIAH
(*Majesty of God*)
1 MAN/1 REFERENCE
1 CHRONICLES 3:24

HODAVIAH
(*Majesty of God*)
3 MEN/3 REFERENCES
Most notably, leader of the half tribe of
    Manasseh.
1 CHRONICLES 5:24; 1 CHRONICLES 9:7;
    EZRA 2:40

HODESH
(*A month*)
1 WOMAN/1 REFERENCE
1 CHRONICLES 8:9

HODEVAH
(*Majesty of God*)
1 MAN/1 REFERENCE
NEHEMIAH 7:43

HODIAH
(*Celebrated*)
1 WOMAN/1 REFERENCE
1 CHRONICLES 4:19

HODIJAH
(*Celebrated*)
2 MEN/5 REFERENCES
Notably, Levite who helped Ezra explain
    the law to exiles returned to Jerusalem.
NEHEMIAH 8:7; NEHEMIAH 10:18

HOGLAH
(*Partridge*)
1 WOMAN/4 REFERENCES
NUMBERS 26:33

HOHAM
1 MAN/1 REFERENCE
Pagan king of Hebron during Joshua's
    conquest of the Promised Land,
    allied with four other rulers
    to attack Gibeon, which had
    deceptively made a peace treaty with
    the Israelites.
JOSHUA 10:3

HOMAM
(*Raging*)
1 MAN/1 REFERENCE
1 CHRONICLES 1:39

HOPHNI
(*Pugilist*)
1 MAN/5 REFERENCES
Son of the high priest Eli. Hophni
    did not know the Lord, misused
    his priestly office, and disobeyed
    the law.
1 SAMUEL 1:3

HORAM
(*High*)
1 MAN/1 REFERENCE
King of Gezer who was killed, along
    with all of his people, by Joshua's
    army during the conquest of the
    Promised Land.
JOSHUA 10:33

HORI
(*Cave dweller*)
2 MEN/4 REFERENCES
GENESIS 36:22; NUMBERS 13:5

HOSAH
(*Hopeful*)
1 MAN/4 REFERENCES
Levite who was chosen by lot to guard
    the west side of the house of the
    Lord.
1 CHRONICLES 16:38

HOSEA
(*Deliverer*)
1 MAN/3 REFERENCES
Minor prophet told by God to marry a prostitute named Gomer. In the Old Testament book that bears his name, Hosea called God's people away from idolatry and back into an intimate relationship with Him.
HOSEA 1:1

HOSHAIAH
(*God has saved*)
2 MEN/3 REFERENCES
Notably, prince of Judah who participated in the dedication of Jerusalem's rebuilt walls. Also, captain of the Israelite forces and father of Azariah, who refused to believe Jeremiah's warning not to escape into Egypt.
NEHEMIAH 12:32; JEREMIAH 42:1

HOSHAMA
(*Jehovah has heard*)
1 MAN/1 REFERENCE
1 CHRONICLES 3:18

HOSHEA
(*Deliverer*)
4 MEN/11 REFERENCES
Most notably, another name of Joshua, successor to Moses as leader of Israel. Also, leader of the tribe of Ephraim in the days of King David.
DEUTERONOMY 32:44; 2 KINGS 15:30;
   1 CHRONICLES 27:20;
   2 NEHEMIAH 10:23

HOTHAM
(*Seal*)
1 MAN/1 REFERENCE
1 CHRONICLES 7:32

HOTHAN
(*Seal*)
1 MAN/1 REFERENCE
1 CHRONICLES 11:44

HOTHIR
(*He has caused to remain*)
1 MAN/2 REFERENCES
1 CHRONICLES 25:4

HUL
(*Circle*)
1 MAN/2 REFERENCES
GENESIS 10:23

HULDAH
(*Weasel*)
1 WOMAN/2 REFERENCES
Prophetess who spoke to King Josiah's messengers about a coming judgment of God on Judah.
2 KINGS 22:14

HUPHAM
(*Protection*)
1 MAN/1 REFERENCE
NUMBERS 26:39

HUPPAH
(*Canopy*)
1 MAN/1 REFERENCE
One of twenty-four priests in David's time who was chosen by lot to serve in the tabernacle.
1 CHRONICLES 24:13

HUPPIM
(*Canopies*)
1 MAN/3 REFERENCES
GENESIS 46:21

HUR
(*White*)
7 MEN/16 REFERENCES
Most notably, Israelite who held up Moses' hand as the battle against the Amalekites raged so Israel could win. Also, Midianite king killed by the Israelites. Also, father of Caleb, who spied out the land of Canaan.
EXODUS 17:10; EXODUS 31:2; NUMBERS 31:8; 1 KINGS 4:8; 1 CHRONICLES 2:50; 1 CHRONICLES 4:1; NEHEMIAH 3:9

HURAI
(*Linen worker*)
1 MAN/1 REFERENCE
One of King David's valiant warriors.
1 CHRONICLES 11:32

HURAM
(*Whiteness*)
3 MEN/12 REFERENCES
Variation of the name Hiram.
1 CHRONICLES 8:5; 2 CHRONICLES 2:3;
    2 CHRONICLES 4:11

HURI
(*Linen worker*)
1 MAN/1 REFERENCE
1 CHRONICLES 5:14

HUSHAH
(*Haste*)
1 MAN/1 REFERENCE
1 CHRONICLES 4:4

HUSHAI
(*Hasty*)
1 MAN/14 REFERENCES
David's friend who remained in
    Jerusalem when Absalom ousted
    the king from the city.
2 SAMUEL 15:32

HUSHAM
(*Hastily*)
1 MAN/4 REFERENCES
King of Edom.
GENESIS 36:34

HUSHIM
(*Hasters*)
2 MEN/1 WOMAN/4 REFERENCES
One of two wives of a Benjamite
    named Shaharaim. He divorced her
    in favor of other wives in Moab.
GENESIS 46:23; 1 CHRONICLES 7:12;
    1 CHRONICLES 8:8

HUZ
(*Consultation*)
1 MAN/1 REFERENCE
Firstborn son of Nahor, Abraham's
    brother.
GENESIS 22:21

HYMENAEUS
(*Nuptial*)
1 MAN/2 REFERENCES
Man whom Paul accused of blasphemy.
1 TIMOTHY 1:20

—I—

IBHAR
(*Choice*)
1 MAN/3 REFERENCES
Son of King David, born in Jerusalem.
2 SAMUEL 5:15

IBNEIAH
(*Built of God*)
1 MAN/1 REFERENCE
1 CHRONICLES 9:8

IBNIJAH
(*Building of God*)
1 MAN/1 REFERENCE
1 CHRONICLES 9:8

IBRI
(*Eberite [Hebrew]*)
1 MAN/1 REFERENCE
Levite worship leader during David's
    reign. Lots were cast to determine
    his duties.
1 CHRONICLES 24:27

IBZAN
(*Splendid*)
1 MAN/2 REFERENCES
Tenth judge of Israel, who led the
    nation for seven years.
JUDGES 12:8

I-CHABOD
(*There is no glory*)
1 MAN/2 REFERENCES
1 SAMUEL 4:21

IDBASH
(*Honeyed*)
1 MAN/1 REFERENCE
1 CHRONICLES 4:3

IDDO

(*Timely, appointed*)

7 MEN/14 REFERENCES

Most notably, leader of the half tribe of Manasseh in the days of King David. Also, prophet who recorded the acts of kings Solomon, Rehoboam, and Abijah.

1 KINGS 4:14; 1 CHRONICLES 6:21; 1 CHRONICLES 27:21; 2 CHRONICLES 9:29; EZRA 5:1; EZRA 8:17; NEHEMIAH 12:4

IGAL

(*Avenger*)

2 MEN/2 REFERENCES

Notably, one of twelve spies sent by Moses to spy out the land of Canaan. Also, one of King David's warriors known as the "mighty men."

NUMBERS 13:7; 2 SAMUEL 23:36

IGDALIAH

(*Magnified of God*)

1 MAN/1 REFERENCE

JEREMIAH 35:4

IGEAL

(*Avenger*)

1 MAN/1 REFERENCE

1 CHRONICLES 3:22

IKKESH

(*Perverse*)

1 MAN/3 REFERENCES

2 SAMUEL 23:36

ILAI

(*Elevated*)

1 MAN/1 REFERENCE

1 CHRONICLES 11:29

IMLA

(*Full*)

1 MAN/2 REFERENCES

Father of Micaiah, prophet in the time of Israel's king Ahab. Same as Imlah.

2 CHRONICLES 18:7

IMLAH

(*Full*)

1 MAN/2 REFERENCES

Father of Micaiah, a prophet in the time of Israel's king Ahab. Same as Imla.

1 KINGS 22:8

IMMANUEL

(*With us is God*)

1 MAN/2 REFERENCES

Prophetic name for a child promised to King Ahaz of Judah. Various Old Testament–era children have been identified as the fulfillment, but this most clearly prophesies the coming of Jesus.

ISAIAH 7:14

IMMER

(*Talkative*)

5 MEN/10 REFERENCES

Most notably, one of twenty-four priests in David's time who was chosen by lot to serve in the tabernacle.

1 CHRONICLES 9:12; 1 CHRONICLES 24:14; EZRA 2:59; NEHEMIAH 3:29; JEREMIAH 20:1

IMNA

(*He will restrain*)

1 MAN/1 REFERENCE

1 CHRONICLES 7:35

IMNAH

(*Prosperity*)

2 MEN/2 REFERENCES

1 CHRONICLES 7:30; 2 CHRONICLES 31:14

IMRAH

(*Interchange*)

1 MAN/1 REFERENCE

1 CHRONICLES 7:36

IMRI

(*Force*)

2 MEN/2 REFERENCES

1 CHRONICLES 9:4; NEHEMIAH 3:2

IPHEDEIAH
(*God will liberate*)
1 MAN/1 REFERENCE
1 CHRONICLES 8:25

IR
(*City*)
1 MAN/1 REFERENCE
1 CHRONICLES 7:12

IRA
(*Wakefulness*)
3 MEN/6 REFERENCES
Most notably, royal official serving
   under Israel's king David. Also,
   commander in King David's army
   overseeing twenty-four thousand
   men in the sixth month of each year.
2 SAMUEL 20:26; 2 SAMUEL 23:26;
   2 SAMUEL 23:28

IRAD
(*Fugitive*)
1 MAN/2 REFERENCES
GENESIS 4:18

IRAM
1 MAN/2 REFERENCES
(*City-wise*)
"Duke of Edom," leader in the family
   line of Esau.
GENESIS 36:43

IRI
(*Urbane*)
1 MAN/1 REFERENCE
1 CHRONICLES 7:7

IRIJAH
(*Fearful of God*)
1 MAN/2 REFERENCES
Sentry who seized the prophet
   Jeremiah, accusing him of deserting
   to the Chaldeans.
JEREMIAH 37:13

IRNAHASH
(*City of a serpent*)
1 MAN/1 REFERENCE
1 CHRONICLES 4:12

IRU
(*City-wise*)
1 MAN/1 REFERENCE
1 CHRONICLES 4:15

ISAAC
(*Laughter*)
1 MAN/132 REFERENCES
Son of Abraham and Sarah whom
   God promised to the long-barren
   couple. Almost sacrificed by his
   father but saved by God when it
   was evident Abraham would fully
   obey His command. Husband of
   Rebekah, and father of two sons,
   Esau and Jacob.
GENESIS 17:19

ISAIAH
(*God has saved*)
1 MAN/32 REFERENCES
Aristocratic prophet of Jerusalem who
   warned against making treaties
   with foreign nations. Isaiah married
   a prophetess and had at least two
   children. Same as Esaias.
2 KINGS 19:2

ISCAH
(*Observant*)
1 WOMAN/1 REFERENCE
GENESIS 11:29

ISCARIOT
(*Inhabitant of Kerioth*)
1 MAN/11 REFERENCES
Name identifying Judas, the disciple
   who betrayed Jesus. Same as Judas.
MATTHEW 10:4

ISHBAH
(*He will praise*)
1 MAN/1 REFERENCE
1 CHRONICLES 4:17

ISHBAK
(*He will leave*)
1 MAN/2 REFERENCES
A son of Abraham by his second wife,
   Keturah.
GENESIS 25:2

ISHBI-BENOB

(*His dwelling is in Nob*)

1 MAN/1 REFERENCE

Philistine giant who planned to kill
King David in battle but was felled
by David's soldier Abishai.

2 SAMUEL 21:16

ISH-BOSHETH

(*Man of shame*)

1 MAN/12 REFERENCES

King Saul's son who was made king
over Israel by Abner, captain of
Saul's army.

2 SAMUEL 2:8

ISHI

(*Saving*)

4 MEN/5 REFERENCES

1 CHRONICLES 2:31; 1 CHRONICLES 4:20;
1 CHRONICLES 4:42; 1 CHRONICLES 5:24

ISHIAH

(*God will lend*)

1 MAN/1 REFERENCE

1 CHRONICLES 7:3

ISHIJAH

(*God will lend*)

1 MAN/1 REFERENCE

EZRA 10:31

ISHMA

(*Desolate*)

1 MAN/1 REFERENCE

1 CHRONICLES 4:3

ISHMAEL

(*God will hear*)

6 MEN/48 REFERENCES

Most notably, son of Hagar, Sarai's
maid, and Abram, born after Sarai
encouraged her husband to have a
child with her maid. God rejected
Ishmael, who was not the son of
His covenant promise, but He
promised to bless Ishmael and make
him fruitful so he would found a
great nation. Also, official who ruled
over the household of Judah's King
Jehoshaphat.

GENESIS 16:11; 2 KINGS 25:23;
1 CHRONICLES 8:38; 2 CHRONICLES
19:11; 2 CHRONICLES 23:1; EZRA 10:22

ISHMAIAH

(*God will hear*)

1 MAN/1 REFERENCE

Leader of the tribe of Zebulun in the
days of King David.

1 CHRONICLES 27:19

ISHMERAI

(*Preservative*)

1 MAN/1 REFERENCE

1 CHRONICLES 8:18

ISHOD

(*Man of renown*)

1 MAN/1 REFERENCE

1 CHRONICLES 7:18

ISHPAN

(*He will hide*)

1 MAN/1 REFERENCE

1 CHRONICLES 8:22

ISHUAH

(*He will level*)

1 MAN/1 REFERENCE

GENESIS 46:17

ISHUAI

(*Level*)

1 MAN/1 REFERENCE

1 CHRONICLES 7:30

ISHUI

(*Level*)

1 MAN/1 REFERENCE

One of three sons of Israel's king
    Saul. Ishui and his brothers died
    with Saul in a battle against the
    Philistines on Mount Gilboa. Same
    as Abinadab.

1 SAMUEL 14:49

ISMACHIAH

(*God will sustain*)

1 MAN/1 REFERENCE

Temple overseer of offerings during the
    reign of King Hezekiah of Judah.

2 CHRONICLES 31:13

ISMAIAH

(*God will hear*)

1 MAN/1 REFERENCE

One of King David's warriors known
    as the "mighty men." Part of an elite
    group called "the thirty."

1 CHRONICLES 12:4

ISPAH

(*He will scratch*)

1 MAN/1 REFERENCE

1 CHRONICLES 8:16

ISRAEL

(*He will rule as God*)

1 MAN/55 REFERENCES

Name given to Jacob by God when
    he wrestled with Him at Peniel.
    Later God again appeared to Jacob,
    confirmed His covenant promises,
    and blessed him. Of his twelve
    sons, Israel loved Joseph more
    than the others, gave him a coat of
    many colors to show his preferred
    status, and put him in a position of
    authority. Israel blessed Joseph's sons,
    Ephraim and Manasseh, taking them
    as his own sons. Same as Jacob.

GENESIS 32:28

ISSACHAR

(*He will bring a reward*)

2 MEN/8 REFERENCES

Notably, Leah and Jacob's fifth son
    and Jacob's ninth son. His mother
    saw him as God's payment to her
    because she gave her servant Zilpah
    to Jacob.

GENESIS 30:18; 1 CHRONICLES 26:5

ISSHIAH

(*God will lend*)

2 MEN/3 REFERENCES

Notably, Levite worship leader during
    David's reign.

1 CHRONICLES 24:21; 1 CHRONICLES 24:25

ISUAH

(*Level*)

1 MAN/1 REFERENCE

1 CHRONICLES 7:30

ISUI

(*Level*)

1 MAN/1 REFERENCE

GENESIS 46:17

ITHAI

(*Near*)

1 MAN/1 REFERENCE

1 CHRONICLES 11:31

ITHAMAR

(*Coast of the palm tree*)

1 MAN/21 REFERENCES

Son of Aaron and his wife, Elisheba,
    who served as a priest. Moses
    became angry at Ithamar because
    he would not eat the sin offering in
    the tabernacle.

EXODUS 6:23

ITHIEL

(*God has arrived*)

2 MEN/3 REFERENCES

Notably, man to whom Agur spoke the
    words of Proverbs 30.

NEHEMIAH 11:7; PROVERBS 30:1

ITHMAH
(*Orphanage*)
1 MAN/1 REFERENCE
One of King David's valiant warriors.
1 CHRONICLES 11:46

ITHRA
(*Excellence*)
1 MAN/1 REFERENCE
2 SAMUEL 17:25

ITHRAN
(*Excellent*)
2 MEN/3 REFERENCES
GENESIS 36:26; 1 CHRONICLES 7:37

ITHREAM
(*Excellence of people*)
1 MAN/2 REFERENCES
Sixth son of David, born to his wife
Eglah in Hebron.
2 SAMUEL 3:5

ITTAI
(*Near*)
2 MEN/8 REFERENCES
Notably, Gittite who remained faithful
to David when Absalom tried to
overthrow the king. David set Ittai
over a third of the people who
followed him out of Jerusalem. Also,
one of King David's warriors known
as the "mighty men."
2 SAMUEL 15:19; 2 SAMUEL 23:29

IZEHAR
(*Anointing*)
1 MAN/1 REFERENCE
NUMBERS 3:19

IZHAR
(*Anointing*)
1 MAN/8 REFERENCES
EXODUS 6:18

IZRAHIAH
(*God will shine*)
1 MAN/2 REFERENCES
1 CHRONICLES 7:3

IZRI
(*Trough*)
1 MAN/1 REFERENCE
One of twenty-four Levite musicians
who was chosen by lot to serve in
the house of the Lord.
1 CHRONICLES 25:11

—J—

JAAKAN
(*To twist*)
1 MAN/1 REFERENCE
DEUTERONOMY 10:6

JAAKOBAH
(*Heel catcher*)
1 MAN/1 REFERENCE
1 CHRONICLES 4:36

JAALA
(*Roe*)
1 MAN/1 REFERENCE
Same as Jaalah.
NEHEMIAH 7:58

JAALAH
(*Roe*)
1 MAN/1 REFERENCE
Same as Jaala.
EZRA 2:56

JAALAM
(*Occult*)
1 MAN/4 REFERENCES
Son of Esau.
GENESIS 36:5

JAANAI
(*Responsive*)
1 MAN/1 REFERENCE
1 CHRONICLES 5:12

JAARE-OREGIM
(*Woods of weavers*)
1 MAN/1 REFERENCE
Father of Elhanan. Same as Jair.
2 SAMUEL 21:19

JAASAU
(*They will do*)
1 MAN/1 REFERENCE
EZRA 10:37

JAASIEL
(*Made of God*)
1 MAN/1 REFERENCE
Leader of the tribe of Benjamin in the
days of King David.
1 CHRONICLES 27:21

JAAZANIAH
(*Heard of God*)
4 MEN/4 REFERENCES
Most notably, captain of the army of
Judah under Nebuchadnezzar's
governor, Gedaliah. Also called
Jezaniah. Also, prince of Judah
whom God described as devising
mischief and giving wicked counsel.
2 KINGS 25:23; JEREMIAH 35:3; EZEKIEL
8:11; EZEKIEL 11:1

JAAZIAH
(*Emboldened of God*)
1 MEN/2 REFERENCES
Levite worship leader during David's
reign. Lots were cast to determine
his duties.
1 CHRONICLES 24:26

JAAZIEL
(*Emboldened of God*)
1 MAN/1 REFERENCE
Levite musician who performed in
celebration when King David
brought the ark of the covenant to
Jerusalem. Same as Aziel.
1 CHRONICLES 15:18

JABAL
(*Stream*)
1 MAN/1 REFERENCE
GENESIS 4:20

JABESH
(*Dry*)
1 MAN/3 REFERENCES
2 KINGS 15:10

JABEZ
(*To grieve*)
1 MAN/3 REFERENCES
Pious man of the line of Judah who
prayed for God's blessing, that He
would enlarge his border, and that
God's hand would be with him and
keep him from harm.
1 CHRONICLES 4:9

JABIN
(*Intelligent*)
2 MEN/8 REFERENCES
Notably, king of Hazor who raised
armies against Joshua and his
invading troops. Also, king of
Canaan who had Sisera as the
captain of his army.
JOSHUA 11:1; JUDGES 4:2

JACHAN
(*Troublesome*)
1 MAN/1 REFERENCE
1 CHRONICLES 5:13

JACHIN
(*He will establish*)
3 MEN/6 REFERENCES
Most notably, one of twenty-four
priests in David's time who was
chosen by lot to serve in the
tabernacle.
GENESIS 46:10; 1 CHRONICLES 9:10;
1 CHRONICLES 24:17

JACOB
(*Supplanter*)
2 MEN/280 REFERENCES
Notably, Isaac and Rebekah's son and
twin brother of Esau who exchanged
a bowl of stew for his brother's birthright. He also gained Isaac's blessing
by deception. God promised him
many descendants and blessed the
earth through them. Jacob married
Laban's daughters, Leah and Rachel.
From them and their handmaids,
Jacob had twelve sons, the founders
of Israel's twelve tribes. He met God,
wrestled with Him, and was renamed
Israel. Same as Israel.
GENESIS 25:26; MATTHEW 1:15

JADA
(*Knowing*)
1 MAN/2 REFERENCES
1 CHRONICLES 2:28

JADAU
(*Praised*)
1 MAN/1 REFERENCE
EZRA 10:43

JADDUA
(*Knowing*)
2 MEN/3 REFERENCES
NEHEMIAH 10:21; NEHEMIAH 12:11

JADON
(*Thankful*)
1 MAN/1 REFERENCE
NEHEMIAH 3:7

JAEL
(*Ibex*)
1 WOMAN/6 REFERENCES
Wife of Heber the Kenite who killed
    the Canaanite commander Sisera
    when he fled to her tent following
    his defeat by the Israelites.
JUDGES 4:17

JAHATH
(*Unity*)
5 MEN/8 REFERENCES
Most notably, Levite worship leader
    during David's reign. Also, Levite
    worship leader who oversaw the
    repair of the temple under King
    Josiah.
1 CHRONICLES 4:2; 1 CHRONICLES 6:20;
    1 CHRONICLES 23:10; 1 CHRONICLES
    24:22; 2 CHRONICLES 34:12

JAHAZIAH
(*God will behold*)
1 MAN/1 REFERENCE
Man who oversaw the Israelites
    who needed to put away "strange"
    (foreign) wives under Ezra.
EZRA 10:15

JAHAZIEL
(*Beheld of God*)
5 MEN/6 REFERENCES
Most notably, a "mighty man" of
    King David. Also, priest who blew
    a trumpet when David brought
    the ark of the Lord to Jerusalem.
    Also, Levite worship leader who
    prophesied before King Jehoshaphat
    of Judah when Edom attacked.
1 CHRONICLES 12:4; 1 CHRONICLES 16:6;
    1 CHRONICLES 23:19; 2 CHRONICLES
    20:14; EZRA 8:5

JAHDAI
(*Jehovah fired*)
1 MAN/1 REFERENCE
1 CHRONICLES 2:47

JAHDIEL
(*Unity of God*)
1 MAN/1 REFERENCE
One of the men leading the half tribe
    of Manasseh.
1 CHRONICLES 5:24

JAHDO
(*His unity, together*)
1 MAN/1 REFERENCE
1 CHRONICLES 5:14

JAHLEEL
(*Wait for God*)
1 MAN/2 REFERENCES
GENESIS 46:14

JAHMAI
(*Hot*)
1 MAN/1 REFERENCE
1 CHRONICLES 7:2

JAHZEEL
(*God will allot*)
1 MAN/2 REFERENCES
Same as Jahziel.
GENESIS 46:24

JAHZERAH
(*Protection*)
1 MAN/1 REFERENCE
1 CHRONICLES 9:12

JAHZIEL
(Allotted of God)
1 MAN/1 REFERENCE
Same as Jahzeel.
1 CHRONICLES 7:13

JAIR
(Enlightener)
4 MEN/9 REFERENCES
Most notably, descendant of Manasseh who captured twenty-three cities of Bashan and named them Havvoth-jair. Also, the eighth judge of Israel, who led the nation for twenty-two years and is known for having thirty sons who rode thirty donkeys.
NUMBERS 32:41; JUDGES 10:3; 1 CHRONICLES 20:5; ESTHER 2:5

JAIRUS
(Enlightener)
1 MAN/2 REFERENCES
Synagogue ruler who asked Jesus to come and heal his daughter. She died before they could reach her, but Jesus brought her back to life.
MARK 5:22

JAKAN
(Tortuous)
1 MAN/1 REFERENCE
Same as Akan or Jaakan.
1 CHRONICLES 1:42

JAKEH
(Obedient)
1 MAN/1 REFERENCE
PROVERBS 30:1

JAKIM
(He will raise)
2 MEN/2 REFERENCES
Most notably, one of twenty-four priests in David's time who was chosen by lot to serve in the tabernacle.
1 CHRONICLES 8:19; 1 CHRONICLES 24:12

JALON
(Lodging)
1 MAN/1 REFERENCE
1 CHRONICLES 4:17

JAMBRES
1 MAN/1 REFERENCE
Opponent of Moses mentioned by the apostle Paul as an example of apostasy.
2 TIMOTHY 3:8

JAMES
3 MEN/42 REFERENCES
Most notably, Jesus' brother, called James the less (younger) who became a leader in the Jerusalem church, and believed by many to be the writer of the book of James in the New Testament. Also, Zebedee's son and John's brother, a fisherman called by Jesus to become a fisher of men as one of His disciples, and years later, executed by Herod Agrippa I. Also, son of Alphaeus and disciple of Jesus.
MATTHEW 4:21; MATTHEW 10:3; MATTHEW 13:55

JAMIN
(Right hand)
3 MEN/6 REFERENCES
Most notably, Levite who helped Ezra to explain the law to exiles who returned to Jerusalem.
GENESIS 46:10; 1 CHRONICLES 2:27; NEHEMIAH 8:7

JAMLECH
(He will make king)
1 MAN/1 REFERENCE
1 CHRONICLES 4:34

JANNA
(Oppressor)
1 MAN/1 REFERENCE
Forebear of Jesus' earthly father, Joseph.
LUKE 3:24

JANNES

(*To cure*)

1 MAN/1 REFERENCE

Opponent of Moses mentioned by
the apostle Paul as an example of
apostasy.

2 TIMOTHY 3:8

JAPHETH

(*Expansion*)

1 MAN/11 REFERENCES

Noah's third son, who joined his family
in the ark.

GENESIS 5:32

JAPHIA

(*Bright*)

2 MEN/4 REFERENCES

Notably, king of Lachish during
Joshua's conquest of the Promised
Land who allied with four other
rulers to attack Gibeon, which had
deceptively made a peace treaty
with the Israelites. Also, son of King
David, born in Jerusalem.

JOSHUA 10:3; 2 SAMUEL 5:15

JAPHLET

(*He will deliver*)

1 MAN/3 REFERENCES

1 CHRONICLES 7:32

JARAH

(*Honey in the comb*)

1 MAN/2 REFERENCES

Same as Jehoadah.

1 CHRONICLES 9:42

JAREB

(*He will contend*)

1 MAN/2 REFERENCES

Assyrian king mentioned in the
prophecies of Hosea.

HOSEA 5:13

JARED

(*A descent*)

1 MAN/6 REFERENCES

Second-longest-lived individual in the
Bible at 962 years. Same as Jered.

GENESIS 5:15

JARESIAH

(*Uncertain*)

1 MAN/1 REFERENCES

1 CHRONICLES 8:27

JARHA

1 MAN/2 REFERENCES

Egyptian servant of Sheshan,
descendant of Abraham through
Jacob's son Judah.

1 CHRONICLES 2:34

JARIB

(*He will contend*)

3 MEN/3 REFERENCES

1 CHRONICLES 4:24; EZRA 8:16;
  EZRA 10:18

JAROAH

(*Born at the new moon*)

1 MAN/1 REFERENCE

1 CHRONICLES 5:14

JASHEN

(*Sleepy*)

1 MAN/1 REFERENCE

2 SAMUEL 23:32

JASHOBEAM

(*People will return*)

2 MEN/3 REFERENCES

Notably, commander in King David's
army, overseeing twenty-four
thousand men in the first month of
each year. One of David's "mighty
men," who once single-handedly
killed three hundred enemy soldiers.

1 CHRONICLES 11:11; 1 CHRONICLES 12:6

JASHUB

(*He will return*)

2 MEN/3 REFERENCES

Notably, descendant of Abraham
through Jacob's son Issachar. Same
as Job.

NUMBERS 26:24; EZRA 10:29

JASHUBI-LEHEM

(*Returner of bread*)

1 MAN/1 REFERENCE

1 CHRONICLES 4:22

JASIEL
(*Made of God*)
1 MAN/1 REFERENCE
One of King David's valiant warriors.
1 CHRONICLES 11:47

JASON
(*About to cure*)
2 MEN/5 REFERENCES
Notably, Christian from Thessalonica who was taken along with other Christians by jealous Jews to the city officials. Also, relative of Paul, living in Rome, who was greeted in the apostle's letter to the Romans.
ACTS 17:5; ROMANS 16:21

JATHNIEL
(*Continued of God*)
1 MAN/1 REFERENCE
1 CHRONICLES 26:2

JAVAN
(*Effervescing*)
1 MAN/4 REFERENCES
Grandson of Noah through his son Japheth.
GENESIS 10:2

JAZIZ
(*He will make prominent*)
1 MAN/1 REFERENCE
Called Jaziz the Hagarite, in charge of King David's flocks.
1 CHRONICLES 27:31

JEATERAI
(*Stepping*)
1 MAN/1 REFERENCE
1 CHRONICLES 6:21

JEBERECHIAH
(*Blessed of God*)
1 MAN/1 REFERENCE
ISAIAH 8:2

JECAMIAH
(*God will rise*)
1 MAN/1 REFERENCE
Descendant of Abraham through Jacob's son Judah, in the line of the nation of Judah's second-to-last king, Jeconiah (also known as Jehoiachin). Same as Jekamiah.
1 CHRONICLES 3:18

JECHOLIAH
(*Jehovah will enable*)
1 WOMAN/1 REFERENCE
Mother of Judah's good king Azariah, also known as Uzziah. Same as Jecoliah.
2 KINGS 15:2

JECHONIAS
(*Jehovah will establish*)
1 MAN/2 REFERENCES
Greek form of the name *Jeconiah*, used in the New Testament.
MATTHEW 1:11

JECOLIAH
(*God will enable*)
1 WOMAN/1 REFERENCE
Mother of Judah's good king Uzziah, also known as Azariah. Same as Jecholiah.
2 CHRONICLES 26:3

JECONIAH
(*God will establish*)
1 MAN/7 REFERENCES
King of Judah and son of King Jehoiakim, carried to Babylon along with his nobles by King Nebuchadnezzar. Same as Coniah, Jechonias, and Jehoiachin.
1 CHRONICLES 3:16

JEDAIAH
(*Praised of God*)
5 MEN/13 REFERENCES
Most notably, rebuilder of the walls of Jerusalem under Nehemiah. Also, one of twenty-four priests in David's time who was chosen by lot to serve in the tabernacle.
1 CHRONICLES 4:37; 1 CHRONICLES 9:10; NEHEMIAH 3:10; NEHEMIAH 11:10; NEHEMIAH 12:7

JEDIAEL
(*Knowing God*)
4 MEN/6 REFERENCES
Most notably, one of King David's valiant warriors. Also, captain of thousands for the tribe of Manasseh, which supported David against Saul.
1 CHRONICLES 7:6; 1 CHRONICLES 11:45; 1 CHRONICLES 12:20; 1 CHRONICLES 26:2

JEDIDAH
(*Beloved*)
1 WOMAN/1 REFERENCE
Mother of Judah's good king Josiah.
2 KINGS 22:1

JEDIDIAH
(*Beloved of God*)
1 MAN/1 REFERENCE
God's special name for Solomon, as delivered by the prophet Nathan.
2 SAMUEL 12:25

JEDUTHUN
(*Laudatory*)
1 MAN/17 REFERENCES
Descendant of Abraham through Jacob's son Levi. One of the key musicians serving in the Jerusalem temple.
1 CHRONICLES 9:16

JEEZER
(*Helpless*)
1 MAN/1 REFERENCE
Descendant of Joseph's son Manasseh and son of Gilead.
NUMBERS 26:30

JEHALELEEL
(*Praising God*)
1 MAN/1 REFERENCE
1 CHRONICLES 4:16

JEHALELEL
(*Praising God*)
1 MAN/1 REFERENCE
2 CHRONICLES 29:12

JEHDEIAH
(*Unity of God*)
2 MEN/2 REFERENCES
Notably, official responsible for King David's herds of donkeys.
1 CHRONICLES 24:20; 1 CHRONICLES 27:30

JEHEZEKEL
(*God will strengthen*)
1 MAN/1 REFERENCE
One of twenty-four priests in David's time, chosen by lot to serve in the tabernacle.
1 CHRONICLES 24:16

JEHIAH
(*God will live*)
1 MAN/1 REFERENCE
A doorkeeper of the ark of the covenant under King David.
1 CHRONICLES 15:24

JEHIEL
(*God will live*)
13 MEN/16 REFERENCES
Most notably, Levite musician who performed in celebration when King David brought the ark of the covenant to Jerusalem. Also, leader of the Gershonites who cared for the precious stones donated for Solomon's temple. Also, tutor to King David's sons. Also, one of King David's valiant warriors.
1 CHRONICLES 9:35 1 CHRONICLES 11:44 1 CHRONICLES 15:18; 1 CHRONICLES 23:8; 1 CHRONICLES 27:32; 2 CHRONICLES 21:2; 2 CHRONICLES 29:14; 2 CHRONICLES 31:13; 2 CHRONICLES 35:8; EZRA 8:9; EZRA 10:2; EZRA 10:21; EZRA 10:26

JEHIELI
(*God will live*)
1 MAN/2 REFERENCES
Levite whose sons were in charge of
the temple treasury.
1 CHRONICLES 26:21

JEHIZKIAH
(*Strengthened of God*)
1 MAN/1 REFERENCE
Man of the tribe of Ephraim who
counseled his nation of Israel
against enslaving fellow Jews from
Judah who were captured in a civil
war. Helped feed and clothe the
prisoners before sending them
home.
2 CHRONICLES 28:12

JEHOADAH
(*Jehovah adorned*)
1 MAN/2 REFERENCES
Descendant of Abraham through
Jacob's son Benjamin, through
the line of King Saul and his son
Jonathan. Same as Jarah.
1 CHRONICLES 8:36

JEHOADDAN
(*Jehovah pleased*)
1 WOMAN/2 REFERENCES
Mother of Amaziah, king of Judah.
2 KINGS 14:2

JEHOAHAZ
(*Jehovah seized*)
3 MEN/23 REFERENCES
Most notably, king of Israel and son of
King Jehu, doing evil in God's sight.
Also, king of Judah, son of King
Josiah. Evil king who reigned only
three months. Same as Shallum.
2 KINGS 10:35; 2 KINGS 23:30;
2 CHRONICLES 21:17

JEHOASH
(*Jehovah fired*)
2 MEN/17 REFERENCES
Another name for Joash. Also, evil
king of Israel, son of King Jehoahaz.
Fought King Amaziah of Judah,
broke down Jerusalem's wall, and
took gold and silver from the temple
and the king.
2 KINGS 11:21; 2 KINGS 13:10

JEHOHANAN
(*Jehovah favored*)
6 MEN/6 REFERENCES
Most notably, military captain of
Judah who stood next to Adnah,
the commander. Also, priest who
helped to dedicate the rebuilt wall of
Jerusalem by giving thanks.
1 CHRONICLES 26:3; 2 CHRONICLES 17:15;
2 CHRONICLES 23:1; EZRA 10:28;
NEHEMIAH 12:13; NEHEMIAH 12:42

JEHOIACHIN
(*Jehovah will establish*)
1 MAN/10 REFERENCES
King of Judah and son of King Jehoiakim, this evil king reigned only three
months before King Nebuchadnezzar of Babylon carried him and the
best of his people to Babylon. In the
thirty-seventh year of Jehoiachin's
captivity, King Evil-merodach
brought him out of prison and gave
him preferential treatment. Same as
Coniah, Jeconiah, and Jeconias.
2 KINGS 24:6

JEHOIADA
(*Jehovah known*)
6 MEN/52 REFERENCES
Most notably, father of Benaiah,
commander in King David's army,
who also served Solomon. Also,
high priest who made a covenant
with the army's leaders to protect
young King Joash.
2 SAMUEL 8:18; 2 KINGS 11:4;
1 CHRONICLES 12:27; 1 CHRONICLES
27:34; NEHEMIAH 3:6; JEREMIAH 29:26

JEHOIAKIM

(*Jehovah will raise*)

I MAN/37 REFERENCES

Originally named Eliakim, Egyptian
pharaoh Necho made him king of
Judah and changed his name to
Jehoiakim. Jehoiakim rebelled, and
when Jeremiah's prophetic warning
words were read to this wicked
king, he burned the scroll they were
written on. Same as Eliakim.

2 KINGS 23:34

JEHOIARIB

(*Jehovah will contend*)

2 MEN/2 REFERENCES

Notably, priest who returned to
Jerusalem after the Babylonian
captivity. Also, one of twenty-
four priests of David's time who
was chosen by lot to serve in the
tabernacle.

I CHRONICLES 9:10; I CHRONICLES 24:7

JEHONADAB

(*Jehovah largessed*)

I MAN/3 REFERENCES

A Rechabite known for spiritual
austerity. Saw destruction of
the temple of Baal, with all the
worshippers in it.

2 KINGS 10:15

JEHONATHAN

(*Jehovah given*)

3 MEN/3 REFERENCES

Most notably, official in charge of King
David's storehouses. Also, Levite
sent by King Jehoshaphat to teach
the law of the Lord throughout the
nation of Judah.

I CHRONICLES 27:25; 2 CHRONICLES 17:8;
NEHEMIAH 12:18

JEHORAM

(*Jehovah raised*)

3 MEN/23 REFERENCES

Most notably, firstborn son of King
Jehoshaphat of Judah. He led his
nation into idolatry. Same as Joram.
Also, king of Israel who did not stop
his nation from worshipping idols.
Also, priest who taught the law of
the Lord throughout Judah.

I KINGS 22:50; 2 KINGS 1:17;
2 CHRONICLES 17:8

JEHOSHABEATH

(*Jehovah sworn*)

I WOMAN/2 REFERENCES

Daughter of Judah's king Jehoram and
sister of Judah's king Ahaziah. After
Ahaziah was killed, Jehoshabeath
saved her infant nephew, Joash,
from a family massacre engineered
by Ahaziah's mother, Athaliah, who
wanted to make herself queen. Same
as Hehosheba.

2 CHRONICLES 22:11

JEHOSHAPHAT

(*Jehovah judged*)

5 MEN/83 REFERENCES

Most notably, official in King David's
court who was his recorder. Also,
king of Judah who inherited the
throne from his father, Asa. Also,
one of King Solomon's twelve
officials over provisions. Also, father
of Jehu, king of Israel.

2 SAMUEL 8:16; I KINGS 4:17;
I KINGS 15:24; 2 KINGS 9:2;
I CHRONICLES 15:24

JEHOSHEBA

(*Jehovah sworn*)

I WOMAN/2 REFERENCES

King Joash's aunt, who protected him
from his wicked grandmother
Athaliah. Same as Jehoshabeath.

2 KINGS 11:2

JEHOSHUA
(*Jehovah saved*)
1 MAN/1 REFERENCE
Variant name for Joshua, son of Nun,
  successor to Moses.
NUMBERS 13:16

JEHOSHUAH
(*Jehovah saved*)
1 MAN/1 REFERENCE
Variant name for Joshua, son of Nun,
  successor to Moses.
1 CHRONICLES 7:27

JEHOZABAD
(*Jehovah endowed*)
3 MEN/4 REFERENCES
Most notably, one of two royal officials
  who conspired to kill Judah's king
  Joash. Also, commander in the army
  of King Jehoshaphat of Israel.
2 KINGS 12:21; 1 CHRONICLES 26:4;
  2 CHRONICLES 17:18

JEHOZADAK
(*Jehovah righted*)
1 MAN/2 REFERENCES
1 CHRONICLES 6:14

JEHU
(*Jehovah [is] He*)
5 MEN/59 REFERENCES
Most notably, prophet who prophesied
  the destruction of Baasha, king of
  Israel, and Baasha's heirs. Also, king
  of Israel anointed to destroy King
  Ahab and his dynasty. Also, "mighty
  man" of King David.
1 KINGS 16:1; 1 KINGS 19:16;
  1 CHRONICLES 2:38; 1 CHRONICLES
  4:35; 1 CHRONICLES 12:3

JEHUBBAH
(*Hidden*)
1 MAN/1 REFERENCE
1 CHRONICLES 7:34

JEHUCAL
(*Potent*)
1 MAN/1 REFERENCE
JEREMIAH 37:3

JEHUDI
(*Descendant of Jehudah*)
1 MAN/4 REFERENCES
JEREMIAH 36:14

JEHUDIJAH
(*Female descendant of Jehudah*)
1 WOMAN/1 REFERENCE
Wife of Ezra.
1 CHRONICLES 4:18

JEHUSH
(*Hasty*)
1 MAN/1 REFERENCE
1 CHRONICLES 8:39

JEIEL
(*Carried away of God*)
8 MEN/11 REFERENCES
Most notably, Levite worship leader
  who played a harp as the ark of
  the covenant was brought into
  Jerusalem.
1 CHRONICLES 5:7; 1 CHRONICLES 15:18;
  2 CHRONICLES 20:14; 2 CHRONICLES
  26:11; 2 CHRONICLES 29:13;
  2 CHRONICLES 35:9; EZRA 8:13;
  EZRA 10:43

JEKAMEAM
(*The people will rise*)
1 MAN/2 REFERENCES
1 CHRONICLES 23:19

JEKAMIAH
(*God will rise*)
1 MAN/2 REFERENCES
Same as Jecamiah.
1 CHRONICLES 2:41

JEKUTHIEL
(*Obedience of God*)
1 MAN/1 REFERENCE
1 CHRONICLES 4:18

JEMIMA
(*Dove*)
1 WOMAN/1 REFERENCE
Oldest daughter of Job, born after God
  restored his fortunes.
JOB 42:14

JEMUEL
(*Day of God*)
1 MAN/2 REFERENCES
Same as Nemuel.
GENESIS 46:10

JEPHTHAE
(*He will open*)
1 MAN/1 REFERENCE
Greek form of the name *Jephthah*, used
in the New Testament.
HEBREWS 11:32

JEPHTHAH
(*He will open*)
1 MAN/29 REFERENCES
Eighth judge of Israel who promised
God that he would give Him
whatever greeted him when he
returned home, should he be
victorious in battle. After winning,
his daughter came to greet him.
Following a two-month reprieve,
Jephthah kept his vow. Same as
Jephthae.
JUDGES 11:1

JEPHUNNEH
(*He will be prepared*)
2 MEN/16 REFERENCES
NUMBERS 13:6; 1 CHRONICLES 7:38

JERAH
(*Month*)
1 MAN/2 REFERENCES
GENESIS 10:26

JERAHMEEL
(*God will be compassionate*)
3 MEN/8 REFERENCES
1 CHRONICLES 2:9; 1 CHRONICLES 24:29;
JEREMIAH 36:26

JERED
(*A descent*)
2 MEN/2 REFERENCES
Second-longest-lived individual in the
Bible at 962 years. Same as Jared.
1 CHRONICLES 1:2; 1 CHRONICLES 4:18

JEREMAI
(*Elevated*)
1 MAN/1 REFERENCE
EZRA 10:33

JEREMIAH
(*God will rise*)
7 MEN/146 REFERENCES
Most notably, prophet of Judah
who had gloomy prophecies,
condemning Judah for idolatry and
calling the nation to repentance.
Same as Jeremias and Jeremy. Also,
leader of the half tribe of Manasseh.
Also, one of King David's mightiest
warriors known as "the thirty."
2 KINGS 23:31; 1 CHRONICLES 5:24;
1 CHRONICLES 12:4; 1 CHRONICLES
12:10; 1 CHRONICLES 12:13;
2 CHRONICLES 35:25; NEHEMIAH 10:2

JEREMIAS
(*God will rise*)
1 MAN/1 REFERENCE
Greek form of the name *Jeremiah*, used
in the New Testament. Same as
Jeremiah.
MATTHEW 16:14

JEREMOTH
(*Elevations*)
5 MEN/5 REFERENCES
Most notably, one of twenty-four
Levite musicians who was chosen by
lot to serve in the house of the Lord.
Same as Jerimoth.
1 CHRONICLES 8:14; 1 CHRONICLES 23:23;
1 CHRONICLES 25:22; EZRA 10:26;
EZRA 10:27;

JEREMY
(*God will rise*)
1 MAN/2 REFERENCES
Latin form of the name *Jeremiah*, used
in the New Testament. Same as
Jeremiah.
MATTHEW 2:17

JERIAH
(*God will throw*)
1 MAN/2 REFERENCES
1 CHRONICLES 23:19

JERIBAI
(*Contentious*)
1 MAN/1 REFERENCE
One of King David's valiant warriors.
1 CHRONICLES 11:46

JERIEL
(*Thrown of God*)
1 MAN/1 REFERENCE
1 CHRONICLES 7:2

JERIJAH
1 MAN/1 REFERENCE
Chief of Hebronites whom King David
gave authority over the Reubenites,
Gadites, and half tribe of Manasseh.
1 CHRONICLES 26:31

JERIMOTH
(*Elevations*)
8 MEN/8 REFERENCES
Most notably, "mighty man" who
supported the future king David
during his conflict with Saul. Also,
leader of the tribe of Naphtali in
the days of King David. Same as
Jeremoth.
1 CHRONICLES 7:7; 1 CHRONICLES 7:8;
1 CHRONICLES 12:5; 1 CHRONICLES
24:30; 1 CHRONICLES 25:4;
1 CHRONICLES 27:19; 2 CHRONICLES
11:18; 2 CHRONICLES 31:13

JERIOTH
(*Curtains*)
1 WOMAN/1 REFERENCE
1 CHRONICLES 2:18

JEROBOAM
(*The people will contend*)
2 MEN/104 REFERENCES
Most notably, servant of King Solomon
who had authority over forced
labor for the tribes of Ephraim and
Manasseh and established idolatrous
worship in Israel. Because of his
disobedience, God cut off all the
men of Jeroboam's household. Also,
king of Israel, son of King Joash,
who continued idolatrous worship.
1 KINGS 11:26; 2 KINGS 13:13

JEROHAM
(*Compassionate*)
7 MEN/10 REFERENCES
Most notably, prince of the tribe of
Dan, assigned to rule by King
David.
1 SAMUEL 1:1; 1 CHRONICLES 8:27;
1 CHRONICLES 9:8; 1 CHRONICLES 9:12;
1 CHRONICLES 12:7; 1 CHRONICLES
27:22; 2 CHRONICLES 23:1

JERUBBAAL
(*Baal will contend*)
1 MAN/14 REFERENCES
Name given to Gideon by his father
after he destroyed the altars to Baal.
JUDGES 6:32

JERUBBESHETH
(*Shame will contend*)
1 MAN/1 REFERENCE
Alternative name for the judge Gideon.
2 SAMUEL 11:21

JERUSHA
(*Possessed [married]*)
1 WOMAN/1 REFERENCE
Mother of Jotham, king of Judah.
2 KINGS 15:33

JERUSHAH
(*Possessed [married]*)
1 WOMAN/1 REFERENCE
Variant spelling of *Jerusha*; mother of
King Jotham of Judah.
2 CHRONICLES 27:1

JESAIAH
(*God has saved*)

2 MEN/2 REFERENCES

1 CHRONICLES 3:21; NEHEMIAH 11:7

JESHAIAH
(*God has saved*)

4 MEN/5 REFERENCES

Most notably, Levite worship leader
under King David.

1 CHRONICLES 25:3; 1 CHRONICLES 26:25;
EZRA 8:7; EZRA 8:19

JESHARELAH
(*Right toward God*)

1 MAN/1 REFERENCE

One of twenty-four Levite musicians
in David's time, chosen by lot to
serve in the house of the Lord.

1 CHRONICLES 25:14

JESHEBEAB
(*People will return*)

1 MAN/1 REFERENCE

One of twenty-four priests in David's
time, chosen by lot to serve in the
tabernacle.

1 CHRONICLES 24:13

JESHER
(*The right*)

1 MAN/1 REFERENCE

1 CHRONICLES 2:18

JESHISHAI
(*Aged*)

1 MAN/1 REFERENCE

1 CHRONICLES 5:14

JESHOHAIAH
(*God will empty*)

1 MAN/1 REFERENCE

1 CHRONICLES 4:36

JESHUA
(*He will save*)

9 MEN/29 REFERENCES

Most notably, high priest who returned
from exile with Zerubbabel and
built the temple altar with him.
Also, another form of the name
Joshua.

1 CHRONICLES 24:11; EZRA 2:2; EZRA
2:6; EZRA 2:36; EZRA 8:33; NEHEMIAH
3:19; NEHEMIAH 8:7; NEHEMIAH 8:17;
NEHEMIAH 10:9

JESIAH
(*God will lend*)

2 MEN/2 REFERENCES

Notably, "mighty man" who supported
the future king David during his
conflict with Saul.

1 CHRONICLES 12:6; 1 CHRONICLES 23:20

JESIMIEL
(*God will place*)

1 MAN/1 REFERENCE

1 CHRONICLES 4:36

JESSE
(*Extant*)

1 MAN/47 REFERENCES

Father of David, who had seven sons
pass before the prophet Samuel
before David was brought before
Samuel and anointed king. Jesus'
earthly lineage stems from Jesse,
through David.

RUTH 4:17

JESUI
(*Level*)

1 MAN/1 REFERENCE

NUMBERS 26:44

JESUS
(*Jehovah saved*)
3 MEN/983 REFERENCES
Most notably, God's Son and humanity's Savior, incarnated within
the womb of Mary and born in
Bethlehem. At about age thirty, He
began His ministry, calling twelve
disciples to follow Him. With them,
He traveled through Israel, preaching about God and healing many
people. Later, Judas betrayed Him,
and Jesus, who had done no wrong,
died for humanity's sin on the cross.
Some time later, after His resurrection, He ascended to heaven and
will someday return for those who
believe in Him. He will establish a
New Jerusalem, where He will live
with them forever. Also, another
form of the name *Joshua*.
MATTHEW 1:1; HEBREWS 4:8;
   COLOSSIANS 4:11

JETHER
(*Superiority*)
5 MEN/8 REFERENCES
Most notably, Gideon's son who
fearfully disobeyed when his
father told him to kill Zebah and
Zalmunna.
JUDGES 8:20; 1 KINGS 2:5; 1 CHRONICLES
   2:32; 1 CHRONICLES 4:17;
   1 CHRONICLES 7:38

JETHETH
1 MAN/2 REFERENCES
A "duke of Edom," a leader in the
family line of Esau.
GENESIS 36:40

JETHRO
(*His excellence*)
1 MAN/10 REFERENCES
Moses' father-in-law, for whom Moses
kept flocks until God called him
to Egypt. For a time, Moses' wife,
Zipporah, and her two sons lived
with Jethro. He advised Moses
to appoint those who could help
him rule over the people. Same as
Hobab.
EXODUS 3:1

JETUR
(*Encircled, enclosed*)
1 MAN/2 REFERENCES
GENESIS 25:15

JEUEL
(*Carried away of God*)
1 MAN/1 REFERENCE
Jewish exile from the tribe of Judah
who resettled Jerusalem.
1 CHRONICLES 9:6

JEUSH
(*Hasty*)
4 MEN/8 REFERENCES
Most notably, son of Esau. Also, son
of Judah's king Rehoboam and a
grandson of Solomon.
GENESIS 36:5; 1 CHRONICLES 7:10;
   1 CHRONICLES 23:10;
   2 CHRONICLES 11:19

JEUZ
(*Counselor*)
1 MAN/1 REFERENCE
1 CHRONICLES 8:10

JEZANIAH
(*Heard of God*)
1 MAN/2 REFERENCES
Captain of Israel's forces under
Nebuchadnezzar's governor
Gedaliah. Same as Jaazaniah.
JEREMIAH 40:8

JEZEBEL
(*Chaste*)

1 WOMAN/22 REFERENCES

Sidonian princess who married King
Ahab of Israel, Jezebel persecuted
Israel's prophets, including Elijah,
after he killed the priests of her god
Baal. God ordered Jehu to strike
Jezebel down. Jehu commanded her
slaves to throw her from a window,
and she died.

1 KINGS 16:31

JEZER
(*Form*)

1 MAN/3 REFERENCES

GENESIS 46:24

JEZIAH
(*Sprinkled of God*)

1 MAN/1 REFERENCE

EZRA 10:25

JEZIEL
(*Sprinkled of God*)

1 MAN/1 REFERENCE

"Mighty man" who supported the
future king David during his
conflict with Saul.

1 CHRONICLES 12:3

JEZLIAH
(*He will draw out*)

1 MAN/1 REFERENCE

1 CHRONICLES 8:18

JEZOAR
(*He will shine*)

1 MAN/1 REFERENCE

1 CHRONICLES 4:7

JEZRAHIAH
(*God will shine*)

1 MAN/1 REFERENCE

Priest who helped to dedicate the
rebuilt wall of Jerusalem by leading
the singing.

NEHEMIAH 12:42

JEZREEL
(*God will sow*)

2 MEN/4 REFERENCES

More notably, firstborn son of the
prophet Hosea whose name
signified the judgment God planned
for the rebellious people of Judah.

1 CHRONICLES 4:3; HOSEA 1:4

JIBSAM
(*Fragrant*)

1 MAN/1 REFERENCE

1 CHRONICLES 7:2

JIDLAPH
(*Tearful*)

1 MAN/1 REFERENCE

Son of Nahor, Abraham's brother.

GENESIS 22:22

JIMNA
(*Prosperity*)

1 MAN/1 REFERENCE

Same as Jimnah.

NUMBERS 26:44

JIMNAH
(*Prosperity*)

1 MAN/1 REFERENCE

Variant spelling of *Jimna*.

GENESIS 46:17

JOAB
(*Jehovah fathered*)

5 MEN/146 REFERENCES

Most notably, commander of David's
army. He obeyed David's command
to put Uriah the Hittite on the front
lines so he would be killed.

1 SAMUEL 26:6; 1 CHRONICLES 2:54;
1 CHRONICLES 4:14; EZRA 2:6;
EZRA 8:9

JOAH
(*Jehovah brothered*)

4 MEN/11 REFERENCES

Most notably, officer of King Hezekiah
of Judah. Also, official under King
Josiah of Judah, whom the king sent
to repair the temple.

2 KINGS 18:18; 1 CHRONICLES 6:21;
1 CHRONICLES 26:4; 2 CHRONICLES 34:8

JOAHAZ
(*Jehovah seized*)
1 MAN / 1 REFERENCE
2 CHRONICLES 34:8

JOANNA
1 MAN / 1 WOMAN / 3 REFERENCES
Notably, wife of one of King Herod's
officials, she followed Jesus and
provided for His financial needs.
LUKE 3:27; LUKE 8:3

JOASH
(*Jehovah hastened*)
8 MEN / 49 REFERENCES
Most notably, king of Judah, son of
King Ahaziah, hidden from his
wicked grandmother Athaliah then
protected by the priest Jehoiada.
He followed the Lord but did not
remove idolatry from the nation.
Same as Jehoash. Also, a king of
Israel. Also, official over stores of oil
under King David. Also, "mighty
man" who supported the future king
David during his conflict with Saul.
JUDGES 6:11; 1 KINGS 22:26; 2 KINGS 11:2;
2 KINGS 13:9; 1 CHRONICLES 4:22;
1 CHRONICLES 7:8; 1 CHRONICLES
27:28; 1 CHRONICLES 12:3

JOATHAM
1 MAN / 2 REFERENCES
MATTHEW 1:9

JOB
(*Hated, persecuted*)
2 MEN / 60 REFERENCES
Notably, righteous man from Uz whom
God tested to prove to Satan that Job
was not faithful to Him because of
His blessings. Job lost his cattle and
servants; then all his children were
killed. Yet he continued to worship
God. When he suffered an affliction, three friends came to share his
misery. At first they were silent but
then accused Job of doing something
wrong. God rebuked his three friends
and restored all of Job's original blessings. Also, same as Jashub.
GENESIS 46:13; JOB 1:1

JOBAB
(*Howler*)
5 MEN / 9 REFERENCES
Most notably, king of Madon who
joined an alliance to attack the
Israelites under Joshua. Also, king
of Edom.
GENESIS 10:29; GENESIS 36:33;
JOSHUA 11:1; 1 CHRONICLES 8:9;
1 CHRONICLES 8:18

JOCHEBED
(*Jehovah gloried*)
1 WOMAN / 2 REFERENCES
Wife of Amram and mother of Moses,
Aaron, and Miriam.
EXODUS 6:20

JOED
(*Appointer*)
1 MAN / 1 REFERENCE
NEHEMIAH 11:7

JOEL
(*Jehovah is his God*)
14 MEN / 20 REFERENCES
Most notably, Old Testament minor
prophet who spoke of the coming
day of the Lord and prophesied
that God would pour out His Spirit
on all flesh in the last days. Also,
firstborn son of the prophet Samuel,
serving as a judge in Beersheba.
Same as Vashni. Also, one of King
David's valiant warriors. Also,
among a group of Levites appointed
by King David to bring the ark of
the covenant from the house of
Obed-edom to Jerusalem.
1 SAMUEL 8:2; 1 CHRONICLES 4:35;
1 CHRONICLES 5:4; 1 CHRONICLES 5:12;
1 CHRONICLES 6:36; 1 CHRONICLES 7:3;
1 CHRONICLES 11:38; 1 CHRONICLES
15:7; 1 CHRONICLES 26:22;
1 CHRONICLES 27:20; 2 CHRONICLES
29:12; EZRA 10:43; NEHEMIAH 11:9;
JOEL 1:1

JOELAH
(*To ascend*)
1 MAN/1 REFERENCE
A "mighty man" who supported the future king David during his conflict with Saul.
1 CHRONICLES 12:7

JOEZER
(*Jehovah is his help*)
1 MAN/1 REFERENCE
"Mighty man" who supported the future king David during his conflict with Saul.
1 CHRONICLES 12:6

JOGLI
(*Exiled*)
1 MAN/1 REFERENCE
Prince of the tribe of Dan when the Israelites entered the Promised Land.
NUMBERS 34:22

JOHA
(*Jehovah revived*)
2 MEN/2 REFERENCES
Notably, one of King David's valiant warriors.
1 CHRONICLES 8:16; 1 CHRONICLES 11:45

JOHANAN
(*Jehovah favored*)
11 MEN/27 REFERENCES
Most notably, rebellious Jewish leader. Also, "mighty man" who supported the future king David during his conflict with Saul. Same as Jonathan.
2 KINGS 25:23; 1 CHRONICLES 3:15;
  1 CHRONICLES 3:24; 1 CHRONICLES 6:9;
  1 CHRONICLES 12:4; 1 CHRONICLES 12:12; 2 CHRONICLES 28:12; EZRA 8:12; EZRA 10:6; NEHEMIAH 6:18;
  NEHEMIAH 12:22

JOHN
4 MEN/133 REFERENCES
Most notably, called "the Baptist." Jesus' cousin who preached repentance in the desert and baptized those who confessed their sins in the Jordan River. He also baptized Jesus and was later imprisoned. Herod promised his stepdaughter whatever she wanted, and her mother, Herodias, pressed her to ask for John the Baptist's head, which Herod reluctantly granted. Also, son of Zebedee and brother of James and became Jesus' disciple when called to leave their fishing boat and follow Him. Known as the disciple whom Jesus loved. Writer of the Gospel, the letters that bear his name, and the book of Revelation. Also, one called Mark. Joined Barnabas and Paul on Paul's first missionary journey but left them at Perga, causing Paul to lose confidence in him for a time.
MATTHEW 3:1; MATTHEW 4:21; ACTS 4:6;
  ACTS 12:12

JOIADA
(*Jehovah knows*)
1 MAN/4 REFERENCES
NEHEMIAH 12:10

JOIAKIM
(*Jehovah will raise*)
1 MAN/4 REFERENCES
NEHEMIAH 12:10

JOIARIB
(*Jehovah will contend*)
3 MEN/5 REFERENCES
Most notably, Jewish exile charged with finding Levites and temple servants to travel to Jerusalem with Ezra.
EZRA 8:16; NEHEMIAH 11:5;
  NEHEMIAH 11:10

JOKIM
(*Jehovah will establish*)
1 MAN/1 REFERENCE
1 CHRONICLES 4:22

JOKSHAN
(*Insidious*)
1 MAN/4 REFERENCES
Son of Abraham by his second wife, Keturah.
GENESIS 25:2

JOKTAN
(*He will be made little*)
1 MAN/6 REFERENCES
GENESIS 10:25

JONA
(*A dove*)
1 MAN/1 REFERENCE
Greek form of the name *Jonah*, used in the New Testament.
JOHN 1:42

JONADAB
(*Jehovah largessed*)
2 MEN/12 REFERENCES
Notably, friend and cousin of David's son Amnon who advised him to pretend to be ill so his half sister Tamar would come to him.
2 SAMUEL 13:3; JEREMIAH 35:6

JONAH
(*A dove*)
1 MAN/19 REFERENCES
Old Testament minor prophet whom God commanded to preach in Nineveh. He fled on a ship headed for Tarshish and was thrown overboard when a tempest struck the ship. He was swallowed by a fish, which later vomited him onto land. He then went to Nineveh and the people repented. Same as Jona and Jonas.
2 KINGS 14:25

JONAN
1 MAN/1 REFERENCE
LUKE 3:30

JONAS
2 MEN/12 REFERENCES
Notably, Greek form of the name *Jonah*, used in the New Testament. Also, father of Simon Peter.
MATTHEW 12:39; JOHN 21:15

JONATHAN
(*Jehovah given*)
14 MEN/121 REFERENCES
Most notably, eldest son of King Saul and close friend of David, making a covenant with him to protect him from his father. Also, scribe in whose home Jeremiah was imprisoned. Also, same as Johanan.
JUDGES 18:30; 1 SAMUEL 13:2; 2 SAMUEL 15:27; 2 SAMUEL 21:21; 2 SAMUEL 23:32; 1 CHRONICLES 2:32; 1 CHRONICLES 27:32; EZRA 8:6; EZRA 10:15; NEHEMIAH 12:11; NEHEMIAH 12:14; NEHEMIAH 12:35; JEREMIAH 37:15; JEREMIAH 40:8

JORAH
(*Rainy*)
1 MAN/1 REFERENCE
EZRA 2:18

JORAI
(*Rainy*)
1 MAN/1 REFERENCE
1 CHRONICLES 5:13

JORAM
(*Jehovah raised*)
4 MEN/29 REFERENCES
Most notably, king of Judah and son of King Jehoshaphat. Also, son of King Ahab and king of Israel. Same as Jehoram.
2 SAMUEL 8:10; 2 KINGS 8:21; 2 KINGS 8:16; 1 CHRONICLES 26:25

JORIM
1 MAN/1 REFERENCE
LUKE 3:29

JORKOAM
(*People will be poured forth*)
1 MAN/1 REFERENCE
1 CHRONICLES 2:44

JOSABAD
(*Jehovah endowed*)
1 MAN/1 REFERENCE
"Mighty man" who supported King
David during his conflict with Saul.
1 CHRONICLES 12:4

JOSAPHAT
1 MAN/2 REFERENCES
MATTHEW 1:8

JOSE
1 MAN/1 REFERENCE
LUKE 3:29

JOSEDECH
(*Jehovah righted*)
1 MAN/6 REFERENCES
HAGGAI 1:1

JOSEPH
(*Let him add*)
11 MEN/250 REFERENCES
Most notably, husband of Mary and
earthly father of Jesus. He was
betrothed to Mary when she conceived Jesus and traveled with her
to Bethlehem, where the child was
born. Also, son of Jacob and Rachel.
Due to his father's favoritism, his
jealous brothers plotted to kill him
but then chose to sell him as a slave.
In Egypt, he was employed by the
captain of Pharaoh's guard and was
falsely accused of impropriety. After
interpreting Pharaoh's dream, he
became second-in-command, car-
rying his country through famine
and eventually reconciling with his
brothers. Also, wealthy man of
Arimathea and member of the
Sanhedrin who became Jesus' disc-
ciple, providing the tomb for Jesus
after His crucifixion.
GENESIS 30:24; NUMBERS 13:7;
1 CHRONICLES 25:2; EZRA 10:42;
NEHEMIAH 12:14; MATTHEW 1:16;
MATTHEW 27:57; LUKE 3:24;
LUKE 3:26; LUKE 3:30; ACTS 1:23

JOSES
3 MEN/6 REFERENCES
Most notably, one of four brothers of
Jesus, as recorded in the Gospels of
Matthew and Mark. Also, son of
one of the Marys who witnessed
Jesus' crucifixion. Also, another
name for Barnabas.
MATTHEW 13:55; MATTHEW 27:56;
ACTS 4:36

JOSHAH
(*Jehovah set*)
1 MAN/1 REFERENCE
1 CHRONICLES 4:34

JOSHAPHAT
(*Jehovah judged*)
1 MAN/1 REFERENCE
One of King David's valiant warriors.
1 CHRONICLES 11:43

JOSHAVIAH
(*Jehovah set*)
1 MAN//1 REFERENCE
One of King David's valiant warriors.
1 CHRONICLES 11:46

JOSHBEKASHAH
(*Hard seat*)
1 MAN/2 REFERENCES
1 CHRONICLES 25:4

JOSHUA
(*Jehovah saved*)
4 MEN/216 REFERENCES
Most notably, son of Nun and Moses'
right-hand man. Spied out Canaan
and came back with a positive
report. For his faith, he was one of
only two men of his generation who
entered the Promised Land. Became
Moses' successor as Israel's leader.
Led the Israelites in defeating
Jericho with trumpets, the ark of the
covenant, and their voices. The walls
fell flat from God's power. Same as
Hoshea and Jesus.
EXODUS 17:9; 1 SAMUEL 6:14; 2 KINGS
23:8; HAGGAI 1:1

JOSIAH
(*Founded of God*)
2 MAN/53 REFERENCES
Notably, son of King Amon of Judah.
He became king when he was eight
years old and followed the Lord
closely through his life.
1 KINGS 13:2; ZECHARIAH 6:10

JOSIAS
(*Founded of God*)
1 MAN/2 REFERENCES
MATTHEW 1:10

JOSIBIAH
(*Jehovah will cause to dwell*)
1 MAN/1 REFERENCE
1 CHRONICLES 4:35

JOSIPHIAH
(*God is adding*)
1 MAN/1 REFERENCE
EZRA 8:10

JOTHAM
(*Jehovah is perfect*)
3 MEN/24 REFERENCES
Most notably, son of Azariah, king of
Judah, who governed for his father,
who had become a leper.
JUDGES 9:5; 2 KINGS 15:5;
1 CHRONICLES 2:47

JOZABAD
(*Jehovah has conferred*)
8 MEN/9 REFERENCES
Most notably, mighty man of valor
who joined David at Ziklag.
1 CHRONICLES 12:20; 2 CHRONICLES
31:13; 2 CHRONICLES 35:9; EZRA 8:33;
EZRA 10:22; EZRA 10:23; NEHEMIAH
8:7; NEHEMIAH 11:16

JOZACHAR
(*Jehovah remembered*)
1 MAN/1 REFERENCE
Servant of King Joash of Judah who
conspired against him and murdered
him.
2 KINGS 12:21

JOZADAK
(*Jehovah righted*)
1 MAN/5 REFERENCES
EZRA 3:2

JUBAL
(*Stream*)
1 MAN/1 REFERENCE
GENESIS 4:21

JUCAL
(*Potent*)
1 MAN/1 REFERENCE
Prince of Judah who urged King
Zedekiah to kill Jeremiah because of
his negative prophecy.
JEREMIAH 38:1

JUDA
(*Judah*)
4 MEN/4 REFERENCES
Most notably, one of four brothers of
Jesus, as recorded in Mark's Gospel.
Same as Judas.
MARK 6:3; LUKE 3:26; LUKE 3:30;
LUKE 3:33

JUDAH
(*Celebrated*)
7 MEN/49 REFERENCES
Most notably, son of Jacob and Leah,
who convinced his brothers not to
kill Joseph but to sell him instead. In
Egypt, Judah spoke up for Benjamin
when he was accused of stealing
Joseph's cup and offered himself in
Benjamin's place. His father's final
blessing described Judah as one
whom his brothers would praise.
GENESIS 29:35; EZRA 3:9; EZRA 10:23;
NEHEMIAH 11:9; NEHEMIAH 12:8;
NEHEMIAH 12:34; NEHEMIAH 12:36

JUDAS
(*Celebrated*)
7 MEN/33 REFERENCES
Most notably, disciple who betrayed
Jesus, usually identified as Judas
Iscariot. Also, one of four brothers
of Jesus, as recorded by Matthew's
Gospel. Same as Juda. Also, "the
brother of James," another of
Jesus' disciples, not to be confused
with Judas Iscariot. Same as Jude,
Lebbaeus, and Thaddaeus. Also,
man of Damascus with whom Saul
stayed while he was blinded. Also,
Greek form of the name *Judah*.
MATTHEW 10:4; MATTHEW 13:55; LUKE
6:16; ACTS 5:37; ACTS 9:11; ACTS
15:22; MATTHEW 1:2

JUDE
1 MAN/1 REFERENCE
Disciple of Jesus, author of the epistle
of Jude, and the brother of James.
Same as Judas, Lebbaeus, and
Thaddaeus.
JUDE 1:1

JUDITH
(*Jew, descendant of Judah*)
1 WOMAN/1 REFERENCE
GENESIS 26:34

JULIA
1 WOMAN/1 REFERENCE
Christian acquaintance of the apostle
Paul, greeted in his letter to the
Romans.
ROMANS 16:15

JULIUS
1 MAN/2 REFERENCES
ACTS 27:1

JUNIA
1 WOMAN/1 REFERENCE
Roman Christian who spent time in
jail with the apostle Paul and who
also may have been related to Paul.
ROMANS 16:7

JUSHABHESED
(*Jehovah is perfect*)
1 MAN/1 REFERENCE
1 CHRONICLES 3:20

JUSTUS
(*Just*)
3 MEN/3 REFERENCES
Most notably, surname of Joseph,
potential apostolic replacement
for Judas Iscariot who lost by lot
to the other candidate, Matthias.
Same as Barsabas. Also, Corinthian
Christian in whose home Paul
stayed. Also, Christian Jew and
fellow worker with the apostle Paul
in Rome.
ACTS 1:23; ACTS 18:7; COLOSSIANS 4:11

—K—

KADMIEL
(*Presence of God*)
3 MEN/8 REFERENCES
EZRA 2:40; EZRA 3:9; NEHEMIAH 9:4

KALLAI
(*Frivolous*)
1 MAN/1 REFERENCE
NEHEMIAH 12:20

KAREAH
(*Bald*)
1 MAN/13 REFERENCES
JEREMIAH 40:8

KEDAR
(*Dusky*)
1 MAN/2 REFERENCES
GENESIS 25:13

KEDEMAH
(*Precedence*)
1 MAN/2 REFERENCES
GENESIS 25:15

KEILAH
(*Enclosing, citadel*)
1 MAN/1 REFERENCE
1 CHRONICLES 4:19

KELAIAH
(*Insignificance*)
1 MAN/1 REFERENCE
Same as Kelita.
EZRA 10:23

KELITA
(*Maiming*)
2 MEN/3 REFERENCES
Same as Kelaiah.
EZRA 10:23; NEHEMIAH 8:7

KEMUEL
(*Raised of God*)
3 MEN/3 REFERENCES
Most notably, prince of the tribe of
    Ephraim when the Israelites entered
    the Promised Land.
GENESIS 22:21; NUMBERS 34:24;
    1 CHRONICLES 27:17

KENAN
(*A nest*)
1 MAN/1 REFERENCE
Sixth-longest-lived person in the Bible,
    at 910 years.
1 CHRONICLES 1:2

KENAZ
(*Hunter*)
4 MEN/11 REFERENCES
GENESIS 36:11; GENESIS 36:42; JOSHUA
    15:17; 1 CHRONICLES 4:15

KEREN-HAPPUCH
(*Horn of cosmetic*)
1 WOMAN/1 REFERENCE
Youngest of three daughters born to
    Job when God restored his fortunes.
JOB 42:14

KEROS
(*Ankled*)
1 MAN/2 REFERENCES
EZRA 2:44

KETURAH
(*Perfumed*)
1 WOMAN/4 REFERENCES
Abraham's concubine and wife, whom
    he may have married following
    Sarah's death, but her children were
    not part of God's promised line.
GENESIS 25:1

KEZIA
(*Cassia*)
1 WOMAN/1 REFERENCE
Second of three daughters born to Job
    when God restored his fortunes.
JOB 42:14

KIRJATH-JEARIM
(*City of forests*)
1 MAN/3 REFERENCES
1 CHRONICLES 2:50

KISH
(*A bow*)
5 MEN/21 REFERENCES
Father of King Saul. Same as Cis.
1 SAMUEL 9:1; 1 CHRONICLES 8:30;
    1 CHRONICLES 23:21; 2 CHRONICLES
    29:12; ESTHER 2:5

KISHI
(*War, battle*)
1 MAN/1 REFERENCE
1 CHRONICLES 6:44

KITTIM
(*Islander*)
1 MAN/2 REFERENCES
GENESIS 10:4

KOHATH
(*Allied*)
1 MAN/32 REFERENCES
GENESIS 46:11

KOLAIAH
(*Voice of God*)
2 MEN/2 REFERENCES
Notably, father of Ahab, a false prophet
    at the time of the Babylonian Exile.
NEHEMIAH 11:7; JEREMIAH 29:21

KORAH
(*To make bald*)
5 MEN/37 REFERENCES

Most notably, descendant of Levi and
Kohath who opposed Moses when
the prophet said all the Israelites
were not holy. Also, descendant of
Abraham through Jacob's son Levi.
Korah's sons are named in the titles
of eleven psalms: 42, 44–49, 84–85,
and 87–88.

GENESIS 36:5; GENESIS 36:16; EXODUS
6:21; 1 CHRONICLES 2:43;
1 CHRONICLES 6:22

KORE
2 MEN/4 REFERENCES
1 CHRONICLES 9:19; 2 CHRONICLES 31:14

KOZ
2 MEN/4 REFERENCES
EZRA 2:61; NEHEMIAH 3:4

KUSHAIAH
(*Entrapped of God*)
1 MAN/1 REFERENCE
1 CHRONICLES 15:17

—L—

LAADAH
1 MAN/1 REFERENCE
1 CHRONICLES 4:21

LAADAN
2 MEN/7 REFERENCES
1 CHRONICLES 7:26; 1 CHRONICLES 23:7

LABAN
(*To be white or to make bricks*)
1 MAN/55 REFERENCES

Called Laban the Syrian, brother of
Rebekah who approved of her
marriage to Isaac. Uncle of Jacob
who employed him for seven years
in exchange for marriage to his
daughter Rachel. Laban tricked
Jacob into marrying his first
daughter, Leah, then offered Rachel
to Jacob for another seven years of
service.

GENESIS 24:29

LAEL
(*Belonging to God*)
1 MAN/1 REFERENCE
Chief of the Gershonites when Moses
led Israel.

NUMBERS 3:24

LAHAD
(*To glow, to be earnest*)
1 MAN/1 REFERENCE
1 CHRONICLES 4:2

LAHMI
(*Foodful*)
1 MAN/1 REFERENCE
Brother of Philistine giant Goliath.
1 CHRONICLES 20:5

LAISH
(*Crushing*)
1 MAN/2 REFERENCES
1 SAMUEL 25:44

LAMECH
1 MAN/12 REFERENCES

Descendant of Cain through Cain's
son Enoch. Lamech's father was
Methuselah, and Lamech was the
father of Noah. Lamech is the first
man whom the Bible records as
having more than one wife.

GENESIS 4:18

LAPIDOTH
(*To shine, or a lamp or flame*)
1 MAN/1 REFERENCE
Husband of Israel's only female judge,
Deborah.

JUDGES 4:4

LAZARUS

1 MAN/11 REFERENCES

Brother of Mary and Martha, and
loved by Jesus. His sisters sent for
Jesus when he became ill, but he
died. After weeping at Lazarus's
tomb, Jesus had the stone removed.
He called Lazarus forth, and
Lazarus walked out. Not to be
confused with the beggar named
Lazarus in Jesus' parable in Luke 16.

JOHN 11:1

LEAH

(*Weary*)

1 WOMAN/34 REFERENCES

Laban's older daughter who was less
beautiful than her sister, Rachel.
Jacob loved Rachel and arranged to
marry her, but Laban insisted that
Jacob marry Leah first, tricking
Jacob into marriage with Leah.
Leah had four children, then later
had two more sons and a daughter.

GENESIS 29:16

LEBANA

(*The white, the moon*)

1 MAN/1 REFERENCE

Same as Lebanah.

NEHEMIAH 7:48

LEBANAH

(*The white, the moon*)

1 MAN/1 REFERENCE

Same as Lebana.

EZRA 2:45

LEBBAEUS

(*Uncertain*)

1 MAN/1 REFERENCE

Also called Thaddaeus, he was one of
Jesus' twelve disciples, as listed by
Matthew. Same as Judas and Jude.

MATTHEW 10:3

LECAH

(*A journey*)

1 MAN/1 REFERENCE

1 CHRONICLES 4:21

LEHABIM

(*Flames*)

1 MAN/2 REFERENCES

GENESIS 10:13

LEMUEL

(*Belonging to God*)

1 MAN/2 REFERENCES

Otherwise unknown king credited with
writing Proverbs 31.

PROVERBS 31:1

LETUSHIM

(*Oppressed*)

1 MAN/1 REFERENCE

GENESIS 25:3

LEUMMIM

(*Night specter*)

1 MAN/1 REFERENCE

GENESIS 25:3

LEVI

(*Attached*)

4 MEN/21 REFERENCES

Most notably, Leah and Jacob's third
child and founder of Israel's priestly
line. Also, son of Alphaeus, tax
collector who became Jesus' disciple.
Same as Matthew.

GENESIS 29:34; MARK 2:14; LUKE 3:24
LUKE 3:29

LIBNI

(*White*)

2 MEN/5 REFERENCES

EXODUS 6:17; 1 CHRONICLES 6:29

LIKHI

(*Learned*)

1 MAN/1 REFERENCE

1 CHRONICLES 7:19

LINUS

1 MAN/1 REFERENCE

Christian whose greetings Paul passed
on to Timothy when Paul wrote his
second letter to the young pastor.

2 TIMOTHY 4:21

LO-AMMI

(*Not my people*)

1 MAN/1 REFERENCE

Third child of the prophet Hosea's adulterous wife, Gomer.

HOSEA 1:9

LOIS

1 WOMAN/1 REFERENCE

Grandmother of the apostle Paul's protégé Timothy.

2 TIMOTHY 1:5

LO-RUHAMAH

(*Not pitied*)

1 WOMAN/2 REFERENCES

Second child of the prophet Hosea's adulterous wife, Gomer.

HOSEA 1:6

LOT

1 MAN/37 REFERENCES

Abram's nephew, who traveled with him to the Promised Land. Although warned not to look back at Sodom, his wife did and was turned into a pillar of salt.

GENESIS 11:27

LOTAN

(*Covering*)

1 MAN/7 REFERENCES

GENESIS 36:20

LUCAS

1 MAN/2 REFERENCES

A variation on the name *Luke*; biblical writer and traveling companion of the apostle Paul.

PHILEMON 1:24

LUCIUS

(*Illuminative*)

2 MEN/2 REFERENCES

Notably, Lucius of Cyrene, prophet or teacher who ministered in Antioch when Paul and Barnabas were chosen for missionary work. Also, relative of Paul who lived in Rome and was greeted in the apostle's letter to the Romans.

ACTS 13:1; ROMANS 16:21

LUD

1 MAN/2 REFERENCES

GENESIS 10:22

LUDIM

(*A Ludite*)

1 MAN/2 REFERENCES

GENESIS 10:13

LUKE

1 MAN/2 REFERENCES

The "beloved physician," probably a Gentile believer who became a companion of Paul. Writer of a Gospel and the book of Acts, he was also an excellent historian, as is shown by the exactness with which he describes the details of the gospel events and the places where they happened. Same as Lucas.

COLOSSIANS 4:14

LYDIA

1 WOMAN/2 REFERENCES

Woman of Thyatira who sold goods dyed with an expensive purple color. After hearing Paul's preaching, she became a Christian believer.

ACTS 16:14

LYSANIAS

(*Grief dispelling*)

1 MAN/1 REFERENCE

Tetrarch of Abilene when John the Baptist began preaching.

LUKE 3:1

LYSIAS

1 MAN/3 REFERENCES

Roman soldier who heard information from Paul's nephew about a plot to kill Paul. Also called Claudius Lysias.

ACTS 23:26

—M—

MAACAH
(*Depression*)
1 MAN/1 WOMAN/2 REFERENCES
Notably, one of David's wives, daughter of Talmai, king of Geshur, and mother of Absalom. Same as Maachah. Also, king who provided soldiers to the Ammonites when they attacked King David.
2 SAMUEL 3:3; 2 SAMUEL 10:6

MAACHAH
(*Depression*)
4 MEN/6 WOMEN/18 REFERENCES
Most notably, mother of King Asa of Judah. Also, one of David's wives who was daughter of Talmai, the king of Geshur, and mother of Absalom. Same as Maacah.
GENESIS 22:24; 1 KINGS 2:39; 1 KINGS 15:2; 1 KINGS 15:13; 1 CHRONICLES 2:48; 1 CHRONICLES 3:2; 1 CHRONICLES 7:15; 1 CHRONICLES 8:29; 1 CHRONICLES 11:43; 1 CHRONICLES 27:16

MAADAI
(*Ornamental*)
1 MAN/1 REFERENCE
EZRA 10:34

MAADIAH
(*Ornament of God*)
1 MAN/1 REFERENCE
Chief priest who went up to Jerusalem with Zerubbabel.
NEHEMIAH 12:5

MAAI
(*Sympathetic*)
1 MAN/1 REFERENCE
Priest who helped to dedicate the rebuilt wall of Jerusalem by playing a musical instrument.
NEHEMIAH 12:36

MAASEIAH
(*Work of God*)
21 MEN/25 REFERENCES
Most notably, Jerusalem's governor who repaired the temple at King Josiah's command. Also, a rebuilder of the walls of Jerusalem under Nehemiah. Also, priest who assisted Ezra in reading the book of the law to the people of Jerusalem. Also, priest who helped to dedicate the rebuilt wall of Jerusalem by giving thanks. Also, priest who gave thanks with a trumpet at the dedication of Jerusalem's rebuilt walls. Also, false prophet against whom Jeremiah prophesied.
1 CHRONICLES 15:18; 2 CHRONICLES 23:1; 2 CHRONICLES 26:11; 2 CHRONICLES 28:7; 2 CHRONICLES 34:8; EZRA 10:18; EZRA 10:21; EZRA 10:22; EZRA 10:30; NEHEMIAH 3:23; NEHEMIAH 8:4; NEHEMIAH 8:7; NEHEMIAH 10:25; NEHEMIAH 11:5; NEHEMIAH 11:7; NEHEMIAH 12:41; NEHEMIAH 12:42; JEREMIAH 21:1; JEREMIAH 29:21; JEREMIAH 35:4; JEREMIAH 32:12

MAASIAI
(*Operative*)
1 MAN/1 REFERENCE
1 CHRONICLES 9:12

MAATH
1 MAN/1 REFERENCE
LUKE 3:26

MAAZ
(*Closure*)
1 MAN/1 REFERENCE
1 CHRONICLES 2:27

MAAZIAH
(*Rescue of God*)
2 MEN/2 REFERENCES
Notably, one of twenty-four priests in David's time, chosen by lot to serve in the tabernacle.
1 CHRONICLES 24:18; NEHEMIAH 10:8

MACHBANAI

(*Native of Machena*)

1 MAN/1 REFERENCE

Warriors from the tribe of Gad who
   left Saul to join David during his
   conflict with the king.

1 CHRONICLES 12:13

MACHBENAH

(*Knoll*)

1 MAN/1 REFERENCE

1 CHRONICLES 2:49

MACHI

(*Pining*)

1 MAN/1 REFERENCE

NUMBERS 13:15

MACHIR

(*Salesman*)

2 MEN/22 REFERENCES

Notably, man who brought food and
   supplies to King David and his
   soldiers as they fled from the army
   of David's son Absalom.

GENESIS 50:23; 2 SAMUEL 9:4

MACHNADEBAI

(*What is like a liberal man?*)

1 MAN/1 REFERENCE

EZRA 10:40

MADAI

(*Mede*)

1 MAN/2 REFERENCES

GENESIS 10:2

MADMANNAH

1 MAN/1 REFERENCE

1 CHRONICLES 2:49

MAGBISH

(*Stiffening*)

1 MAN/1 REFERENCE

EZRA 2:30

MAGDALENE

(*Woman of Magdala*)

1 WOMAN/12 REFERENCES

Surname of Mary.

MATTHEW 27:56

MAGDIEL

(*Preciousness of God*)

1 MAN/2 REFERENCES

GENESIS 36:43

MAGOG

1 MAN/2 REFERENCES

GENESIS 10:2

MAGOR-MISSABIB

(*Afright from around*)

1 MAN/1 REFERENCE

JEREMIAH 20:3

MAGPIASH

(*Exterminator of the moth*)

1 MAN/1 REFERENCE

Jewish leader who renewed the
   covenant under Nehemiah.

NEHEMIAH 2:10

MAHALAH

(*Sickness*)

1 MAN/1 REFERENCE

1 CHRONICLES 7:18

MAHALALEEL

(*Praise of God*)

2 MEN/7 REFERENCES

GENESIS 5:12; NEHEMIAH 11:4

MAHALATH

(*Sickness*)

2 WOMEN/2 REFERENCES

GENESIS 28:9; 2 CHRONICLES 11:18

MAHALI

(*Sick*)

1 MAN/1 REFERENCE

EXODUS 6:19

MAHARAI

(*Hasty*)

1 MAN/3 REFERENCES

Commander in King David's army
   overseeing twenty-four thousand
   men in the tenth month of each year.

2 SAMUEL 23:28

MAHATH
(*Erasure*)
2 MEN/3 REFERENCES
1 CHRONICLES 6:35; 2 CHRONICLES 31:13

MAHAZIOTH
(*Visions*)
1 MAN/2 REFERENCES
1 CHRONICLES 25:4

MAHER-SHALAL-HASH-BAZ
(*Hasting is he to the booty*)
1 MAN/2 REFERENCES
Son of the prophet Isaiah, named at
God's command to describe the
Assyrian attack on Damascus and
Samaria.
ISAIAH 8:1

MAHLAH
(*Sickness*)
1 WOMAN/4 REFERENCES
One of Zelophehad's five daughters
who received his inheritance because
he had no sons.
NUMBERS 26:33

MAHLI
(*Sick*)
2 MEN/11 REFERENCES
NUMBERS 3:20; 1 CHRONICLES 6:47

MAHLON
(*Sick*)
1 MAN/4 REFERENCES
Son of Naomi and her husband,
Elimelech. Died in Moab, forcing
Naomi and his wife, Ruth, to return
to Bethlehem.
RUTH 1:2

MAHOL
(*Dancing*)
1 MAN/1 REFERENCE
1 KINGS 4:31

MALACHI
(*Ministrative*)
1 MAN/1 REFERENCE
Writer of the last book of the Old
Testament, who lived in the time of
Nehemiah and Ezra.
MALACHI 1:1

MALCHAM
1 MAN/1 REFERENCE
1 CHRONICLES 8:9

MALCHIAH
(*King of [appointed by] God*)
7 MEN/9 REFERENCES
Most notably, man who repaired
Jerusalem's walls under Nehemiah.
Also, priest who assisted Ezra in
reading the book of the law to the
people of Jerusalem.
1 CHRONICLES 6:40; EZRA 10:25; EZRA
10:31; NEHEMIAH 3:14; NEHEMIAH
3:31; NEHEMIAH 8:4; JEREMIAH 38:1

MALCHIEL
(*King of [appointed by] God*)
1 MAN/3 REFERENCES
GENESIS 46:17

MALCHIJAH
(*King of [appointed by] God*)
5 MEN/6 REFERENCES
Most notably, one of twenty-four
priests in David's time who was
chosen by lot to serve in the
tabernacle. Also, priest who helped
to dedicate the rebuilt walls of
Jerusalem by giving thanks.
1 CHRONICLES 9:12; 1 CHRONICLES
24:9; EZRA 10:25; NEHEMIAH 3:11;
NEHEMIAH 10:3

MALCHIRAM
(*King of a high one [or exaltation]*)
1 MAN/1 REFERENCE
1 CHRONICLES 3:18

MALCHI-SHUA

1 MAN/3 REFERENCES

Son of King Saul. Same as
Melchi-shua.

1 CHRONICLES 8:33

MALCHUS

1 MAN/1 REFERENCE

High priest's servant whose ear
Simon Peter cut off when Jesus was
arrested.

JOHN 18:10

MALELEEL

1 MAN/1 REFERENCE

LUKE 3:37

MALLOTHI

(*I have talked, loquacious*)

1 MAN/2 REFERENCES

1 CHRONICLES 25:4

MALLUCH

(*Regnant*)

5 MEN/6 REFERENCES

Most notably, priest who renewed the
covenant under Nehemiah.

1 CHRONICLES 6:44; EZRA 10:29;
EZRA 10:32; NEHEMIAH 10:4;
NEHEMIAH 10:27

MAMRE

(*Lusty [meaning "vigorous"]*)

1 MAN/2 REFERENCES

Amorite ally of Abram who went with
him to recover Abram's nephew Lot
from the king of Sodom.

GENESIS 14:13

MANAEN

(*Uncertain*)

1 MAN/1 REFERENCE

Prophet or teacher at Antioch
when Barnabas and Saul were
commissioned as missionaries.

ACTS 13:1

MANAHATH

(*Rest*)

1 MAN/2 REFERENCES

GENESIS 36:23

MANASSEH

(*Causing to forget*)

5 MEN/55 REFERENCES

Most notably, elder child of Joseph and
Asenath who was adopted, with his
brother, Ephraim, by Joseph's father,
Jacob. Also, priest of the tribe of
Dan, who worshipped idols, in the
period of the judges. Also, king of
Judah and son of King Hezekiah, he
was an evil ruler who led his nation
into idolatry, burning his sons as
offerings to the idols. He repented
and commanded his nation to
follow God.

GENESIS 41:51; JUDGES 18:30; 2 KINGS
20:21; EZRA 10:30; EZRA 10:33

MANASSES

(*Causing to forget*)

1 MAN/2 REFERENCES

Greek form of *Manasseh*.

MATTHEW 1:10

MANOAH

(*Rest*)

1 MAN/18 REFERENCES

Father of Samson, who received
instructions from an angel as to
what to do when his child was born.

JUDGES 13:2

MAOCH

(*Oppressed*)

1 MAN/1 REFERENCE

1 SAMUEL 27:2

MAON

(*A residence*)

1 MAN/2 REFERENCES

1 CHRONICLES 2:45

MARA

(*Bitter*)

1 WOMAN/1 REFERENCE

Name Naomi gave herself after the
men of her family died and she felt
that God had dealt bitterly with her.

RUTH 1:20

MARCUS

1 MAN/3 REFERENCES
Latin form of *Mark*.
COLOSSIANS 4:10

MARESHAH

(*Summit*)
2 MEN/2 REFERENCES
1 CHRONICLES 2:42; 1 CHRONICLES 4:21

MARK

1 MAN/5 REFERENCES
Nephew of Barnabas and fellow
missionary with Barnabas and Saul.
Writer of the Gospel that bears his
name. Same as Marcus.
ACTS 12:12

MARSENA

1 MAN/1 REFERENCE
One of seven Persian princes serving
under King Ahasuerus.
ESTHER 1:14

MARTHA

(*Mistress*)
1 WOMAN/13 REFERENCES
Sister of Lazarus and Mary who asked
Jesus to tell Mary to help her serve.
He told her that Mary had chosen
better in listening to His teaching.
LUKE 10:38

MARY

7 WOMEN/54 REFERENCES
Most notably, a virgin who received
news from an angel that she would
bear the Messiah and traveled to
Bethlehem with Joseph, where
Jesus was born. Mary stood by the
cross and saw her son crucified.
Also, Mary Magdalene, who had
seven devils cast out of her by Jesus
and was present throughout the
crucifixion of Jesus, and one of the
group of women who went to the
tomb to anoint His body. She saw
the angels who reported that Jesus
had risen from the dead and went
to tell the disciples. As she wept
at the tomb, Jesus appeared to her
and spoke her name. Also, Mary,
the mother of James and Joses, with
Mary Magdalene and other women
at the crucifixion of Jesus and at the
tomb following His resurrection.
Also, sister of Lazarus and Martha
who listened at Jesus' feet while
her sister became sidetracked with
household matters.
MATTHEW 1:16; MATTHEW 27:56;
    MATTHEW 27:56; JOHN 19:25; LUKE
    10:39; ACTS 12:12; ROMANS 16:6

MASH

1 MAN/1 REFERENCE
GENESIS 10:23

MASSA

(*Burden*)
1 MAN/2 REFERENCES
Son of Ishmael.
GENESIS 25:14

MATHUSALA

1 MAN/1 REFERENCE
LUKE 3:37

MATRED

(*Propulsive*)
1 WOMAN/2 REFERENCES
GENESIS 36:39

MATRI

1 MAN/1 REFERENCE
1 SAMUEL 10:21

MATTAN

2 MEN/3 REFERENCES
Priest of Baal killed by the people
of Judah after Jehoiada made a
covenant between them, King Joash,
and God.
2 KINGS 11:18; JEREMIAH 38:1

MATTANIAH

(*Gift of God*)

9 MEN/16 REFERENCES

Most notably, king who began to rule
in his uncle Jehoiachin's place when
Nebuchadnezzar, king of Babylon,
conquered Judah. Renamed
Zedekiah.

2 KINGS 24:17; 1 CHRONICLES 9:15;
1 CHRONICLES 25:4; 2 CHRONICLES
29:13; EZRA 10:26; EZRA 10:27; EZRA
10:30; EZRA 10:37; NEHEMIAH 13:13

MATTATHA

(*Gift of God*)

1 MAN/1 REFERENCE

LUKE 3:31

MATTATHAH

(*Gift of God*)

1 MAN/1 REFERENCE

EZRA 10:33

MATTATHIAS

(*Gift of God*)

2 MEN/2 REFERENCES

LUKE 3:25; LUKE 3:26

MATTENAI

(*Liberal*)

3 MEN/2 REFERENCES

EZRA 10:33; EZRA 10:37;
NEHEMIAH 12:19

MATTHAN

1 MAN/2 REFERENCES

MATTHEW 1:15

MATTHAT

(*Gift of God*)

2 MEN/2 REFERENCES

LUKE 3:24; LUKE 3:29

MATTHEW

1 MAN/5 REFERENCES

Tax collector (or publican), also called
Levi, who left his tax booth to
follow Jesus. Although Matthew
does not list himself as the writer
of the Gospel named after him,
the early church ascribed it to him.
Same as Levi.

MATTHEW 9:9

MATTHIAS

1 MAN/2 REFERENCES

Apostolic replacement for Judas
Iscariot.

ACTS 1:23

MATTITHIAH

(*Gift of God*)

5 MEN/8 REFERENCES

Most notably, Levite musician who
performed in celebration when King
David brought the ark of the covenant to Jerusalem. Also, priest who
assisted Ezra in reading the book of
the law to the people of Jerusalem.
Also, Levite official in charge of
goods baked in the temple sanctuary.

1 CHRONICLES 9:31; 1 CHRONICLES 15:18;
1 CHRONICLES 25:3; EZRA 10:43;
NEHEMIAH 8:4

MEBUNNAI

(*Built up*)

1 MAN/1 REFERENCE

One of King David's warriors known
as the "mighty men."

2 SAMUEL 23:27

MEDAD

(*Loving, affectionate*)

1 MAN/2 REFERENCES

Man who prophesied after God sent
the Israelites quail to eat in the
wilderness.

NUMBERS 11:26

MEDAN

(*Discord, strife*)

1 MAN/2 REFERENCES

Son of Abraham by his second wife, Keturah.

GENESIS 25:2

MEHETABEEL

(*Bettered of God*)

1 MAN/1 REFERENCE

NEHEMIAH 6:10

MEHETABEL

(*Bettered of God*)

1 WOMAN/2 REFERENCES

GENESIS 36:39

MEHIDA

(*Junction*)

1 MAN/2 REFERENCES

EZRA 2:52

MEHIR

(*Price*)

1 MAN/1 REFERENCE

1 CHRONICLES 4:11

MEHUJAEL

(*Smitten of God*)

1 MAN/2 REFERENCES

GENESIS 4:18

MEHUMAN

1 MAN/1 REFERENCE

Eunuch serving the Persian king Ahasuerus in Esther's time.

ESTHER 1:10

MEHUNIM

(*A Muenite or inhabitant of Maon*)

1 MAN/1 REFERENCE

EZRA 2:50

MELATIAH

(*God has delivered*)

1 MAN/1 REFERENCE

Repaired Jerusalem's walls under Nehemiah.

NEHEMIAH 3:7

MELCHI

(*My king*)

2 MEN/2 REFERENCES

LUKE 3:24; LUKE 3:28

MELCHIAH

(*King of [appointed by] God*)

1 MAN/1 REFERENCE

JEREMIAH 21:1

MELCHISEDEC

(*King of right*)

1 MAN/9 REFERENCES

King and high priest of Salem who blessed Abram. The writer of Hebrews refers to Jesus as high priest "after the order of Melchisedec," since He was not a priest from the line of Levi. Same as Melchizedek.

HEBREWS 5:6

MELCHI-SHUA

(*King of wealth*)

1 MAN/2 REFERENCES

Son of King Saul, killed by the Philistines along with his father and two brothers. Same as Malchi-shua.

1 SAMUEL 14:49

MELCHIZEDEK

(*King of right*)

1 MAN/2 REFERENCES

Hebrew form of the name *Melchisedec*.

GENESIS 14:18

MELEA

1 MAN/1 REFERENCE

LUKE 3:31

MELECH

(*King*)

1 MAN/2 REFERENCES

1 CHRONICLES 8:35

MELICU

(*Regnant*)

1 MAN/1 REFERENCE

NEHEMIAH 12:14

MELZAR

1 MAN/2 REFERENCES

Babylonian official in charge of Daniel
and his three friends.

DANIEL 1:11

MEMUCAN

1 MAN/3 REFERENCES

One of seven Persian princes serving
under King Ahasuerus.

ESTHER 1:14

MENAHEM

(*Comforter*)

1 MAN/8 REFERENCES

King of Israel who usurped the throne
from King Shallum. During his ten-
year reign, the idolatrous Menahem
did evil.

2 KINGS 15:14

MENAN

1 MAN/1 REFERENCE

LUKE 3:31

MEONOTHAI

(*Habitative*)

1 MAN/1 REFERENCE

1 CHRONICLES 4:14

MEPHIBOSHETH

(*Dispeller of shame*)

2 MEN/15 REFERENCES

Notably, grandson of King Saul and
son of Jonathan. When David took
the throne of Israel, he treated the
lame Mephibosheth kindly because
of his friendship with Jonathan.
Same as Merib-baal. Also, one
of King Saul's sons whom David
handed over to the Gibeonites, who
sought vengeance on Saul's house.

2 SAMUEL 4:4; 2 SAMUEL 21:8

MERAB

(*Increase*)

1 WOMAN/3 REFERENCES

King Saul's firstborn daughter who
was promised to David but married
another man.

1 SAMUEL 14:49

MERAIAH

(*Rebellion*)

1 MAN/1 REFERENCE

Priest in the days of the high priest
Joiakim.

NEHEMIAH 12:12

MERAIOTH

(*Rebellious*)

3 MEN/7 REFERENCES

1 CHRONICLES 6:6; 1 CHRONICLES 9:11;
NEHEMIAH 12:15

MERARI

(*Bitter*)

1 MAN/39 REFERENCES

Levi's third son, in charge of the
boards, bars, pillars, sockets,
and vessels of the tabernacle.

GENESIS 46:11

MERED

(*Rebellion*)

1 MAN/2 REFERENCES

1 CHRONICLES 4:17

MEREMOTH

(*Heights*)

3 MEN/6 REFERENCES

Most notably, priest's son who weighed
the valuable utensils that King
Artaxerxes of Persia and his officials
had given Ezra to take back to
Jerusalem's temple. Also, priest
who renewed the covenant under
Nehemiah.

EZRA 8:33; EZRA 10:36; NEHEMIAH 10:5

MERES

1 MAN/1 REFERENCE

One of seven Persian princes serving
under King Ahasuerus.

ESTHER 1:14

MERIB-BAAL

(*Quarreler of Baal*)

1 MAN/4 REFERENCES

Same as Mephibosheth.

1 CHRONICLES 8:34

MERODACH-BALADAN

1 MAN/1 REFERENCE

King of Babylon during the reign of
King Hezekiah of Judah.

ISAIAH 39:1

MESHA

(*Safety*)

3 MEN/3 REFERENCES

King of Moab at the time of King
Jehoram of Israel.

2 KINGS 3:4; 1 CHRONICLES 2:42;
1 CHRONICLES 8:9

MESHACH

1 MAN/15 REFERENCES

Babylonian name for Mishael, one
of Daniel's companions in exile.
Survived the fiery furnace when cast
there for not bowing down to an
idol. Same as Mishael.

DANIEL 1:7

MESHECH

2 MEN/3 REFERENCES

GENESIS 10:2; 1 CHRONICLES 1:17

MESHELEMIAH

(*Ally of God*)

1 MAN/4 REFERENCES

1 CHRONICLES 9:21

MESHEZABEEL

(*Delivered of God*)

2 MEN/3 REFERENCES

Notably, Levite who renewed the
covenant under Nehemiah.

NEHEMIAH 3:4; NEHEMIAH 10:21

MESHILLEMITH

(*Reconciliation*)

1 MAN/1 REFERENCE

1 CHRONICLES 9:12

MESHILLEMOTH

(*Reconciliations*)

2 MEN/2 REFERENCES

2 CHRONICLES 28:12; NEHEMIAH 11:13

MESHOBAB

(*Returned*)

1 MAN/1 REFERENCE

1 CHRONICLES 4:34

MESHULLAM

(*Allied*)

21 MEN/25 REFERENCES

Most notably, descendant of Benjamin
and a chief of that tribe who lived in
Jerusalem. Also, man who repaired
Jerusalem's walls under Nehemiah.
Also, priest who assisted Ezra in
reading the book of the law to the
people of Jerusalem. Also, priest
who helped to dedicate Jerusalem's
rebuilt walls.

2 KINGS 22:3; 1 CHRONICLES 3:19;
1 CHRONICLES 5:13; 1 CHRONICLES
8:17; 1 CHRONICLES 9:7; 1 CHRONICLES
9:8; 1 CHRONICLES 9:11; 1 CHRONICLES
9:12; 2 CHRONICLES 34:12; EZRA 8:16;
EZRA 10:15; EZRA 10:29; NEHEMIAH
3:4; NEHEMIAH 3:6; NEHEMIAH 8:4;
NEHEMIAH 10:7; NEHEMIAH 10:20;
NEHEMIAH 11:7; NEHEMIAH 12:13;
NEHEMIAH 12:16; NEHEMIAH 12:25

MESHULLEMETH

(*A mission or a favorable release*)

1 WOMAN/1 REFERENCE

Mother of King Amon of Judah.

2 KINGS 21:19

METHUSAEL

(*Man who is of God*)

1 MAN/2 REFERENCES

GENESIS 4:18

METHUSELAH

(*Man of a dart*)

1 MAN/6 REFERENCES

Descendant of Seth who lived for 969
years, the longest-recorded life span
in the Bible.

GENESIS 5:21

MEUNIM

(*A Meunite*)

1 MAN/1 REFERENCE

NEHEMIAH 7:52

MEZAHAB
(*Water of gold*)
1 WOMAN/2 REFERENCES
GENESIS 36:39

MIAMIN
(*From the right hand*)
2 MEN/2 REFERENCES
Notably, chief priest who went up to
Jerusalem with Zerubbabel.
EZRA 10:25; NEHEMIAH 12:5

MIBHAR
(*Select, the best*)
1 MAN/1 REFERENCE
One of King David's warriors known
as the "mighty men."
1 CHRONICLES 11:38

MIBSAM
(*Fragrant*)
2 MEN/3 REFERENCES
Notably, fourth son of Ishmael.
GENESIS 25:13; 1 CHRONICLES 4:25

MIBZAR
(*Fortification, castle, or fortified city*)
1 MAN/2 REFERENCES
GENESIS 36:42

MICAH
(*Who is like God?*)
7 MEN/31 REFERENCES
Most notably, Micah the Morasthite,
the Old Testament minor prophet
who ministered during the reign of
Hezekiah, king of Judah.
JUDGES 17:1; 1 CHRONICLES 5:5;
    1 CHRONICLES 8:34; 1 CHRONICLES
    9:15; 1 CHRONICLES 23:20;
    2 CHRONICLES 34:20; JEREMIAH 26:18

MICAIAH
1 MAN/18 REFERENCES
Prophet whom King Ahab of Israel
hated because he never prophesied
anything good to him. When King
Jehoshaphat asked Ahab for a
prophet who would tell the truth,
Ahab called for Micaiah.
1 KINGS 22:8

MICHA
3 MEN/4 REFERENCES
Most notably, son of Mephibosheth
and grandson of King Saul's son
Jonathan.
2 SAMUEL 9:12; NEHEMIAH 10:11;
    NEHEMIAH 11:17

MICHAEL
(*Who is like God?*)
10 MEN/10 REFERENCES
Most notably, mighty man of valor who
defected to David at Ziklag. Also,
son of Judah's king Jehoshaphat.
NUMBERS 13:13; 1 CHRONICLES 5:13;
    1 CHRONICLES 5:14; 1 CHRONICLES
    6:40; 1 CHRONICLES 7:3;
    1 CHRONICLES 8:16; 1 CHRONICLES
    12:20; 1 CHRONICLES 27:18;
    2 CHRONICLES 21:2; EZRA 8:8

MICHAH
(*Who is like God?*)
1 MAN/3 REFERENCES
Levite worship leader during David's
reign. Lots were cast to determine
his duties.
1 CHRONICLES 24:24

MICHAIAH
(*Who is like God?*)
4 MEN/1 WOMAN/7 REFERENCES
Most notably, prince of Judah sent by
King Jehoshaphat to teach the law
of the Lord throughout the nation.
Also, mother of King Abijah of
Judah. Also, father of Achbor. Same
as Micah. Also, priest who helped
to dedicate the rebuilt walls of
Jerusalem by giving thanks.
2 KINGS 22:12; 2 CHRONICLES 13:12;
    2 CHRONICLES 17:7; NEHEMIAH 12:35;
    JEREMIAH 36:11

MICHAL

(*Rivulet*)

1 WOMAN/18 REFERENCES

Daughter of King Saul and wife of
David. To win her, David killed two
hundred of the enemy, fulfilling
the king's request twice over. She
warned her husband and let him
out a window when Saul sought to
kill David.

1 SAMUEL 14:49

MICHRI

(*Salesman*)

1 MAN/1 REFERENCE

1 CHRONICLES 9:8

MIDIAN

(*Brawling, contentious*)

1 MAN/4 REFERENCES

Son of Abraham by his second wife,
Keturah.

GENESIS 25:2

MIJAMIN

2 MEN/2 REFERENCES

Notably, one of twenty-four priests in
David's time who was chosen by
lot to serve in the tabernacle. Also,
priest who renewed the covenant
under Nehemiah.

1 CHRONICLES 24:9; NEHEMIAH 10:7

MIKLOTH

(*Rods*)

2 MEN/4 REFERENCES

Notably, one of David's officers who
served him during the second
month.

1 CHRONICLES 8:32; 1 CHRONICLES 27:4

MIKNEIAH

(*Possession of God*)

1 MAN/2 REFERENCES

Levite musician who performed in
celebration when King David
brought the ark of the covenant to
Jerusalem.

1 CHRONICLES 15:18

MILALAI

(*Talkative*)

1 MAN/1 REFERENCE

Priest who helped to dedicate the
rebuilt walls of Jerusalem by playing
a musical instrument.

NEHEMIAH 12:36

MILCAH

(*Queen*)

2 WOMEN/11 REFERENCES

Notably, wife of Nahor, Abraham's
brother. Also, one of Zelophehad's
five daughters who received his
inheritance because he had no sons.
Each had to marry within their
tribe, Manasseh.

GENESIS 11:29; NUMBERS 26:33

MINIAMIN

(*From the right hand*)

2 MEN/3 REFERENCES

Notably, priest in the time of King
Hezekiah. Also, priest who
helped dedicate the rebuilt wall of
Jerusalem by giving thanks.

2 CHRONICLES 31:15; NEHEMIAH 12:17

MIRIAM

(*Rebelliously*)

2 WOMEN/15 REFERENCES

Notably, sister of Moses and Aaron and
a prophetess of Israel.

EXODUS 15:20; 1 CHRONICLES 4:17

MIRMA

(*Deceiving, fraud*)

1 MAN/1 REFERENCE

1 CHRONICLES 8:10

MISHAEL

(*Who is what God is?*)

3 MEN/8 REFERENCES

Most notably, friend of the prophet
    Daniel who would not defile
    himself by eating the king's meat.
    Along with two others, he would
    not worship an idol and was cast
    into the fiery furnace by King
    Nebuchadnezzar. Also called
    Meshach. Also, priest who assisted
    Ezra in reading the book of the law
    to the people of Jerusalem.

EXODUS 6:22; DANIEL 1:6; NEHEMIAH 8:4

MISHAM

(*Inspection*)

1 MAN/1 REFERENCE

1 CHRONICLES 8:12

MISHMA

(*A report, hearing*)

1 MAN/4 REFERENCES

GENESIS 25:14

MISHMANNAH

(*Fatness*)

1 MAN/1 REFERENCE

One of several warriors from the tribe
    of Gad who left Saul to join David
    during his conflict with
    the king.

1 CHRONICLES 12:10

MISPERETH

(*Enumeration*)

1 MAN/1 REFERENCE

NEHEMIAH 7:7

MITHREDATH

1 MAN/2 REFERENCES

Treasurer for Cyrus, king of Persia.
    Joined in writing a letter of
    complaint to King Artaxerxes about
    the rebuilding of Jerusalem.

EZRA 1:8

MIZPAR

(*Number*)

1 MAN/1 REFERENCE

EZRA 2:2

MIZRAIM

(*Upper and Lower Egypt*)

1 MAN/4 REFERENCES

GENESIS 10:6

MIZZAH

(*To faint with fear*)

1 MAN/3 REFERENCES

GENESIS 36:13

MNASON

1 MAN/1 REFERENCE

Elderly Christian from Cyprus who
    accompanied Paul to Jerusalem.

ACTS 21:16

MOAB

(*From her [the mother's] father*)

1 MAN/1 REFERENCE

Forefather of the Moabites.

GENESIS 19:37

MOADIAH

(*Assembly of God*)

1 MAN/1 REFERENCE

Priest under the leadership of Joiakim
    following the return from exile.

NEHEMIAH 12:17

MOLID

(*Genitor*)

1 MAN/1 REFERENCE

1 CHRONICLES 2:29

MORDECAI

2 MEN/60 REFERENCES

Most notably, an exiled Jew and cousin
    of Queen Esther, wife of the Persian
    king Ahasuerus. He discovered a
    plot against the Jews, set up by the
    king's scheming counselor, Haman,
    and warned Esther, encouraging
    her to confront the king. Mordecai
    received all of Haman's household
    as a reward.

EZRA 2:2; ESTHER 2:5

MOSES
(*Drawing out* [*of the water*], *rescued*)
1 MAN/848 REFERENCES
Old Testament prophet through
whom God gave Israel the law.
When Pharaoh commanded that
all male newborn Israelites should
be killed, Moses' mother placed
him in a basket in the Nile River,
where he was found by an Egyptian
princess, who raised him. Later, as
God's prophet in Egypt, Moses
confronted Pharaoh. Following the
Exodus, God gave Moses the Ten
Commandments and other laws.
Moses and his people wandered in
the desert for forty years. He died
on Mount Nebo just before Israel
entered the Promised Land.
EXODUS 2:10

MOZA
2 MEN/5 REFERENCES
1 CHRONICLES 2:46; 1 CHRONICLES 8:36

MUPPIM
(*Wavings*)
1 MAN/1 REFERENCE
GENESIS 46:21

MUSHI
(*Sensitive*)
1 MAN/8 REFERENCES
EXODUS 6:19

—N—

NAAM
(*Pleasure*)
1 MAN/1 REFERENCE
Son of Caleb.
1 CHRONICLES 4:15

NAAMAH
(*Pleasantness*)
2 WOMEN/4 REFERENCES
Notably, mother of King Rehoboam.
GENESIS 4:22; 1 KINGS 14:21

NAAMAN
(*Pleasantness*)
4 MEN/17 REFERENCES
Most notably, leprous captain of the
Syrian army who came to the
prophet Elisha for healing. Angered
that Elisha told him to wash seven
times in the Jordan River, he had
to be persuaded to obey. When
he did, he was healed. Also, son
of Benjamin and a descendant of
Abraham.
GENESIS 46:21; NUMBERS 26:40;
1 CHRONICLES 8:7; 2 KINGS 5:1

NAARAH
(*Girl*)
1 WOMAN/3 REFERENCES
1 CHRONICLES 4:5

NAARAI
(*Youthful*)
1 MAN/1 REFERENCE
One of King David's valiant warriors.
1 CHRONICLES 11:37

NAASHON
(*Enchanter*)
1 MAN/1 REFERENCE
EXODUS 6:23

NAASSON
1 MAN/3 REFERENCES
MATTHEW 1:4

NABAL
(*Dolt*)
1 MAN/22 REFERENCES
First husband of Abigail, Nebal refused
to give David and his men anything
in return for their protection of his
lands during David's battles with
Saul. Abigail generously provided
them with food; ten days later Nabal
died.
1 SAMUEL 25:3

NABOTH

(*Fruits*)

1 MAN/22 REFERENCES

Owner of a vineyard that was coveted by King Ahab of Israel. After Naboth refused to trade it, Queen Jezebel had him stoned, and Ahab took possession of his land.

1 KINGS 21:1

NACHON

(*Prepared*)

1 MAN/1 REFERENCE

2 SAMUEL 6:6

NACHOR

(*Snorer*)

2 MEN/2 REFERENCES

Notably, brother of Abraham. Same as Nahor.

JOSHUA 24:2; LUKE 3:34

NADAB

(*Liberal*)

4 MEN/20 REFERENCES

Most notably, son of Jeroboam, king of Israel, who inherited Jeroboam's throne and did evil and made his country sin. Also, son of Aaron who, along with his brother Abihu, offered strange fire before the Lord. God sent fire from His presence to consume them, and they died.

EXODUS 6:23; 1 KINGS 14:20;
    1 CHRONICLES 2:28;
    1 CHRONICLES 8:30

NAGGE

1 MAN/1 REFERENCE

LUKE 3:25

NAHAM

1 MAN/1 REFERENCE

1 CHRONICLES 4:19

NAHAMANI

(*Consolatory*)

1 MAN/1 REFERENCE

NEHEMIAH 7:7

NAHARAI

(*Snorer*)

1 MAN/1 REFERENCE

One of King David's valiant warriors. Same as Nahari.

1 CHRONICLES 11:39

NAHARI

(*Snorer*)

1 MAN/1 REFERENCE

One of King David's valiant warriors. Same as Naharai.

2 SAMUEL 23:37

NAHASH

3 MEN/9 REFERENCES

Most notably, king of the Ammonites.

1 SAMUEL 11:1; 2 SAMUEL 10:2;
    2 SAMUEL 17:25

NAHATH

(*Quiet*)

3 MEN/5 REFERENCES

Most notably, temple overseer during the reign of King Hezekiah of Judah.

GENESIS 36:13; 1 CHRONICLES 6:26;
    2 CHRONICLES 31:13

NAHBI

(*Occult*)

1 MAN/1 REFERENCE

One of the twelve spies sent by Moses to spy out Canaan.

NUMBERS 13:14

NAHOR

(*Snorer*)

2 MEN/17 REFERENCES

Notably, grandfather of Abraham. Also, brother of Abraham and son of Terah, and married Milcah. Same as Nachor.

GENESIS 11:22; GENESIS 11:26

NAHSHON
(*Enchanter*)
1 MAN/9 REFERENCES
Captain and prince of the tribe of
Judah, appointed by God through
Moses.
NUMBERS 1:7

NAHUM
(*Comfortable*)
1 MAN/1 REFERENCE
Old Testament minor prophet who
preached to Judah after Assyria had
captured Israel.
NAHUM 1:1

NAOMI
(*Pleasant*)
1 WOMAN/21 REFERENCES
Elimelech's wife and mother-in-law to
Ruth. Naomi and her family moved
to Moab during a famine. Following
the deaths of her husband and two
sons, Naomi and Ruth returned to
Bethlehem, impoverished.
RUTH 1:2

NAPHISH
(*Refreshed*)
1 MAN/2 REFERENCES
Son of Ishmael.
GENESIS 25:15

NAPHTALI
(*My wrestling*)
1 MAN/8 REFERENCES
Son of Jacob and founder of one of
Israel's twelve tribes.
GENESIS 30:8

NARCISSUS
(*Narcissus [flower]*)
1 MAN/1 REFERENCE
Head of a household of believers and
greeted by Paul in his letter to the
Romans.
ROMANS 16:11

NATHAN
(*Given*)
10 MEN/43 REFERENCES
Most notably, prophet who confronted
King David about his sin with
Bath-sheba. Also, son of King
David. Also, Jewish exile charged
with finding Levites and temple
servants to travel to Jerusalem with
Ezra. Also, one who will mourn at
the piercing of the Messiah when
God defends Jerusalem.
2 SAMUEL 5:14; 2 SAMUEL 7:2; 2 SAMUEL
23:36; 1 KINGS 4:5; 1 KINGS 4:5;
1 CHRONICLES 2:36; 1 CHRONICLES
11:38; EZRA 8:16; EZRA 10:39;
ZECHARIAH 12:12

NATHANAEL
1 MAN/6 REFERENCES
Jesus' disciple from Cana, described by
Him as an Israelite in whom there
was no guile. Nathanael recognized
Jesus as the Son of God and fol-
lowed Him. Probably the same as
Bartholomew.
JOHN 1:45

NATHAN-MELECH
(*Given of the king*)
1 MAN/1 REFERENCE
Court official under King Josiah of
Judah.
2 KINGS 23:11

NAUM
1 MAN/1 REFERENCE
LUKE 3:25

NEARIAH
(*Servant of God*)
2 MEN/3 REFERENCES
Notably, captain over the sons of
Simeon during the reign of King
Hezekiah of Judah.
1 CHRONICLES 3:22; 1 CHRONICLES 4:42

NEBAI
(*Fruitful*)
1 MAN/1 REFERENCE
Israelite who signed an agreement
    declaring that exiles from Babylon
    would repent and obey God.
NEHEMIAH 10:19

NEBAIOTH
(*Fruitfulness*)
1 MAN/1 REFERENCE
A variant spelling of *Nebajoth*.
1 CHRONICLES 1:29

NEBAJOTH
(*Fruitfulness*)
1 MAN/3 REFERENCES
Ishmael's firstborn son. Same as
    Nebaioth.
GENESIS 25:13

NEBAT
(*Regard*)
1 MAN/25 REFERENCES
Father of King Jeroboam.
1 KINGS 11:26

NEBO
1 MAN/1 REFERENCE
EZRA 10:43

NEBUCHADNEZZAR
1 MAN/60 REFERENCES
King of Babylon who besieged
    Jerusalem, took its king, and brought
    Judah's people into exile, including
    the prophet Daniel, who interpreted
    the king's dream. Daniel and his
    friends Shadrach, Meshach, and
    Abednego refused to worship an
    idol, so Nebuchadnezzar had them
    thrown into a fiery furnace, but they
    were not consumed. Amazed, the
    king declared that no one should
    speak against their God. Same as
    Nebuchadrezzar.
2 KINGS 24:1

NEBUCHADREZZAR
1 MAN/31 REFERENCES
King of Babylon. A variant spelling of
    Nebuchadnezzar.
JEREMIAH 21:2

NEBUSHASBAN
1 MAN/1 REFERENCE
Babylonian official who, at King
    Nebuchadnezzar's command,
    showed kindness to the prophet
    Jeremiah.
JEREMIAH 39:13

NEBUZAR-ADAN
1 MAN/15 REFERENCES
Captain of the guard for King
    Nebuchadnezzar of Babylon and
    carried Israelite captives to Babylon.
2 KINGS 25:8

NECHO
1 MAN/3 REFERENCES
King of Egypt who attacked
    Carchemish.
2 CHRONICLES 35:20

NEDABIAH
(*Largesse of God*)
1 MAN/1 REFERENCE
1 CHRONICLES 3:18

NEHEMIAH
(*Consolation of God*)
3 MEN/8 REFERENCES
Notably, cupbearer sent at his own
    request by Persian King Artaxerxes
    to rebuild Jerusalem, where he ruled
    as governor and rebuilt the walls.
    Also, man who repaired Jerusalem's
    walls under Nehemiah.
EZRA 2:2; NEHEMIAH 1:1; NEHEMIAH 3:16

NEHUM
(*Comforted*)
1 MAN/1 REFERENCE
NEHEMIAH 7:7

NEHUSHTA
(*Copper*)
1 WOMAN/1 REFERENCE
Mother of King Jehoiachin of Judah.
2 KINGS 24:8

NEKODA
(*Distinction, marked*)
2 MEN/4 REFERENCES
EZRA 2:48; EZRA 2:60

NEMUEL
(*Day of God*)
2 MEN/3 REFERENCES
Notably, Reubenite counted in the
census taken by Moses and Aaron.
Same as Jemuel.
NUMBERS 26:9; NUMBERS 26:12

NEPHEG
(*To spring forth, a sprout*)
2 MEN/4 REFERENCES
Notably, son of King David.
EXODUS 6:21; 2 SAMUEL 5:15

NEPHISHESIM
(*To scatter, expansions*)
1 MAN/1 REFERENCE
NEHEMIAH 7:52

NEPHUSIM
(*To scatter, expansions*)
1 MAN/1 REFERENCE
EZRA 2:50

NER
(*Lamp*)
1 MAN/16 REFERENCES
Grandfather of King Saul and father
of Abner.
1 SAMUEL 14:50

NEREUS
(*Wet*)
1 MAN/1 REFERENCE
Christian whom Paul greeted in his
letter to the church at Rome.
ROMANS 16:15

NERGAL-SHAREZER
2 MEN/3 REFERENCES
Notably, prince of Babylon who
besieged Jerusalem during the reign
of King Zedekiah of Judah. Also,
another Babylonian prince who took
part in the destruction of Jerusalem
under King Nebuchadnezzar.
JEREMIAH 39:3; JEREMIAH 39:3

NERI
1 MAN/1 REFERENCE
LUKE 3:27

NERIAH
(*Light of God*)
1 MAN/10 REFERENCES
JEREMIAH 32:12

NETHANEEL
(*Given of God*)
10 MEN/14 REFERENCES
Most notably, head of the tribe of
Issachar during Israel's wandering.
Also, priest who blew a trumpet
before the ark of the covenant when
David brought it to Jerusalem. Also,
prince of Judah who taught the law
of the Lord throughout the nation. Also,
chief Levite who provided for
the first Passover celebration under
King Josiah of Judah. Also, priest
who helped to dedicate the rebuilt
walls of Jerusalem by playing a
musical instrument.
NUMBERS 1:8; 1 CHRONICLES 2:14;
1 CHRONICLES 15:24; 1 CHRONICLES
24:6; 1 CHRONICLES 26:4;
2 CHRONICLES 17:7; 2 CHRONICLES
35:9; EZRA 10:22; NEHEMIAH 12:21;
NEHEMIAH 12:36

NETHANIAH
(*Given of God*)
4 MEN/20 REFERENCES
Most notably, Levite sent by King
Jehoshaphat to teach the law of
the Lord throughout the nation of
Judah.
2 KINGS 25:23; 1 CHRONICLES 25:2;
2 CHRONICLES 17:8; JEREMIAH 36:14

NEZIAH
(*Conspicuous*)
1 MAN/2 REFERENCES
EZRA 2:54

NICANOR
(*Victorious*)
1 MAN/1 REFERENCE
One of seven men selected to serve
needy Christians in Jerusalem.
ACTS 6:5

NICODEMUS
(*Victorious among his people*)
1 MAN/5 REFERENCES
Member of the Jewish Sanhedrin who
came to Jesus by night to question
Him about His miracles and was
told he must be born again. When
the Pharisees wanted to arrest Jesus,
Nicodemus stood up for Him. He
provided the spices with which
Jesus' body was wrapped after His
death.
JOHN 3:1

NICOLAS
(*Victorious over the people*)
1 MAN/1 REFERENCE
One of seven men selected to serve
needy Christians in Jerusalem.
ACTS 6:5

NIGER
(*Black*)
1 MAN/1 REFERENCE
Prophet and teacher in the church at
Antioch in the time of the apostle
Paul. Also called Simeon.
ACTS 13:1

NIMROD
1 MAN/4 REFERENCES
Built the city of Nineveh.
GENESIS 10:8

NIMSHI
(*Extricated*)
1 MAN/5 REFERENCES
1 KINGS 19:16

NOADIAH
(*Convened of God*)
1 MAN/1 WOMAN/2 REFERENCES
Notably, Levite who weighed the
temple vessels after the Babylonian
exile. Also, prophetess who opposed
Nehemiah as he rebuilt Jerusalem's
walls.
EZRA 8:33; NEHEMIAH 6:14

NOAH
(*Rest*)
1 MAN/1 WOMAN/53 REFERENCES
Notably, the man God chose to build
an ark that would save both animals
and people. Same as Noe. Also, one
of Zelophehad's five daughters who
received his inheritance because he
had no sons.
GENESIS 5:29; NUMBERS 26:33

NOBAH
(*A bark*)
1 MAN/2 REFERENCES
Man who took Kenath and its villages
for his inheritance when Moses
divided the Promised Land between
the tribes.
NUMBERS 32:42

NOE
(*Noah*)
1 MAN/5 REFERENCES
Greek spelling of *Noah*, used in the
New Testament.
MATTHEW 24:37

NOGAH
(*Brilliancy*)
1 MAN/2 REFERENCES
Son of King David.
1 CHRONICLES 3:7

NOHAH
(*Quietude*)
1 MAN/1 REFERENCE
Benjamin's fourth son.
1 CHRONICLES 8:2

NON
(*Perpetuity*)
1 MAN/1 REFERENCE
Variant spelling of *Nun*; father of the
Israelite leader Joshua.
1 CHRONICLES 7:27

NUN
(*Perpetuity*)
1 MAN/29 REFERENCES
Father of the Israelite leader Joshua.
Same as Non.
EXODUS 33:11

NYMPHAS
(*Nymph given*)
1 WOMAN/1 REFERENCE
Colossian Christian who had a house
church in her home.
COLOSSIANS 4:15

—O—

OBADIAH
(*Serving God*)
13 MEN/20 REFERENCES
Most notably, Old Testament minor
prophet who spoke God's words
against Edom. Also, "governor" of
the household of King Ahab of
Israel and a man who feared God.
Also, ruler of the tribe of Zebulun in
the days of King David. Also, prince
of Judah sent by King Jehoshaphat
to teach the law of the Lord
throughout the nation.
1 KINGS 18:3; 1 CHRONICLES 3:21;
    1 CHRONICLES 7:3; 1 CHRONICLES 8:38;
    1 CHRONICLES 9:16; 1 CHRONICLES
    12:9; 1 CHRONICLES 27:19;
    2 CHRONICLES 17:7; 2 CHRONICLES
    34:12; EZRA 8:9; NEHEMIAH 10:5;
    NEHEMIAH 12:25; OBADIAH 1:1

OBAL
1 MAN/1 REFERENCE
GENESIS 10:28

OBED
(*Serving*)
5 MEN/13 REFERENCES
Most notably, one of King David's
warriors known as the "mighty
men."
RUTH 4:17; 1 CHRONICLES 2:37;
    1 CHRONICLES 11:47; 1 CHRONICLES
    26:7; 2 CHRONICLES 23:1

OBED-EDOM
(*Worker of Edom*)
3 MEN/20 REFERENCES
Most notably, owner of a house where
the ark of the covenant was kept
for three months before David
brought it to Jerusalem. Also,
Levite musician who performed
in celebration when King David
brought the ark of the covenant to
Jerusalem.
2 SAMUEL 6:10; 1 CHRONICLES 15:18;
    2 CHRONICLES 25:24

OBIL
(*Mournful*)
1 MAN/1 REFERENCE
Servant of King David who was in
charge of the royal camels.
1 CHRONICLES 27:30

OCRAN
(*Muddler*)
1 MAN/5 REFERENCES
NUMBERS 1:13

ODED
(*Reiteration*)
2 MEN/3 REFERENCES
Notably, prophet who warned the
Israelites not to enslave their fellow
Jewish citizens.
2 CHRONICLES 15:1; 2 CHRONICLES 28:9

OG
(*Round*)
1 MAN/22 REFERENCES
Amorite king of Bashan, whom Moses
defeated after Israel failed to enter
the Promised Land.
NUMBERS 21:33

OHAD
(*Unity*)
1 MAN/2 REFERENCES
GENESIS 46:10

OHEL
(*A tent*)
1 MAN/1 REFERENCE
1 CHRONICLES 3:20

OLYMPAS
(*Olympian bestowed or heaven descended*)
1 MAN/1 REFERENCE
Christian whom Paul greeted in his letter to the church at Rome.
ROMANS 16:15

OMAR
(*Talkative*)
1 MAN/3 REFERENCES
GENESIS 36:11

OMRI
(*Heaping*)
4 MEN/18 REFERENCES
Most notably, commander of Israel's army under King Elah, he later became king and did evil, causing Israel to sin. Also, ruler of the tribe of Issachar under David.
1 KINGS 16:16; 1 CHRONICLES 7:8; 1 CHRONICLES 9:4; 1 CHRONICLES 27:18

ON
(*Ability, power, wealth*)
1 MAN/1 REFERENCE
NUMBERS 16:1

ONAM
(*Strong*)
2 MEN/4 REFERENCES
GENESIS 36:23; 1 CHRONICLES 2:26

ONAN
(*Strong*)
1 MAN/8 REFERENCES
GENESIS 38:4

ONESIMUS
(*Profitable*)
1 MAN/2 REFERENCES
Slave of Philemon. He fled his master and met Paul, who led him to Christ.
COLOSSIANS 4:9

ONESIPHORUS
(*Profit bearer*)
1 MAN/2 REFERENCES
Ephesian Christian whose household refreshed Paul.
2 TIMOTHY 1:16

OPHIR
1 MAN/2 REFERENCES
GENESIS 10:29

OPHRAH
(*Female fawn*)
1 MAN/1 REFERENCE
1 CHRONICLES 4:14

OREB
(*Mosquito*)
1 MAN/5 REFERENCES
Prince of Midian who was killed by the tribe of Ephraim when Gideon called the tribe to fight that nation.
JUDGES 7:25

OREN
1 MAN/1 REFERENCE
1 CHRONICLES 2:25

ORNAN
(*Strong*)
1 MAN/12 REFERENCES
Same as Araunah.
1 CHRONICLES 21:15

ORPAH
(*Mane*)
1 WOMAN/2 REFERENCES
Naomi's daughter-in-law who did not follow her to Bethlehem.
RUTH 1:4

OSEE

1 MAN/1 REFERENCE

Greek form of the name *Hoshea*.

ROMANS 9:25

OSHEA

(*Deliverer*)

1 MAN/2 REFERENCES

Variant spelling of the name *Joshua*.

NUMBERS 13:8

OTHNI

(*To force, forcible*)

1 MAN/1 REFERENCE

1 CHRONICLES 26:7

OTHNIEL

(*Force of God*)

1 MAN/6 REFERENCES

Caleb's brother who delivered Israel
    from the king of Mesopotamia and
    judged Israel for forty years.

JOSHUA 15:17

OZEM

(*To be strong, strength*)

2 MEN/2 REFERENCES

Notably, sixth son of Jesse and brother
    of King David.

1 CHRONICLES 2:15; 1 CHRONICLES 2:25

OZIAS

1 MAN/2 REFERENCES

MATTHEW 1:8

OZNI

(*Having quick ears*)

1 MAN/1 REFERENCE

NUMBERS 26:16

—P—

PAARAI

(*Yawning*)

1 MAN/1 REFERENCE

One of King David's warriors known
    as the "mighty men."

2 SAMUEL 23:35

PADON

(*Ransom*)

1 MAN/2 REFERENCES

EZRA 2:44

PAGIEL

(*Accident of God*)

1 MAN/5 REFERENCES

Chief of the tribe of Asher who helped
    Moses take a census of Israel.

NUMBERS 1:13

PAHATH-MOAB

(*Pit of Moab*)

3 MEN/6 REFERENCES

Most notably, Jewish leader who
    renewed the covenant under
    Nehemiah.

EZRA 2:6; EZRA 8:4; NEHEMIAH 10:14

PALAL

(*Judge*)

1 MAN/1 REFERENCE

Man who repaired Jerusalem's walls
    under Nehemiah.

NEHEMIAH 3:25

PALLU

(*Distinguished*)

1 MAN/4 REFERENCES

EXODUS 6:14

PALTI

(*Delivered*)

1 MAN/1 REFERENCE

Spy from the tribe of Benjamin who
    reported that Israel could not take
    the Promised Land.

NUMBERS 13:9

PALTIEL

(*Deliverance of God*)

1 MAN/1 REFERENCE

Prince of the tribe of Issachar when the
    Israelites entered the Promised Land.

NUMBERS 34:26

PARMASHTA

1 MAN/1 REFERENCE

ESTHER 9:9

PARMENAS
(*Constant*)

1 MAN/1 REFERENCE

One of seven men selected to serve
    needy Christians in Jerusalem.

ACTS 6:5

PARNACH

1 MAN/1 REFERENCE

NUMBERS 34:25

PAROSH
(*A flea*)

4 MEN/5 REFERENCES

EZRA 2:3; EZRA 10:25; NEHEMIAH 3:25;
    NEHEMIAH 10:14

PARSHANDATHA

1 MAN/1 REFERENCE

ESTHER 9:7

PARUAH
(*Blossomed*)

1 MAN/1 REFERENCE

1 KINGS 4:17

PASACH
(*Divider*)

1 MAN/1 REFERENCE

1 CHRONICLES 7:33

PASEAH
(*Limping*)

3 MEN/3 REFERENCES

Most notably, prince of Judah who
    sought to have King Zedekiah kill
    Jeremiah because of his negative
    prophecy.

1 CHRONICLES 4:12; EZRA 2:49;
    NEHEMIAH 3:6

PASHUR
(*Liberation*)

4 MEN/14 REFERENCES

Most notably, priest and "chief
    governor" of the temple who
    responded to Jeremiah's prophecies
    by hitting him and putting him in
    the stocks near the temple. Also,
    priest who renewed the covenant
    under Nehemiah.

1 CHRONICLES 9:12; NEHEMIAH 10:3;
    JEREMIAH 20:1; JEREMIAH 21:1

PATROBAS
(*Father's life*)

1 MAN/1 REFERENCE

Christian whom Paul greeted in his
    letter to the church at Rome.

ROMANS 16:14

PAUL
(*Little*)

1 MAN/157 REFERENCES

Latin form of the name Saul; God's
    chosen apostle to the Gentiles who
    zealously persecuted Christians
    until he became one himself as
    he traveled to Damascus and
    was confronted by Jesus. He
    communicated with the churches
    through his epistles to the Romans,
    Corinthians, Galatians, Colossians,
    and Thessalonians and a letter
    to Titus. During his time of
    imprisonment, he wrote additional
    epistles that became scripture:
    Ephesians, Philippians, the letters
    to Timothy, and Philemon. Same
    as Saul.

ACTS 13:9

PAULUS
(*Little*)

1 MAN/1 REFERENCE

Sergius Paulus was a proconsul of
    Cyprus who called on Barnabas and
    Saul to share their faith with him.

ACTS 13:7

PEDAHEL
(*God has ransomed*)
1 MAN/1 REFERENCE
Prince of the tribe of Naphtali when
the Israelites entered the Promised
Land.
NUMBERS 34:28

PEDAHZUR
(*A rock [God] has ransomed*)
1 MAN/5 REFERENCES
NUMBERS 1:10

PEDAIAH
(*God has ransomed*)
6 MEN/8 REFERENCES
Most notably, priest who assisted Ezra
in reading the book of the law to the
people of Jerusalem. Nehemiah also
appointed him one of the temple
treasurers. Also, man who repaired
Jerusalem's walls under Nehemiah.
2 KINGS 23:36; 1 CHRONICLES 3:18;
1 CHRONICLES 27:20; NEHEMIAH 3:25;
NEHEMIAH 8:4; NEHEMIAH 11:7

PEKAH
(*Watch*)
1 MAN/11 REFERENCES
Captain of King Pekahiah of Israel,
he conspired against his king,
killed him, and usurped his throne.
2 KINGS 15:25

PEKAHIAH
(*God has answered*)
1 MAN/3 REFERENCES
Evil ruler of Israel who succeeded his
father, Menahem, as king.
2 KINGS 15:22

PELAIAH
(*God has distinguished*)
3 MEN/3 REFERENCES
Most notably, Levite who helped Israel
to understand the law after Ezra
read it to them.
1 CHRONICLES 3:24; NEHEMIAH 8:7;
NEHEMIAH 10:10

PELALIAH
(*God has judged*)
1 MAN/1 REFERENCE
NEHEMIAH 11:12

PELATIAH
(*God has delivered*)
4 MEN/5 REFERENCES
Most notably, Jewish leader who
renewed the covenant under
Nehemiah. Also, prince of Judah
and a wicked counselor who died
while Ezekiel prophesied against
Jerusalem.
1 CHRONICLES 3:21; 1 CHRONICLES 4:42;
NEHEMIAH 10:22; EZEKIEL 11:1

PELEG
(*Earthquake*)
1 MAN/7 REFERENCES
Same as Phalec.
GENESIS 10:25

PELET
(*Escape*)
2 MEN/2 REFERENCES
Notably, "mighty man" who supported
the future king David during his
conflict with Saul.
1 CHRONICLES 2:47; 1 CHRONICLES 12:3

PELETH
(*To flee, swiftness*)
1 MAN/2 REFERENCES
NUMBERS 16:1

PENINNAH
(*A pearl, round*)
1 WOMAN/3 REFERENCES
Elkanah's wife who had children and
provoked his other wife, Hannah,
who was barren.
1 SAMUEL 1:2

PENUEL
(*Face of God*)
2 MEN/2 REFERENCES
1 CHRONICLES 4:4; 1 CHRONICLES 8:25

PERESH

1 MAN/1 REFERENCE
1 CHRONICLES 7:16

PEREZ

(*A break*)

2 MEN/3 REFERENCES
Same as Pharez and Phares.
1 CHRONICLES 27:3; NEHEMIAH 11:4

PERIDA

(*Dispersion*)

1 MAN/1 REFERENCE
Same as Peruda.
NEHEMIAH 7:57

PERSIS

1 WOMAN/1 REFERENCE
Christian whom Paul greeted and
  commended in his letter to the
  church at Rome.
ROMANS 16:12

PERUDA

(*Dispersions*)

1 MAN/1 REFERENCE
Same as Perida.
EZRA 2:55

PETER

(*A piece of rock*)

1 MAN/162 REFERENCES
Jesus' disciple, also called Simon Peter
  and Simon Bar-Jonah, who was
  called from his fishing to become a
  fisher of men. He walked on water
  and was the first to call Jesus "the
  Christ." Peter cut off the ear of the
  high priest's servant at Jesus' arrest
  then denied Jesus three times. He
  wrote the books of 1 and 2 Peter.
  Same as Cephas.
MATTHEW 4:18

PETHAHIAH

(*God has opened*)

4 MEN/4 REFERENCES
Most notably, one of twenty-four
  priests in David's time who was
  chosen by lot to serve in the
  tabernacle. Also, Levite who led a
  revival among the Israelites in the
  time of Nehemiah.
1 CHRONICLES 24:16; EZRA 10:23;
  NEHEMIAH 9:5; NEHEMIAH 11:24

PETHUEL

(*Enlarged of God*)

1 MAN/1 REFERENCE
Father of the Old Testament minor
  prophet Joel.
JOEL 1:1

PEULTHAI

(*Laborious*)

1 MAN/1 REFERENCE
1 CHRONICLES 26:5

PHALEC

1 MAN/1 REFERENCE
Same as Peleg.
LUKE 3:35

PHALLU

(*Distinguished*)

1 MAN/1 REFERENCE
GENESIS 46:9

PHALTI

(*Delivered*)

1 MAN/1 REFERENCE
Michal's second husband, to whom
  Saul married her after David fled.
  Same as Phaltiel.
1 SAMUEL 25:44

PHALTIEL

(*Deliverance of God*)

1 MAN/1 REFERENCE
Michal's second husband, from whom
  King David claimed her. Same as
  Phalti.
2 SAMUEL 3:15

PHANUEL

1 MAN/1 REFERENCE

Father of the prophetess Anna, who saw the baby Jesus in the temple.

LUKE 2:36

PHARAOH-HOPHRA

1 MAN/1 REFERENCE

King of Egypt who Jeremiah prophesied would be given into the hands of his enemies.

JEREMIAH 44:30

PHARAOH-NECHO

1 MAN/1 REFERENCE

King of Egypt against whom Jeremiah prophesied God would take vengeance. Same as Pharaoh-nechoh.

JEREMIAH 46:2

PHARAOH-NECHOH

1 MAN/4 REFERENCES

King of Egypt who fought Assyria and King Josiah of Judah. Same as Pharaoh-necho.

2 KINGS 23:29

PHARES

1 MAN/3 REFERENCES

Same as Pharez and Perez.

MATTHEW 1:3

PHAREZ

1 MAN/12 REFERENCES

Same as Phares and Perez.

GENESIS 38:29

PHAROSH

(*A flea*)

1 MAN/1 REFERENCE

EZRA 8:3

PHASEAH

(*Limping*)

1 MAN/1 REFERENCE

NEHEMIAH 7:51

PHEBE

(*Bright*)

1 WOMAN/1 REFERENCE

Believer whom Paul recommended that the Roman church assist.

ROMANS 16:1

PHICHOL

(*Mouth of all*)

1 MAN/3 REFERENCES

Commander of the Philistine king Abimelech's army in the time of Abraham and Isaac.

GENESIS 21:22

PHILEMON

(*Friendly*)

1 MAN/1 REFERENCE

Christian owner of the escaped slave Onesimus.

PHILEMON 1:1

PHILETUS

(*Amiable*)

1 MAN/1 REFERENCE

False teacher who opposed Paul, teaching that Christians would not be physically resurrected.

2 TIMOTHY 2:17

PHILIP

(*Fond of horses*)

3 MEN/36 REFERENCES

Most notably, one of seven men selected to serve needy Christians in Jerusalem. He preached to the Ethiopian eunuch and baptized him. Also called Philip the evangelist. Also, disciple of Jesus who introduced the soon-to-be-disciple Nathanael to Him. Also, one called Herod Philip I, the tetrarch of Iturea, and Trachonitis was a son of Herod the Great. His wife, Herodias, left him and married his half brother, Herod.

MATTHEW 10:3; MATTHEW 14:3;
ACTS 6:5

PHILOLOGUS
(*Fond of words*)
1 MAN/1 REFERENCE
Christian whom Paul greeted in his
letter to the church at Rome.
ROMANS 16:15

PHINEHAS
(*Mouth of a serpent*)
3 MEN/25 REFERENCES
Most notably, son of the high priest
Eli who did not know the Lord.
He misused his priestly office and
disobeyed the law.
EXODUS 6:25; 1 SAMUEL 1:3; EZRA 8:33

PHLEGON
(*Blazing*)
1 MAN/1 REFERENCE
Christian whom Paul greeted in his
letter to the church at Rome.
ROMANS 16:14

PHURAH
(*Foliage*)
1 MAN/2 REFERENCES
Servant of Gideon.
JUDGES 7:10

PHUT
1 MAN/2 REFERENCES
A grandson of Noah through his son
Ham.
GENESIS 10:6

PHUVAH
(*A blast*)
1 MAN/1 REFERENCE
GENESIS 46:13

PHYGELLUS
(*Fugitive*)
1 MAN/1 REFERENCE
Asian Christian who turned away from
Paul.
2 TIMOTHY 1:15

PILATE
(*Close pressed*)
1 MAN/56 REFERENCES
Procurator (governor) of Judea before
whom Jesus appeared after His
trial before the Jewish religious
authorities. Pilate understood
He was innocent but, out of fear,
allowed the Jewish leaders to
condemn Jesus. Same as Pontius
Pilate.
MATTHEW 27:2

PILDASH
1 MAN/1 REFERENCE
GENESIS 22:22

PILEHA
(*Slicing*)
1 MAN/1 REFERENCE
Jewish leader who renewed the
covenant under Nehemiah.
NEHEMIAH 10:24

PILTAI
(*A Paltite or descendant of Palti*)
1 MAN/1 REFERENCE
Chief priest under Joiakim in the days
of Zerubbabel.
NEHEMIAH 12:17

PINON
(*Perplexity*)
1 MAN/2 REFERENCES
GENESIS 36:41

PIRAM
(*Wildly*)
1 MAN/1 REFERENCE
JOSHUA 10:3

PISPAH
(*Dispersion*)
1 MAN/1 REFERENCE
1 CHRONICLES 7:38

PITHON
(*Expansive*)
1 MAN/2 REFERENCES
1 CHRONICLES 8:35

POCHERETH
(*To entrap*)
1 MAN/2 REFERENCES
EZRA 2:57

PONTIUS PILATE
(*Pontius, "bridged"; Pilate, "close pressed"*)
1 MAN/4 REFERENCES
Pilate's family name and first name.
Same as Pilate.
MATTHEW 27:2

PORATHA
1 MAN/1 REFERENCE
ESTHER 9:8

PORCIUS FESTUS
(*Porcius, "swinish"; Festus, "festal"*)
1 MAN/1 REFERENCE
Governor of Judea who heard Paul's
case and sent him to Caesar. Also
called Festus.
ACTS 24:27

POTIPHAR
1 MAN/2 REFERENCES
Officer of Pharaoh and captain of
Pharaoh's guard, Potiphar became
master to the enslaved Joseph.
GENESIS 37:36

POTIPHERAH
1 MAN/3 REFERENCES
Egyptian priest of On and father-in-
law of Joseph.
GENESIS 41:45

PRISCA
1 WOMAN/1 REFERENCE
With her husband, Aquila, she was a
coworker of Paul. Same as Priscilla.
2 TIMOTHY 4:19

PRISCILLA
1 WOMAN/5 REFERENCES
Wife of Aquila. This tent-making
couple worked with the apostle Paul
in their craft and in spreading the
gospel and founded a house church
in their home. Same as Prisca.
ACTS 18:2

PROCHORUS
(*Before the dance*)
1 MAN/1 REFERENCE
One of seven men selected to serve
needy Christians in Jerusalem.
ACTS 6:5

PUA
(*A blast*)
1 MAN/1 REFERENCE
Same as Puah.
NUMBERS 26:23

PUAH
(*A blast*)
2 MEN/1 WOMAN/3 REFERENCES
Same as Pua. Also, Hebrew midwife
who did not obey the command of
the king of Egypt to kill all male
Israelite babies.
1 CHRONICLES 7:1; JUDGES 10:1;
EXODUS 1:15

PUBLIUS
(*Popular*)
1 MAN/2 REFERENCES
Chief official of Melita who housed
Paul and his companions after they
were shipwrecked on their way to
Rome.
ACTS 28:7

PUDENS
(*Modest*)
1 MAN/1 REFERENCE
Christian to whom Paul sent greetings
when he wrote Timothy.
2 TIMOTHY 4:21

PUL
1 MAN/3 REFERENCES
King of Assyria who exacted tribute
from Israel then brought the nation
into exile. Possibly the same as
Tiglath-pileser.
2 KINGS 15:19

PUT
1 MAN/1 REFERENCE
1 CHRONICLES 1:8

PUTIEL
(*Contempt of God*)
1 MAN/1 REFERENCE
EXODUS 6:25

QUARTUS
(*Fourth*)
1 MAN/1 REFERENCE
Christian in Corinth who sent his greetings to fellow believers in Paul's letter to Rome.
ROMANS 16:23

RAAMAH
(*Mane*)
1 MAN/4 REFERENCES
GENESIS 10:7

RAAMIAH
(*God has shaken*)
1 MAN/1 REFERENCE
NEHEMIAH 7:7

RABMAG
(*Chief magician*)
1 MAN/2 REFERENCES
Babylonian prince who took part in the destruction of Jerusalem under King Nebuchadnezzar but showed kindness to the prophet Jeremiah.
JEREMIAH 39:3

RABSARIS
(*Chief eunuch*)
2 MEN/3 REFERENCES
Notably, Babylonian prince who took part in the destruction of Jerusalem under King Nebuchadnezzar but showed kindness to the prophet Jeremiah. Also, Assyrian military commander who participated in King Sennacherib's failed attempt to take Jerusalem in the days of King Hezekiah and the prophet Isaiah.
JEREMIAH 39:3; 2 KINGS 18:17

RAB-SHAKEH
(*Chief butler*)
1 MAN/16 REFERENCES
Assyrian field commander sent by King Sennacherib to attack King Hezekiah at Jerusalem. Same as Rabshakeh.
2 KINGS 18:17

RABSHAKEH
(*Chief butler*)
1 MAN/16 REFERENCES
Variant spelling of the name of the Assyrian military commander Rab-shakeh.
ISAIAH 36:2

RACHAB
(*Proud*)
1 WOMAN/1 REFERENCE
Greek form of the name *Rahab*, used in the New Testament.
MATTHEW 1:5

RACHEL
(*Ewe*)
1 WOMAN/47 REFERENCES
Daughter of Laban and wife of Jacob, promised to Jacob for seven years' work. But Laban deceived Jacob, giving her sister, Leah, to him in marriage and requiring Jacob to work another seven years to receive Rachel as his bride. Leah had children, but Rachel remained barren. Finally God enabled Rachel to conceive, and she bore Joseph and Benjamin. Same as Rahel.
GENESIS 29:6

RADDAI
(*Domineering*)
1 MAN/1 REFERENCE
Fifth son of Jesse and older brother of King David.
1 CHRONICLES 2:14

RAGAU
(*Friend*)
1 MAN/1 REFERENCE
Greek form of the name *Reu*, used in the New Testament.
LUKE 3:35

RAGUEL
(*Friend of God*)
1 MAN/1 REFERENCE
Father-in-law of Moses. Same as Reuel and Jethro.
NUMBERS 10:29

RAHAB
(*Proud*)
1 WOMAN/7 REFERENCES
Prostitute of Jericho who hid the two spies whom Joshua sent to look over the city before Israel attacked it. When Jericho fell to Joshua's troops, he kept the spies' promise to spare her and her family. Same as Rachab.
JOSHUA 2:1

RAHAM
(*Pity*)
1 MAN/1 REFERENCE
1 CHRONICLES 2:44

RAHEL
(*Ewe*)
1 WOMAN/1 REFERENCE
Variant spelling of the name of Jacob's wife Rachel.
JEREMIAH 31:15

RAKEM
(*Parti-colored*)
1 MAN/1 REFERENCE
1 CHRONICLES 7:16

RAM
(*High*)
3 MEN/7 REFERENCES
RUTH 4:19; 1 CHRONICLES 2:25; JOB 32:2

RAMIAH
(*God has raised*)
1 MAN/1 REFERENCE
EZRA 10:25

RAMOTH
(*Elevations*)
1 MAN/1 REFERENCE
EZRA 10:29

RAPHA
(*Giant*)
2 MEN/2 REFERENCES
1 CHRONICLES 8:2; 1 CHRONICLES 8:37

RAPHU
(*Cured*)
1 MAN/1 REFERENCE
NUMBERS 13:9

REAIA
(*God has seen*)
1 MAN/1 REFERENCE
1 CHRONICLES 5:5

REAIAH
(*God has seen*)
2 MEN/3 REFERENCES
1 CHRONICLES 4:2; EZRA 2:47

REBA
(*A fourth*)
1 MAN/2 REFERENCES
Midianite king killed by the Israelites at God's command.
NUMBERS 31:8

REBECCA
(*Fettering by beauty*)
1 WOMAN/1 REFERENCE
Greek form of the name *Rebekah*, used in the New Testament.
ROMANS 9:10

REBEKAH
(*Fettering by beauty*)
1 WOMAN/30 REFERENCES
Wife for Abraham's son, Isaac, discovered by Abraham's servant as she watered his camels. She agreed to marry Isaac and traveled to her new home. She was at first barren, but then conceived twins Esau and Jacob. Same as Rebecca.
GENESIS 22:23

RECHAB
(*Rider*)
3 MEN/13 REFERENCES
Most notably, leader of one of the
raiding bands of Saul's son Ish-
bosheth. Also, father of Jonadab,
who commanded his descendants
not to drink wine.
2 SAMUEL 4:2; 2 KINGS 10:15;
NEHEMIAH 3:14

REELAIAH
(*Fearful of God*)
1 MAN/1 REFERENCE
EZRA 2:2

REGEM
(*Stone heap*)
1 MAN/1 REFERENCE
1 CHRONICLES 2:47

REGEM-MELECH
(*King's heap*)
1 MAN/1 REFERENCE
Messenger sent to the prophet
Zechariah to ask if the Jews should
fast over their exile in Babylon.
ZECHARIAH 7:2

REHABIAH
(*God has enlarged*)
1 MAN/5 REFERENCES
1 CHRONICLES 23:17

REHOB
(*Width*)
2 MEN/3 REFERENCES
Notably, father of Hadadezer, king
of Zobah, whom King David
conquered. Also, Jewish leader
who renewed the covenant under
Nehemiah.
2 SAMUEL 8:3; NEHEMIAH 10:11

REHOBOAM
(*A people has enlarged*)
1 MAN/50 REFERENCES
Son of King Solomon who inherited
the kingdom of Israel. Same as
Roboam.
1 KINGS 11:43

REHUM
(*Compassionate*)
4 MEN/8 REFERENCES
Most notably, officer of the Persian
king Artaxerxes who joined
in opposition to Zerubbabel's
rebuilding of the temple in
Jerusalem. Also, Levite who repaired
the walls of Jerusalem under
Nehemiah. Also, Jewish leader
who renewed the covenant under
Nehemiah.
EZRA 2:2; EZRA 4:8; NEHEMIAH 3:17;
NEHEMIAH 10:25

REI
(*Social*)
1 MAN/1 REFERENCE
Friend of King David who did not join
in the attempted coup of David's
son Adonijah.
1 KINGS 1:8

REKEM
(*Parti-colored*)
2 MEN/4 REFERENCES
Notably, Midianite king killed by the
Israelites at God's command to
Moses.
NUMBERS 31:8; 1 CHRONICLES 2:43

REMALIAH
(*God has bedecked*)
1 MAN/13 REFERENCES
Father of King Pekah of Israel.
2 KINGS 15:25

REPHAEL
(*God has cured*)
1 MAN/1 REFERENCE
1 CHRONICLES 26:7

REPHAH
(*To sustain*)
1 MAN/1 REFERENCE
1 CHRONICLES 7:25

REPHAIAH
(*God has cured*)
5 MEN/5 REFERENCES
Most notably, city official of Jerusalem
and rebuilder of the walls under
Nehemiah.
1 CHRONICLES 3:21; 1 CHRONICLES 4:42;
1 CHRONICLES 7:2; 1 CHRONICLES 9:43;
NEHEMIAH 3:9

RESHEPH
(*Lightning*)
1 MAN/1 REFERENCE
1 CHRONICLES 7:25

REU
(*Friend*)
1 MAN/5 REFERENCES
Same as Ragau.
GENESIS 11:18

REUBEN
(*See ye a son*)
1 MAN/26 REFERENCES
Jacob and Leah's first son. Brother of
Joseph who was sorrowful when he
learned his brothers had sold Joseph
as a slave; Reuben had hoped to
return him to their father.
GENESIS 29:32

REUEL
(*Friend of God*)
4 MEN/10 REFERENCES
Most notably, father-in-law of Moses.
Same as Raguel and Jethro. Also,
son of Esau.
GENESIS 36:4; EXODUS 2:18; NUMBERS
2:14; 1 CHRONICLES 9:8

REUMAH
(*Raised*)
1 WOMAN/1 REFERENCE
GENESIS 22:24

REZIA
(*Delight*)
1 MAN/1 REFERENCE
1 CHRONICLES 7:39

REZIN
(*Delight*)
2 MEN/10 REFERENCES
Notably, king of Syria who attacked
Judah during the reigns of kings
Jotham and Ahaz.
2 KINGS 15:37; EZRA 2:48

REZON
(*Prince*)
1 MAN/1 REFERENCE
Rebel leader in Damascus who became
King Solomon's adversary.
1 KINGS 11:23

RHESA
(*God has cured*)
1 MAN/1 REFERENCE
LUKE 3:27

RHODA
(*Rose*)
1 WOMAN/1 REFERENCE
Young woman serving in the Jerusalem
home of Mary, mother of John
Mark, who responded to a knock
at the gate. She heard the voice of
Peter, and in her excitement, she
forgot to let Peter in, returning
instead to those who were praying
for his release.
ACTS 12:13

RIBAI
(*Contentious*)
1 MAN/2 REFERENCES
2 SAMUEL 23:29

RIMMON
(*Pomegranate*)
1 MAN/3 REFERENCES
2 SAMUEL 4:2

RINNAH
(*Creaking*)
1 MAN/1 REFERENCE
1 CHRONICLES 4:20

RIPHATH
1 MAN/2 REFERENCES
GENESIS 10:3

RIZPAH
(*Hot stone*)
1 WOMAN/4 REFERENCES
Concubine of Saul.
2 SAMUEL 3:7

ROBOAM
(*A people has enlarged*)
1 MAN/2 REFERENCES
Greek form of the name *Rehoboam*,
    used in the New Testament. Son of
    Solomon and first king of Judah, the
    southern portion of divided Israel.
MATTHEW 1:7

ROHGAH
(*Outcry*)
1 MAN/1 REFERENCE
1 CHRONICLES 7:34

ROMAMTI-EZER
(*I have raised up a help*)
1 MAN/2 REFERENCES
1 CHRONICLES 25:4

ROSH
(*To shake the head*)
1 MAN/1 REFERENCE
GENESIS 46:21

RUFUS
(*Red*)
2 MEN/2 REFERENCES
Notably, son of Simon, man from
    Cyrene forced by Roman soldiers to
    carry Jesus' cross to Golgotha, the
    crucifixion site. Also, acquaintance
    whom the apostle Paul greeted in
    his letter to the Romans.
MARK 15:21; ROMANS 16:13

RUTH
(*Friend*)
1 WOMAN/13 REFERENCES
Moabite daughter-in-law of Naomi,
    married to Naomi's son Mahlon.
    After Mahlon's death, she returned
    to Bethlehem with Naomi. There she
    gleaned barley in Boaz's field and she
    married him, her kinsman-redeemer.
RUTH 1:4

—S—

SABTA
1 MAN/1 REFERENCE
Same as Sabtah.
1 CHRONICLES 1:9

SABTAH
1 MAN/1 REFERENCE
Same as Sabta.
GENESIS 10:7

SABTECHA
1 MAN/1 REFERENCE
Same as Sabtechah.
1 CHRONICLES 1:9

SABTECHAH
1 MAN/1 REFERENCE
Same as Sabtecha.
GENESIS 10:7

SACAR
(*Recompense*)
2 MEN/2 REFERENCES
1 CHRONICLES 11:35; 1 CHRONICLES 26:4

SADOC
(*Just*)
1 MAN/2 REFERENCES
MATTHEW 1:14

SALA
(*Spear*)
1 MAN/1 REFERENCE
Greek form of the name *Salah*, used in
    the New Testament.
LUKE 3:35

SALAH
(*Spear*)
1 MAN/1 REFERENCE
Same as Sala.
GENESIS 10:24

SALATHIEL
(*I have asked God*)
1 MAN/4 REFERENCES
1 CHRONICLES 3:17

SALLAI
(*Weighed*)
2 MEN/2 REFERENCES
Notably, man chosen by lot to resettle Jerusalem after the Babylonian Exile. Also, priest who returned to Jerusalem with Zerubbabel.
NEHEMIAH 11:8; NEHEMIAH 12:20

SALLU
(*Weighed*)
2 MEN/3 REFERENCES
Notably, man chosen by lot to resettle Jerusalem after the Babylonian Exile. Also, exiled priest who returned to Judah under Zerubbabel.
1 CHRONICLES 9:7; NEHEMIAH 12:7

SALMA
(*Clothing*)
1 MAN/4 REFERENCES
Father of Boaz and a descendant of Abraham through Jacob's son Judah. Same as Salmon.
1 CHRONICLES 2:11

SALMON
(*Clothing*)
1 MAN/5 REFERENCES
Father of Boaz and a forefather of Jesus. Same as Salma.
RUTH 4:20

SALOME
(*Welfare*)
1 WOMAN/2 REFERENCES
Follower of Jesus who witnessed His death on the cross and later brought spices to anoint His body—only to find it gone due to His resurrection.
MARK 15:40

SALU
(*Weighed*)
1 MAN/1 REFERENCE
NUMBERS 25:14

SAMGAR-NEBO
1 MAN/1 REFERENCE
Babylonian prince who took part in the destruction of Jerusalem under King Nebuchadnezzar.
JEREMIAH 39:3

SAMLAH
(*Dress*)
1 MAN/4 REFERENCES
King of Edom.
GENESIS 36:36

SAMSON
(*Sunlight*)
1 MAN/39 REFERENCES
Twelfth judge of Israel who was to follow a Nazarite vow, which included not cutting his hair, the source of his strength. His wife, Delilah, betrayed him after he revealed his secret to her. His hair was shaved, but as his hair grew, his strength returned. While bound by the Philistines, he leaned on the pillars of the temple and brought it down, killing the worshippers and himself.
JUDGES 13:24

SAMUEL
(*Heard of God*)
1 MAN/142 REFERENCES
Prophet and judge of Israel. After Samuel's birth, his mother gave him to Eli to raise in the temple. God spoke to him; Samuel mistakenly thought Eli called, but Eli told him that it was God's voice. Anointed Saul king and later anointed David king in Saul's place. Same as Shemuel.
1 SAMUEL 1:20

SANBALLAT
1 MAN/10 REFERENCES
One of Nehemiah's opponents who plotted to fight against Jerusalem as he rebuilt the walls.
NEHEMIAH 2:10

SAPH

(*Containing*)

1 MAN/1 REFERENCE

2 SAMUEL 21:18

SAPPHIRA

(*Sapphire*)

1 WOMAN/1 REFERENCE

Wife of Ananias who lied to the
apostle Peter and was struck dead.

ACTS 5:1

SARA

(*Female noble*)

1 WOMAN/2 REFERENCES

Greek form of the name *Sarah*, used in
the New Testament.

HEBREWS 11:1

SARAH

(*Female noble*)

2 WOMEN/41 REFERENCES

Notably, the name God gave Sarai,
wife of Abram (Abraham), after
He promised she would bear a child.
When she was over ninety years old,
she bore Isaac.

GENESIS 17:15; NUMBERS 26:46

SARAI

(*Controlling*)

1 WOMAN/17 REFERENCES

Barren wife of Abram who traveled
with her husband to Canaan at
God's calling. Sarai had no children,
so she gave her maid, Hagar, to
Abram to bear children for her; but
Hagar despised Sarai and fled. God
changed her name to Sarah, and she
gave birth to a son who would be
the father of a multitude.

GENESIS 11:29

SARAPH

(*Burning*)

1 MAN/1 REFERENCE

1 CHRONICLES 4:22

SARGON

1 MAN/1 REFERENCE

King of Assyria in the days of the
prophet Isaiah.

ISAIAH 20:1

SARSECHIM

1 MAN/1 REFERENCE

Babylonian prince who took part in the
destruction of Jerusalem under King
Nebuchadnezzar.

JEREMIAH 39:3

SARUCH

(*Tendril*)

1 MAN/1 REFERENCE

LUKE 3:35

SAUL

(*Asked*)

3 MEN/422 REFERENCES

Most notably, anointed king of Israel
by the prophet Samuel, he fought
the Philistines throughout his reign.
He wrongly made a burnt offering,
and the consequence was that his
kingdom would not be established
forever. Because of his sin, God
rejected him as Israel's king. Samuel
anointed David king, and Saul
became increasingly jealous of
and attempted to kill him. In fear,
he consulted a witch, then soon
died in battle. Also, zealous Jew
who witnessed the martyrdom of
Stephen and persecuted Christians.
He was temporarily blinded and
turned to Christ, preaching His
message and traveling on missionary
journeys, at which time scripture
begins to call him Paul.

GENESIS 36:37; 1 SAMUEL 9:2; ACTS 7:58

SCEVA

(*Left-handed*)

1 MAN/1 REFERENCE

Jewish chief priest in Ephesus whose
seven sons were beaten by a demon-
possessed man during an attempted
exorcism.

ACTS 19:14

SEBA
1 MAN/2 REFERENCES
GENESIS 10:7

SECUNDUS
(*Second*)
1 MAN/1 REFERENCE
Man from Thessalonica who was a
traveling companion of the apostle
Paul.
ACTS 20:4

SEGUB
(*Aloft*)
2 MEN/3 REFERENCES
1 KINGS 16:34; 1 CHRONICLES 2:21

SEIR
(*Rough*)
1 MAN/2 REFERENCES
GENESIS 36:20

SELED
(*Exultation*)
1 MAN/2 REFERENCES
1 CHRONICLES 2:30

SEM
1 MAN/1 REFERENCE
Greek form of the name *Shem*, used in
the New Testament.
LUKE 3:36

SEMACHIAH
(*Supported of God*)
1 MAN/1 REFERENCE
1 CHRONICLES 26:7

SEMEI
(*Famous*)
1 MAN/1 REFERENCE
LUKE 3:26

SENNACHERIB
1 MAN/13 REFERENCES
King of Assyria who attacked and
captured Judah's fortified cities
during King Hezekiah's reign.
2 KINGS 18:13

SENUAH
(*Pointed*)
1 MAN/1 REFERENCE
Father of man chosen by lot to resettle
Jerusalem after the Babylonian Exile.
NEHEMIAH 11:9

SEORIM
(*Barley*)
1 MAN/1 REFERENCE
One of twenty-four priests in David's
time who was chosen by lot to serve
in the tabernacle.
1 CHRONICLES 24:8

SERAH
(*Superfluity*)
1 WOMAN/2 REFERENCES
GENESIS 46:17

SERAIAH
(*God has prevailed*)
9 MEN/20 REFERENCES
Most notably, scribe in King David's
court. Also, high priest during
King Zedekiah's reign. Also,
priest who renewed the covenant
under Nehemiah. Also, priest who
resettled Jerusalem following the
Babylonian Exile.
2 SAMUEL 8:17; 2 KINGS 25:18;
2 KINGS 25:23; 1 CHRONICLES 4:13;
1 CHRONICLES 4:35; EZRA 2:2;
NEHEMIAH 11:11; JEREMIAH 36:26;
JEREMIAH 51:59

SERED
(*Trembling*)
1 MAN/2 REFERENCES
GENESIS 46:14

SERGIUS
1 MAN/1 REFERENCE
Roman ruler of Cyprus during the
apostle Paul's first missionary
journey. Asked Paul and Barnabas
to share the word of God with him.
A false prophet interfered, but after
Paul pronounced blindness on him,
Sergius came to faith.
ACTS 13:7

SERUG
(*Tendril*)
1 MAN/5 REFERENCES
GENESIS 11:20

SETH
(*Substituted*)
1 MAN/8 REFERENCES
Adam and Eve's third son, whom Eve
    bore after Abel was killed by his
    brother Cain. Same as Sheth.
GENESIS 4:25

SETHUR
(*Hidden*)
1 MAN/1 REFERENCE
One of twelve spies sent by Moses to
    spy out the land of Canaan.
NUMBERS 13:13

SHAAPH
(*Fluctuation*)
1 CHRONICLES 2:47

SHAASHGAZ
1 MAN/1 REFERENCE
Eunuch serving Persian king
    Ahasuerus, overseeing the king's
    harem, including the future queen
    Esther.
ESTHER 2:14

SHABBETHAI
(*Restful*)
3 MEN/3 REFERENCES
Most notably, Levite who helped Ezra
    to explain the law to exiles returned
    to Jerusalem. Also, Levite who
    oversaw the outside of the Jerusalem
    temple in the time of Nehemiah.
EZRA 10:15; NEHEMIAH 8:7;
    NEHEMIAH 11:16

SHACHIA
(*Captivation*)
1 MAN/1 REFERENCE
1 CHRONICLES 8:10

SHADRACH
1 MAN/15 REFERENCES
Babylonian name for Hananiah, one
    of Daniel's companions in exile.
    Survived being cast into a fiery
    furnace when he refused to bow to
    an idol.
DANIEL 1:7

SHAGE
1 MAN/1 REFERENCE
1 CHRONICLES 11:34

SHAHARAIM
(*Double dawn*)
1 MAN/1 REFERENCE
1 CHRONICLES 8:8

SHALLUM
(*Retribution*)
14 MEN/27 REFERENCES
Most notably, fifth-to-last king of
    the northern kingdom of Israel,
    obtained the throne by assassinating
    King Zachariah. Also, husband of
    the prophetess Huldah during the
    reign of King Josiah. Also, fourth
    son of Judah's king Josiah who
    inherited the throne from his father.
    Same as Jehoahaz. Also, city official
    who, with the aid of his daughters,
    helped to rebuild the walls of
    Jerusalem under Nehemiah.
2 KINGS 15:10; 2 KINGS 22:14;
    1 CHRONICLES 2:40; 1 CHRONICLES
    3:15; 1 CHRONICLES 4:25;
    1 CHRONICLES 6:12; 1 CHRONICLES
    7:13; 1 CHRONICLES 9:17;
    2 CHRONICLES 28:12; EZRA 10:24;
    EZRA 10:42; NEHEMIAH 3:12;
    JEREMIAH 32:7; JEREMIAH 35:4

SHALLUN
(*Retribution*)
1 MAN/1 REFERENCE
Rebuilder of the walls of Jerusalem,
    repaired the Fountain Gate.
NEHEMIAH 3:15

SHALMAI
(*Clothed*)
1 MAN/2 REFERENCES
EZRA 2:46

SHALMAN
1 MAN/1 REFERENCE
Variant spelling of the name
Shalmaneser, king of Assyria.
HOSEA 10:14

SHALMANESER
1 MAN/2 REFERENCES
King of Assyria who imprisoned King
Hoshea of Israel and besieged and
captured Samaria and brought Israel
into exile. Same as Shalman.
2 KINGS 17:3

SHAMA
(*Obedient*)
1 MAN/1 REFERENCE
One of King David's valiant warriors.
1 CHRONICLES 11:44

SHAMARIAH
1 MAN/1 REFERENCE
Son of Judah's king Rehoboam and a
grandson of Solomon.
2 CHRONICLES 11:19

SHAMED
(*Preserved*)
1 MAN/1 REFERENCE
1 CHRONICLES 8:12

SHAMER
(*Preserved*)
2 MEN/2 REFERENCES
1 CHRONICLES 6:46; 1 CHRONICLES 7:34

SHAMGAR
1 MAN/2 REFERENCES
Third judge of Israel who killed six
hundred Philistines with an ox goad.
JUDGES 3:31

SHAMHUTH
(*Desolation*)
1 MAN/1 REFERENCE
Commander in King David's army
overseeing twenty-four thousand
men in the fifth month of each year.
1 CHRONICLES 27:8

SHAMIR
(*Observed*)
1 MAN/1 REFERENCE
1 CHRONICLES 24:24

SHAMMA
(*Desolation*)
1 MAN/1 REFERENCE
1 CHRONICLES 7:37

SHAMMAH
(*Consternation*)
4 MEN/8 REFERENCES
Most notably, third son of Jesse and an
older brother of King David who
served as a soldier in King Saul's
army. Same as Shimea and Shimeah.
Also, one of King David's warriors
known as the "mighty men." Also,
one of King David's valiant warriors.
GENESIS 36:13; 1 SAMUEL 16:9; 2 SAMUEL
23:11; 2 SAMUEL 23:25

SHAMMAI
(*Destructive*)
3 MEN/6 REFERENCES
1 CHRONICLES 2:28; 1 CHRONICLES 2:44;
1 CHRONICLES 4:17

SHAMMOTH
(*Ruins*)
1 MAN/1 REFERENCE
One of King David's valiant warriors.
1 CHRONICLES 11:27

SHAMMUA
(*Renowned*)
4 MEN/4 REFERENCES
Most notably, son of King David. Same
as Shammuah. Also, one of twelve
spies sent by Moses to spy out the
land of Canaan.
NUMBERS 13:4; 1 CHRONICLES 14:4;
NEHEMIAH 11:17; NEHEMIAH 12:18

SHAMMUAH

(*Renowned*)

1 MAN/1 REFERENCE

Son of King David. Same as Shammua.

2 SAMUEL 5:14

SHAMSHERAI

(*Sunlike*)

1 MAN/1 REFERENCE

1 CHRONICLES 8:26

SHAPHAM

(*Baldly*)

1 MAN/1 REFERENCE

1 CHRONICLES 5:12

SHAPHAN

(*Rock-rabbit*)

4 MEN/30 REFERENCES

Most notably, scribe for King Josiah of Judah.

2 KINGS 22:3; 2 KINGS 22:12; JEREMIAH 29:3; EZEKIEL 8:11

SHAPHAT

(*Judge*)

5 MEN/8 REFERENCES

Most notably, one of twelve spies sent by Moses to spy out the land of Canaan. Also, father of the prophet Elisha. Also, King David's chief shepherd over herds in the valleys.

NUMBERS 13:5; 1 KINGS 19:16; 1 CHRONICLES 3:22; 1 CHRONICLES 5:12; 1 CHRONICLES 27:29

SHARAI

(*Hostile*)

1 MAN/1 REFERENCE

EZRA 10:40

SHARAR

(*Hostile*)

1 MAN/1 REFERENCE

2 SAMUEL 23:33

SHAREZER

1 MAN/2 REFERENCES

Son of the Assyrian king Sennacherib who, with his brother Adrammelech, killed his father.

2 KINGS 19:37

SHASHAI

(*Whitish*)

1 MAN/1 REFERENCE

EZRA 10:40

SHASHAK

(*Pedestrian*)

1 MAN/2 REFERENCES

1 CHRONICLES 8:14

SHAUL

(*Asked*)

3 MEN/7 REFERENCES

Most notably, king of Edom in the days before Israel had a king.

GENESIS 46:10; 1 CHRONICLES 1:48; 1 CHRONICLES 6:24

SHAVSHA

(*Joyful*)

1 MAN/1 REFERENCE

Scribe serving in the government of King David.

1 CHRONICLES 18:16

SHEAL

(*Request*)

1 MAN/1 REFERENCE

EZRA 10:29

SHEALTIEL

(*I have asked God*)

1 MAN/9 REFERENCES

Father of Zerubbabel, governor of Judah after the Babylonian Exile.

EZRA 3:2

SHEARIAH

(*God has stormed*)

1 MAN/2 REFERENCES

1 CHRONICLES 8:38

SHEAR-JASHUB
(*A remnant will return*)
1 MAN/1 REFERENCE
Son of Isaiah who joined the prophet
in delivering a message to Judah's
king Ahaz.
ISAIAH 7:3

SHEBA
5 MEN/15 REFERENCES
Most notably, Israelite who rebelled
against King David.
GENESIS 10:7; GENESIS 10:28; GENESIS
25:3; 2 SAMUEL 20:1;
1 CHRONICLES 5:13

SHEBANIAH
(*God has grown*)
4 MEN/7 REFERENCES
Most notably, priest who blew a
trumpet before the ark of the
covenant when David brought it to
Jerusalem. Also, one of a group of
Levites who led a revival among the
Israelites in the time of Nehemiah.
Also, priest who renewed the
covenant under Nehemiah. Also,
Levite who renewed the covenant
under Nehemiah.
1 CHRONICLES 15:24; NEHEMIAH 9:4;
NEHEMIAH 10:4; NEHEMIAH 10:12

SHEBER
(*Fracture*)
1 MAN/1 REFERENCE
1 CHRONICLES 2:48

SHEBNA
(*Growth*)
2 MEN/9 REFERENCES
Most notably, scribe for King
Hezekiah of Judah who spoke to
King Sennacherib's representative
and also later took a message to
the prophet Isaiah. Also, treasurer
(steward) Isaiah prophesied against
for building himself a kingly tomb.
2 KINGS 18:18; ISAIAH 22:15

SHEBUEL
(*Captive of God*)
2 MEN/3 REFERENCES
1 CHRONICLES 23:16; 1 CHRONICLES 25:4

SHECANIAH
(*God has dwelt*)
2 MEN/2 REFERENCES
Notably, one of twenty-four priests in
David's time who was chosen by
lot to serve in the tabernacle. Also,
priest in the time of King Hezekiah
who helped to distribute freewill
offerings to his fellow priests.
1 CHRONICLES 24:11; 2 CHRONICLES 31:15

SHECHANIAH
(*God has dwelt*)
7 MEN/8 REFERENCES
Most notably, priest who returned to
Jerusalem under Zerubbabel.
1 CHRONICLES 3:21; EZRA 8:3; EZRA
8:5; EZRA 10:2; NEHEMIAH 3:29;
NEHEMIAH 6:18; NEHEMIAH 12:3

SHECHEM
(*Neck*)
3 MEN/19 REFERENCES
Most notably, prince of the city
of Shechem who raped Jacob's
daughter, Dinah, then wanted
to marry her. Simeon and Levi
attacked the city; killed Shechem,
his father, and all the males of the
city; and brought Dinah home.
GENESIS 34:2; NUMBERS 26:31;
1 CHRONICLES 7:19

SHEDEUR
(*Spreader of light*)
1 MAN/5 REFERENCES
NUMBERS 1:5

SHEHARIAH
(*God has sought*)
1 MAN/1 REFERENCE
1 CHRONICLES 8:26

SHELAH
(*Request*)
2 MEN/11 REFERENCES
Notably, son of Jacob's son Judah.
GENESIS 38:5; 1 CHRONICLES 1:18

SHELEMIAH
(*Thank-offering of God*)
9 MEN/10 REFERENCES
Most notably, Levite who was chosen
by lot to guard the east side of the
house of the Lord. Also, priest
whom Nehemiah made treasurer
to distribute the portions of the
Levites. Also, man whom King
Jehoiakim ordered to imprison the
prophet Jeremiah and his scribe.
1 CHRONICLES 26:14; EZRA 10:39; EZRA
10:41; NEHEMIAH 3:30; NEHEMIAH
13:13; JEREMIAH 36:14; JEREMIAH
36:26; JEREMIAH 37:3; JEREMIAH 37:13

SHELEPH
(*Extract*)
1 MAN/2 REFERENCES
GENESIS 10:26

SHELESH
(*Triplet*)
1 MAN/1 REFERENCE
1 CHRONICLES 7:35

SHELOMI
(*Peaceable*)
1 MAN/1 REFERENCE
NUMBERS 34:27

SHELOMITH
(*Peaceableness, pacification*)
5 MEN/2 WOMEN/9 REFERENCES
Most notably, Levite chief appointed
under King David. Same as
Shelomoth. Also, Levite in charge
of the treasures that were dedicated
to the temple. Also, son of Judah's
king Rehoboam and grandson of
Solomon.
LEVITICUS 24:11; 1 CHRONICLES 3:19;
1 CHRONICLES 23:9; 1 CHRONICLES
23:18; 1 CHRONICLES 26:25;
2 CHRONICLES 11:20; EZRA 8:10

SHELOMOTH
(*Pacification*)
1 MAN/1 REFERENCE
Same as Shelomith.
1 CHRONICLES 24:22

SHELUMIEL
(*Peace of God*)
1 MAN/5 REFERENCES
Man of the tribe of Simeon who
helped Aaron take a census.
NUMBERS 1:6

SHEM
(*Name*)
1 MAN/17 REFERENCES
Eldest son of Noah, he joined Noah in
the ark. Same as Sem.
GENESIS 5:32

SHEMA
(*Heard*)
4 MEN/5 REFERENCES
Most notably, priest who assisted Ezra
in reading the book of the law to the
people of Jerusalem.
1 CHRONICLES 2:43; 1 CHRONICLES 5:8;
1 CHRONICLES 8:13; NEHEMIAH 8:4

SHEMAAH
(*Annunciation*)
1 MAN/1 REFERENCE
1 CHRONICLES 12:3

SHEMAIAH
(*God has heard*)
25 MEN/41 REFERENCES
Most notably, prophet who told King
Rehoboam not to fight Israel when
it revolted against him. Also, one
of a group of Levites appointed by
King David to bring the ark of the
covenant from the house of Obed-
edom to Jerusalem. Also, one of a
group of Levites who cleansed the
Jerusalem temple during the revival
in King Hezekiah's reign. Also, one
of a group who distributed sacrificial
animals to fellow Levites preparing
to celebrate the Passover under King
Josiah. Also, man who repaired

Jerusalem's walls under Nehemiah. Also, priest who renewed the covenant under Nehemiah.

1 Kings 12:22; 1 Chronicles 3:22; 1 Chronicles 4:37; 1 Chronicles 5:4; 1 Chronicles 9:14; 1 Chronicles 9:16; 1 Chronicles 15:8; 1 Chronicles 24:6; 1 Chronicles 26:4; 2 Chronicles 17:8; 2 Chronicles 29:14; 2 Chronicles 31:15; 2 Chronicles 35:9; Ezra 8:13; Ezra 8:16; Ezra 10:21; Ezra 10:31; Nehemiah 3:29; Nehemiah 6:10; Nehemiah 10:8; Nehemiah 12:36; Nehemiah 12:42; Jeremiah 26:20; Jeremiah 29:24; Jeremiah 36:12

SHEMARIAH
(*God has guarded*)
3 MEN/3 REFERENCES
Most notably, "mighty man" who supported the future king David during his conflict with Saul.
1 Chronicles 12:5; Ezra 10:32; Ezra 10:41

SHEMEBER
(*Illustrious*)
1 MAN/1 REFERENCE
King of Zeboiim in the days of Abram.
Genesis 14:2

SHEMER
(*Preserved*)
1 MAN/1 REFERENCE
Owner of the hill of Samaria, which he sold to King Omri of Israel.
1 Kings 16:24

SHEMIDA
(*Name of knowing*)
1 MAN/2 REFERENCES
Same as Shemidah.
Numbers 26:32

SHEMIDAH
(*Name of knowing*)
1 MAN/1 REFERENCE
Same as Shemida.
1 Chronicles 7:19

SHEMIRAMOTH
(*Name of heights*)
2 MEN/4 REFERENCES
Notably, Levite musician who performed in celebration when King David brought the ark of the covenant to Jerusalem. Also, Levite sent by King Jehoshaphat to teach the law of the Lord throughout the nation of Judah.
1 Chronicles 15:18; 2 Chronicles 17:8

SHEMUEL
(*Heard of God*)
3 MEN/3 REFERENCES
Most notably, prince of the tribe of Simeon when the Israelites entered the Promised Land. Also, alternative name for the prophet Samuel.
Numbers 34:20; 1 Chronicles 6:33; 1 Chronicles 7:2

SHENAZAR
1 MAN/1 REFERENCE
1 Chronicles 3:18

SHEPHATHIAH
(*God has judged*)
1 MAN/1 REFERENCE
1 Chronicles 9:8

SHEPHATIAH
(*God has judged*)
9 MEN/12 REFERENCES
Notably, fifth son of David, born to his wife Abital. Also, "mighty man" who supported the future king David during his conflict with Saul. Also, leader of the tribe of Simeon in the days of King David. Also, son of Judah's king Jehoshaphat.
2 Samuel 3:4; 1 Chronicles 12:5; 1 Chronicles 27:16; 2 Chronicles 21:2; Ezra 2:4; Ezra 2:57; Ezra 8:8; Nehemiah 11:4; Jeremiah 38:1

SHEPHI
(*Baldness*)
1 MAN/1 REFERENCE
Same as Shepho.
1 Chronicles 1:40

SHEPHO
(*Baldness*)
1 MAN/1 REFERENCE
Same as Shephi.
GENESIS 36:23

SHEPHUPHAN
(*Serpentlike*)
1 MAN/1 REFERENCE
1 CHRONICLES 8:5

SHERAH
(*Kindred*)
1 WOMAN/1 REFERENCE
1 CHRONICLES 7:24

SHEREBIAH
(*God has brought heat*)
2 MEN/8 REFERENCES
Most notably, Levite whom Ezra
    called to serve in the temple upon
    his return to Jerusalem. Also, Levite
    who renewed the covenant under
    Nehemiah.
EZRA 8:18; NEHEMIAH 10:12

SHERESH
(*Root*)
1 MAN/1 REFERENCE
1 CHRONICLES 7:16

SHEREZER
1 MAN/1 REFERENCE
Man sent by the people of Bethel to
    the prophet Zechariah to seek God's
    favor.
ZECHARIAH 7:2

SHESHAI
(*Whitish*)
1 MAN/3 REFERENCES
One of the children of Anak, killed
    after Joshua's death when Judah
    battled the Canaanites.
NUMBERS 13:22

SHESHAN
(*Lily*)
1 MAN/4 REFERENCES
1 CHRONICLES 2:31

SHESHBAZZAR
1 MAN/4 REFERENCES
Another name for Zerubbabel, the
    leader of exiles who returned from
    Babylon to Judah.
EZRA 1:8

SHETH
(*Substituted*)
2 MEN/2 REFERENCES
Notably, leader of Moab mentioned in
    one of Balaam's prophecies. Also,
    variant spelling of the name *Seth*;
    Adam's third son.
NUMBERS 24:17; 1 CHRONICLES 1:1

SHETHAR
1 MAN/1 REFERENCE
One of seven Persian princes serving
    under King Ahasuerus.
ESTHER 1:14

SHETHAR-BOZNAI
1 MAN/4 REFERENCES
Persian official who objected to the
    rebuilding of the Jewish temple.
EZRA 5:3

SHEVA
(*False*)
2 MEN/2 REFERENCES
Notably, scribe serving in the
    government of King David.
2 SAMUEL 20:25; 1 CHRONICLES 2:49

SHILHI
(*Armed*)
1 MAN/2 REFERENCES
Grandfather of Judah's king
    Jehoshaphat.
1 KINGS 22:42

SHILLEM
(*Requital*)
1 MAN/2 REFERENCES
GENESIS 46:24

SHILONI
(*Inhabitant of Shiloh*)
1 MAN/1 REFERENCE
Jewish exile from the tribe of Judah
who resettled Jerusalem.
NEHEMIAH 11:5

SHILSHAH
(*Triplication*)
1 MAN/1 REFERENCE
1 CHRONICLES 7:37

SHIMEA
(*Annunciation*)
4 MEN/4 REFERENCES
Most notably, brother of King David.
Same as Shimeah, Shammah, and
Shimma. Also, son of King David,
born in Jerusalem to Bath-sheba
(also known as Bath-shua).
1 CHRONICLES 3:5; 1 CHRONICLES 6:30;
1 CHRONICLES 6:39;
1 CHRONICLES 20:7

SHIMEAH
(*Annunciation*)
2 MEN/4 REFERENCES
Notably, brother of King David. Same
as Shimea, Shammah, and Shimma.
2 SAMUEL 13:3; 1 CHRONICLES 8:32

SHIMEAM
(*Annunciation*)
1 MAN/1 REFERENCE
Cousin of King Saul.
1 CHRONICLES 9:38

SHIMEATH
(*Annunciation*)
1 WOMAN/2 REFERENCES
Mother of Zabad, royal official who
conspired to kill Judah's king Joash.
2 KINGS 12:21

SHIMEI
(*Famous*)
18 MEN/42 REFERENCES
Most notably, relative of King Saul
who cursed King David when
he fled Jerusalem. Later Shimei
apologized to David, who pardoned
him. Same as Shimi. Also, one of
King Solomon's twelve officials
over provisions. Also, King David's
official who was in charge of the
vineyards. Also, Levite appointed
by King Hezekiah to care for the
temple contributions. Also, head
of a household whom Zechariah
prophesied would be set apart before
the day of the Lord.
NUMBERS 3:18; 2 SAMUEL 16:5; 1 KINGS
1:8; 1 KINGS 4:18; 1 CHRONICLES 3:19;
1 CHRONICLES 4:26; 1 CHRONICLES 5:4;
1 CHRONICLES 6:29; 1 CHRONICLES
23:9; 1 CHRONICLES 25:17;
1 CHRONICLES 27:27; 2 CHRONICLES
29:14; 2 CHRONICLES 31:12; EZRA
10:23; EZRA 10:33; EZRA 10:38;
ESTHER 2:5; ZECHARIAH 12:13

SHIMEON
(*Hearing*)
1 MAN/1 REFERENCE
EZRA 10:31

SHIMHI
(*Famous*)
1 MAN/1 REFERENCE
1 CHRONICLES 8:21

SHIMI
(*Famous*)
1 MAN/1 REFERENCE
Same as Shimei.
EXODUS 6:17

SHIMMA
(*Annunciation*)
1 MAN/1 REFERENCE
Third son of Jesse and an older brother
of David. Same as Shammah,
Shimea, and Shimeah.
1 CHRONICLES 2:13

SHIMON
(*Desert*)
1 MAN/1 REFERENCE
1 CHRONICLES 4:20

SHIMRATH
(*Guardship*)
1 MAN/1 REFERENCE
1 CHRONICLES 8:21

SHIMRI
(*Watchful*)
3 MEN/3 REFERENCES
Most notably, among the Levites
    who cleansed the Jerusalem
    temple during the revival in King
    Hezekiah's reign.
1 CHRONICLES 4:37; 1 CHRONICLES 11:45;
    2 CHRONICLES 29:13

SHIMRITH
(*Female guard*)
1 WOMAN/1 REFERENCE
Mother of Jehozabad, a royal official
    who conspired to kill Judah's king
    Joash. Same as Shomer.
2 CHRONICLES 24:26

SHIMROM
(*Guardianship*)
1 MAN/1 REFERENCE
Same as Shimron.
1 CHRONICLES 7:1

SHIMRON
(*Guardianship*)
1 MAN/4 REFERENCES
Same as Shimrom.
GENESIS 46:13

SHIMSHAI
(*Sunny*)
1 MAN/4 REFERENCES
Scribe who wrote King Artaxerxes a
    letter objecting to the rebuilding of
    Jerusalem.
EZRA 4:8

SHINAB
(*Father has turned*)
1 MAN/1 REFERENCE
King of Admah in the days of
    Abraham.
GENESIS 14:2

SHIPHI
(*Copious*)
1 MAN/1 REFERENCE
1 CHRONICLES 4:37

SHIPHRAH
(*Brightness*)
1 WOMAN/1 REFERENCE
Hebrew midwife who did not obey the
    command of the king of Egypt to
    kill all male Israelite babies.
EXODUS 1:15

SHIPHTAN
(*Judgelike*)
1 MAN/1 REFERENCE
NUMBERS 34:24

SHISHA
(*Whiteness*)
1 MAN/1 REFERENCE
1 KINGS 4:3

SHISHAK
1 MAN/7 REFERENCES
King of Egypt to whom Jeroboam fled
    when Solomon discovered he had
    been anointed king over the ten
    northern tribes.
1 KINGS 11:40

SHITRAI
(*Magisterial*)
1 MAN/1 REFERENCE
King David's chief shepherd over herds
    in Sharon.
1 CHRONICLES 27:29

SHIZA
1 MAN/1 REFERENCE
1 CHRONICLES 11:42

SHOBAB
(*Rebellious*)
2 MEN/4 REFERENCES
Notably, son of King David.
2 SAMUEL 5:14; 1 CHRONICLES 2:18

SHOBACH
(*Thicket*)
1 MAN/2 REFERENCES
Captain in the Syrian army of King
  Hadarezer. Same as Shophach.
2 SAMUEL 10:16

SHOBAI
(*Captor*)
1 MAN/2 REFERENCES
EZRA 2:42

SHOBAL
(*Overflowing*)
3 MEN/9 REFERENCES
GENESIS 36:20; 1 CHRONICLES 2:50;
  1 CHRONICLES 4:1

SHOBEK
(*Forsaking*)
1 MAN/1 REFERENCE
Jewish leader who renewed the
  covenant under Nehemiah.
NEHEMIAH 10:24

SHOBI
(*Captor*)
1 MAN/1 REFERENCE
Man who brought food and supplies to
  King David and his soldiers as they
  fled from the army of David's son
  Absalom, who was staging a coup.
2 SAMUEL 17:27

SHOHAM
(*To blanch*)
1 MAN/1 REFERENCE
1 CHRONICLES 24:27

SHOMER
(*Keeper*)
1 MAN/1 WOMAN/2 REFERENCES
Same as Shimrith.
2 KINGS 12:21; 1 CHRONICLES 7:32

SHOPHACH
(*Poured*)
1 MAN/2 REFERENCES
Captain in the Syrian army of King
  Hadarezer. Same as Shobach.
1 CHRONICLES 19:16

SHUA
(*A cry*)
2 WOMEN/2 REFERENCES
Same as Shuah.
1 CHRONICLES 2:3; 1 CHRONICLES 7:32

SHUAH
(*Dell*)
2 MEN/1 WOMAN/5 REFERENCES
Notably, son of Abraham by his second
  wife, Keturah. Also, same as Shua.
GENESIS 25:2; GENESIS 38:2;
  1 CHRONICLES 4:11

SHUAL
(*Jackal*)
1 MAN/1 REFERENCE
1 CHRONICLES 7:36

SHUBAEL
(*God has favored*)
2 MEN/3 REFERENCES
Notably, one of twenty-four Levite
  musicians who was chosen by lot to
  serve in the house of the Lord.
1 CHRONICLES 24:20; 1 CHRONICLES 25:20

SHUHAM
(*Humbly*)
1 MAN/1 REFERENCE
NUMBERS 26:42

SHUNI
(*Rest*)
1 MAN/2 REFERENCES
GENESIS 46:16

SHUPHAM
(*Serpentlike*)
1 MAN/1 REFERENCE
NUMBERS 26:39

SHUPPIM
(*Serpents*)
2 MEN/3 REFERENCES
Notably, Levite who was chosen by lot
to guard the west side of the house
of the Lord.
1 CHRONICLES 7:12; 1 CHRONICLES 26:16

SHUTHELAH
(*Crash of breakage*)
2 MEN/4 REFERENCES
NUMBERS 26:35; 1 CHRONICLES 7:21

SIA
(*Converse*)
1 MAN/1 REFERENCE
Same as Siaha.
NEHEMIAH 7:47

SIAHA
(*Converse*)
1 MAN/1 REFERENCE
Same as Sia.
EZRA 2:44

SIBBECAI
(*Corpselike*)
1 MAN/2 REFERENCES
Commander in King David's army
overseeing twenty-four thousand
men in the eighth month of each
year. Same as Sibbechai.
1 CHRONICLES 11:29

SIBBECHAI
1 MAN/2 REFERENCES
One of King David's valiant warriors.
Same as Sibbecai.
2 SAMUEL 21:18

SIDON
(*Fishery*)
1 MAN/1 REFERENCE
GENESIS 10:15

SIHON
(*Tempestuous*)
1 MAN/37 REFERENCES
Amorite king whom the Israelites
defeated when he would not let
them pass through his land as they
turned back before the Promised
Land.
NUMBERS 21:21

SILAS
(*Sylvan*)
1 MAN/13 REFERENCES
Prophet chosen by the Jerusalem
Council to accompany Paul and
Barnabas to the Gentiles. Same as
Silvanus.
ACTS 15:22

SILVANUS
(*Sylvan*)
2 MEN/4 REFERENCES
Notably, Latin name for Silas, who
accompanied Paul on his missionary
journeys. Also, a "faithful brother" by
whom Peter wrote the epistle of
1 Peter.
2 CORINTHIANS 1:19; 1 PETER 5:12

SIMEON
(*Hearing*)
5 MEN/18 REFERENCES
Most notably, devout man at the
Jerusalem temple who held the
eight-day-old Jesus when His
parents brought Him to the temple
to present Him to the Lord. Also,
second son of Jacob and Leah. Also,
prophet and teacher in the church
at Antioch during the apostle Paul's
ministry. Also called Niger. Also,
variant name for the apostle Simon
Peter.
GENESIS 29:33; LUKE 2:25; LUKE 3:30;
ACTS 13:1; ACTS 15:14

SIMON
(*Hearing*)
9 MEN/76 REFERENCES

Most notably, disciple whom Jesus
surnamed Peter, also called Simon
Bar-jona. Also, one of Jesus' twelve
disciples, called "the Canaanite"
and "Zelotes" (the Zealot). Also,
one of four brothers of Jesus, as
recorded by Matthew's and Mark's
Gospels. Also, man from Cyrene
whom the Romans forced to carry
Jesus' cross to the crucifixion site.
Also, Pharisee who invited Jesus to
eat in his home and thought Jesus
should have known that the woman
who anointed him with oil was a
sinner. Also, sorcerer who became a
Christian. Also, tanner of Joppa who
lived by the sea and lodged Peter.

MATTHEW 4:18; MATTHEW 10:4;
MATTHEW 13:55; MATTHEW 26:6;
MATTHEW 27:32; LUKE 7:40; JOHN
6:71; ACTS 8:9; ACTS 9:43

SIMRI
(*Watchful*)
1 MAN/1 REFERENCE
1 CHRONICLES 26:10

SIPPAI
(*Basinlike*)
1 MAN/1 REFERENCE

Philistine warrior killed by one of King
David's soldiers.

1 CHRONICLES 20:4

SISAMAI
1 MAN/2 REFERENCES
1 CHRONICLES 2:40

SISERA
2 MEN/21 REFERENCES

Notably, captain under Jabin, king of
Canaan, who fled to the tent of Jael,
the wife of Heber the Kenite. She
encouraged him to come in then
killed him by nailing a tent peg into
his temple.

JUDGES 4:2; EZRA 2:53

SO
1 MAN/1 REFERENCE

King of Egypt approached by Israel's
last king, Hoshea, for aid against the
Assyrian Empire.

2 KINGS 17:4

SOCHO
(*Entwine*)
1 MAN/1 REFERENCE
1 CHRONICLES 4:18

SODI
(*Confidant*)
1 MAN/1 REFERENCE
NUMBERS 13:10

SOLOMON
(*Peaceful*)
1 MAN/306 REFERENCES

Son of King David and Bath-sheba
who became king over Israel
and was blessed with wisdom,
understanding, wealth, and honor.
He dedicated the temple with a
prayer and benediction. Had seven
hundred wives and three hundred
concubines; when he was old, his
wives turned his heart away from
God and he did evil, building pagan
altars and worshipping there.

2 SAMUEL 5:14

SOPATER
(*Of a safe father*)
1 MAN/1 REFERENCE

Man from Berea and traveling
companion of the apostle Paul.

ACTS 20:4

SOPHERETH
(*Scribe*)
1 MAN/2 REFERENCES
EZRA 2:55

SOSIPATER
(*Of a safe father*)
1 MAN/1 REFERENCE

Relative of Paul who lived in Rome,
greeted in the apostle's letter to the
Romans.

ROMANS 16:21

SOSTHENES
(*Of safe strength*)
2 MEN/2 REFERENCES
Notably, chief ruler of the synagogue
at Corinth. Also, coworker of
Paul, named in the greeting of
the apostle's first letter to the
Corinthians.
ACTS 18:17; 1 CORINTHIANS 1:1

SOTAI
(*Roving*)
1 MAN/2 REFERENCES
EZRA 2:55

STACHYS
(*Head of grain*)
1 MAN/1 REFERENCE
Christian acquaintance of the apostle
Paul in Rome.
ROMANS 16:9

STEPHANAS
1 MAN/3 REFERNCES
Corinthian Christian whose household,
the first converts in Achaia, was
baptized by Paul.
1 CORINTHIANS 1:16

STEPHEN
(*Wreathe*)
1 MAN/7 REFERENCES
Man of the Jewish church ordained
to care for the physical needs of
church members. He was accused of
blasphemy and, after witnessing to
the Jewish council, was stoned by an
angry mob that included Saul.
ACTS 6:5

SUAH
(*Wipe away*)
1 MAN/1 REFERENCE
1 CHRONICLES 7:36

SUSANNA
(*Lily*)
1 WOMAN/1 REFERENCE
Woman who followed Jesus and
provided for His financial needs.
LUKE 8:3

SUSI
(*Horselike*)
1 MAN/1 REFERENCE
NUMBERS 13:11

SYNTYCHE
(*Accident*)
1 WOMAN/1 REFERENCE
Christian woman of Philippi who
had conflict with another church
member, Euodias.
PHILIPPIANS 4:2

—T—

TABBAOTH
(*Rings*)
1 MAN/2 REFERENCES
EZRA 2:43

TABEAL
(*Pleasing to God*)
1 MAN/1 REFERENCE
Father of a man whom Syria and Israel
wanted to make king over Judah in
Ahaz's place.
ISAIAH 7:6

TABEEL
(*Pleasing to God*)
1 MAN/1 REFERENCE
Man who tried to stop the rebuilding
of Jerusalem's wall.
EZRA 4:7

TABITHA
(*The gazelle*)
1 WOMAN/2 REFERENCES
Christian of Joppa who did many good
works. When she died, her friends
called Peter, who raised her back to
life. Same as Dorcas.
ACTS 9:36

TABRIMON
(*Pleasing to Rimmon*)
1 MAN/1 REFERENCE
1 KINGS 15:18

TAHAN
(*Station*)
2 MEN/2 REFERENCES
NUMBERS 26:35; 1 CHRONICLES 7:25

TAHATH
(*Bottom*)
3 MEN/4 REFERENCES
1 CHRONICLES 6:24; 1 CHRONICLES 7:20;
    1 CHRONICLES 7:20

TAHPENES
1 WOMAN/3 REFERENCES
Queen of Egypt during the rule of
    Solomon and sister-in-law of
    Solomon's adversary Hadad the
    Edomite.
1 KINGS 11:19

TAHREA
(*Earth*)
1 MAN/1 REFERENCE
1 CHRONICLES 9:41

TALMAI
(*Ridged*)
2 MEN/6 REFERENCES
Notably, one of the children of Anak
    who was killed after Joshua's death
    when Judah battled the Canaanites.
    Also, king of Geshur.
NUMBERS 13:22; 2 SAMUEL 3:3

TALMON
(*Oppressive*)
1 MAN/5 REFERENCES
1 CHRONICLES 9:17

TAMAH
1 MAN/1 REFERENCE
NEHEMIAH 7:55

TAMAR
(*Palm tree*)
3 WOMEN/22 REFERENCES
Most notably, daughter of King David
    and half sister of Amnon, who raped
    her. Her full brother Absalom heard
    of it and later had his servants kill
    Amnon. Also, daughter-in-law of
    Jacob. Same as Thamar. Also, the
    only daughter of Absalom, son of
    King David.
GENESIS 38:6; 2 SAMUEL 13:1;
    2 SAMUEL 14:27

TANHUMETH
(*Compassion*)
1 MAN/2 REFERENCES
2 KINGS 25:23

TAPHATH
(*Drop of ointment*)
1 WOMAN/1 REFERENCE
Daughter of Solomon and the wife
    of one of the king's commissary
    officers.
1 KINGS 4:11

TAPPUAH
(*Apple*)
1 MAN/1 REFERENCE
1 CHRONICLES 2:43

TAREA
(*Earth*)
1 MAN/1 REFERENCE
1 CHRONICLES 8:35

TARSHISH
(*Topaz*)
2 MEN/3 REFERENCES
Notably, one of seven Persian princes
    serving under King Ahasuerus.
GENESIS 10:4; ESTHER 1:14

TARTAN
1 MAN/2 REFERENCES
Assyrian military commander who
    conquered the city of Ashdod and
    participated in King Sennacherib's
    failed attempt to take Jerusalem in
    the days of King Hezekiah and the
    prophet Isaiah.
2 KINGS 18:17

TATNAI
1 MAN/4 REFERENCES
Governor who objected to the
    rebuilding of Jerusalem's temple and
    wrote the Persian king Darius, who
    commanded Tatnai to let the work
    continue.
EZRA 5:3

TEBAH
(*Massacre*)
1 MAN/1 REFERENCE
Nephew of Abraham.
GENESIS 22:24

TEBALIAH
(*God has dipped*)
1 MAN/1 REFERENCE
1 CHRONICLES 26:11

TEHINNAH
(*Graciousness*)
1 MAN/1 REFERENCE
1 CHRONICLES 4:12

TEKOA
(*Trumpet*)
1 MAN/2 REFERENCES
1 CHRONICLES 2:24

TELAH
(*Breach*)
1 MAN/1 REFERENCE
1 CHRONICLES 7:25

TELEM
(*Oppression*)
1 MAN/1 REFERENCE
EZRA 10:24

TEMA
1 MAN/4 REFERENCES
GENESIS 25:15

TEMAN
(*South*)
1 MAN/5 REFERENCES
GENESIS 36:11

TEMENI
(*South*)
1 MAN/1 REFERENCE
1 CHRONICLES 4:6

TERAH
1 MAN/11 REFERENCES
Father of Abram (Abraham), Nahor, and Haran.
GENESIS 11:24

TERESH
1 MAN/2 REFERENCES
One of two palace doorkeepers who conspired to kill their king, Ahasuerus of Persia. The plot was uncovered by Mordecai, and both were hanged.
ESTHER 2:21

TERTIUS
(*Third*)
1 MAN/1 REFERENCE
Assistant of Paul who wrote down the apostle's message to the Romans.
ROMANS 16:22

TERTULLUS
1 MAN/2 REFERENCES
Orator from Jerusalem who accused the apostle Paul before the Roman governor in Caesarea.
ACTS 24:1

THADDAEUS
1 MAN/2 REFERENCES
One of Jesus' twelve disciples, as listed by Matthew and Mark. Matthew mentions that Thaddaeus's surname was Lebbaeus. Called "Judas, the brother of James" in Luke's Gospel and the book of Acts. Same as Judas and Jude.
MATTHEW 10:3

THAHASH
(*Antelope*)
1 MAN/1 REFERENCE
GENESIS 22:24

THAMAH
1 MAN/1 REFERENCE
EZRA 2:53

THAMAR
(*Palm tree*)
1 WOMAN/1 REFERENCE
Greek form of the name *Tamar*, used in the New Testament.
MATTHEW 1:3

THARA

1 MAN/1 REFERENCE

Greek form of the name *Terah*, used in
the New Testament.

LUKE 3:34

THARSHISH

(*Topaz*)

1 MAN/1 REFERENCE

1 CHRONICLES 7:10

THEOPHILUS

(*Friend of God*)

1 MAN/2 REFERENCES

Otherwise unknown person for whom
Luke wrote his Gospel and the
book of Acts.

LUKE 1:3

THEUDAS

1 MAN/1 REFERENCE

False Jewish messiah who attracted
four hundred people. They scattered
when he was killed.

ACTS 5:36

THOMAS

(*The twin*)

1 MAN/12 REFERENCES

Jesus' disciple who doubted the other
disciples' story of seeing Jesus
resurrected, not believing until he
saw the Master himself.

MATTHEW 10:3

TIBERIUS

(*Pertaining to the Tiber River*)

1 MAN/1 REFERENCE

Roman emperor who was ruling when
John the Baptist and Jesus began
their ministries.

LUKE 3:1

TIBNI

(*Strawlike*)

1 MAN/3 REFERENCES

1 KINGS 16:21

TIDAL

(*Fearfulness*)

1 MAN/2 REFERENCES

"King of nations" in the days of
Abraham.

GENESIS 14:1

TIGLATH-PILESER

1 MAN/3 REFERENCES

King of Assyria who conquered the
land of Naphtali and Galilee and
took the Israelites captive. Same as
Tilgath-pilneser and possibly Pul.

2 KINGS 15:29

TIKVAH

(*Cord*)

2 MEN/2 REFERENCES

Same as Tikvath.

2 KINGS 22:14; EZRA 10:15

TIKVATH

(*Cord*)

1 MAN/1 REFERENCE

Same as Tikvah.

2 CHRONICLES 34:22

TILGATH-PILNESER

1 MAN/3 REFERENCES

Variant spelling of the name of the
Assyrian king Tiglath-pileser.

1 CHRONICLES 5:6

TILON

(*Suspension*)

1 MAN/1 REFERENCE

1 CHRONICLES 4:20

TIMAEUS

(*Foul*)

1 MAN/1 REFERENCE

MARK 10:46

TIMNA

(*Restraint*)

1 MAN/2 WOMEN/4 REFERENCES

GENESIS 36:12; GENESIS 36:22;
1 CHRONICLES 1:36

TIMNAH
(*Restraint*)
1 MAN/2 REFERENCES
GENESIS 36:40

TIMON
(*Valuable*)
1 MAN/1 REFERENCE
One of seven men selected to serve
    needy Christians in Jerusalem.
ACTS 6:5

TIMOTHEUS
(*Dear to God*)
1 MAN/18 REFERENCES
Alternative name for Timothy, the
    apostle Paul's coworker.
ACTS 16:1

TIMOTHY
(*Dear to God*)
1 MAN/8 REFERENCES
Coworker of the apostle Paul and
    young pastor who was like a son
    to him. His name is joined with
    Paul's in the introductory greetings
    of 2 Corinthians and Philemon,
    and Paul also wrote two epistles of
    guidance to him.
2 CORINTHIANS 1:1

TIRAS
(*Fearful*)
1 MAN/2 REFERENCES
GENESIS 10:2

TIRHAKAH
1 MAN/2 REFERENCES
King of Ethiopia in the time of Judah's
    king Hezekiah.
2 KINGS 19:9

TIRHANAH
1 MAN/1 REFERENCE
1 CHRONICLES 2:48

TIRIA
(*Fearful*)
1 MAN/1 REFERENCE
1 CHRONICLES 4:16

TIRSHATHA
1 MAN/5 REFERENCES
Title of the governor of Judea, used to
    describe Nehemiah.
EZRA 2:63

TIRZAH
(*Delightsomeness*)
1 WOMAN/4 REFERENCES
One of five daughters of Zelophehad,
    who inherited their father's land,
    a right normally reserved for sons.
NUMBERS 26:33

TITUS
1 MAN/14 REFERENCES
The apostle Paul's highly trusted Greek
    coworker who traveled with him
    and whom Paul sent to Corinth
    with a letter of rebuke for the
    church. When Titus was in Crete,
    Paul wrote him an epistle on church
    leadership.
2 CORINTHIANS 2:13

TOAH
(*To depress*)
1 MAN/1 REFERENCE
Same as Tohu.
1 CHRONICLES 6:34

TOB-ADONIJAH
(*Pleasing to Adonijah*)
1 MAN/1 REFERENCE
Levite sent by King Jehoshaphat
    to teach the law of the Lord
    throughout the nation of Judah.
2 CHRONICLES 17:8

TOBIAH
(*Goodness of Jehovah*)
2 MEN/15 REFERENCES
Notably, Ammonite who resisted
    the rebuilding of Jerusalem under
    Governor Nehemiah.
EZRA 2:60; NEHEMIAH 2:10

TOBIJAH
(*Goodness of Jehovah*)
2 MEN/3 REFERENCES
Notably, Levite sent by King
Jehoshaphat to teach the law of
the Lord throughout the nation of
Judah.
2 CHRONICLES 17:8; ZECHARIAH 6:10

TOGARMAH
1 MAN/4 REFERENCES
GENESIS 10:3

TOHU
(*Abasement*)
1 MAN/1 REFERENCE
Same as Toah.
1 SAMUEL 1:1

TOI
(*Error*)
1 MAN/3 REFERENCES
King of Hamath who sent
congratulations and gifts to King
David for defeating Toi's enemy
Hadadezer. Same as Tou.
2 SAMUEL 8:9

TOLA
(*Worm*)
2 MEN/6 REFERENCES
Notably, seventh judge of Israel who
led the nation for twenty-three
years.
GENESIS 46:13; JUDGES 10:1

TOU
(*Error*)
1 MAN/2 REFERENCES
Variant spelling of the name of the
Assyrian king Toi.
1 CHRONICLES 18:9

TROPHIMUS
(*Nutritive*)
1 MAN/3 REFERENCES
Gentile believer and coworker of the
apostle Paul.
ACTS 20:4

TRYPHENA
(*Luxurious*)
1 WOMAN/1 REFERENCE
Christian woman in Rome
commended by the apostle Paul.
ROMANS 16:12

TRYPHOSA
(*Luxuriating*)
1 WOMAN/1 REFERENCE
Christian woman in Rome
commended by the apostle Paul.
ROMANS 16:12

TUBAL
1 MAN/2 REFERENCES
GENESIS 10:2

TUBAL-CAIN
(*Offspring of Cain*)
1 MAN/2 REFERENCES
First recorded metalworker in the
Bible.
GENESIS 4:22

TYCHICUS
(*Fortunate*)
1 MAN/7 REFERENCES
Asian coworker of Paul who
accompanied him to Macedonia
Also sent on missions to the
Ephesians and Colossians and
perhaps to Crete.
ACTS 20:4

TYRANNUS
(*Tyrant*)
1 MAN/1 REFERENCE
Ephesian teacher who allowed the
apostle Paul to debate Christianity
in his school.
ACTS 19:9

—U—

UCAL
(*Devoured*)
1 MAN/1 REFERENCE
Man to whom Agur spoke the words
of Proverbs 30.
PROVERBS 30:1

UEL
(*Wish of God*)
1 MAN/1 REFERENCE
EZRA 10:34

ULAM
(*Solitary*)
2 MEN/4 REFERENCES
1 CHRONICLES 7:16; 1 CHRONICLES 8:39

ULLA
(*Burden*)
1 MAN/1 REFERENCE
1 CHRONICLES 7:39

UNNI
(*Afflicted*)
2 MEN/3 REFERENCES
Notably, Levite musician who
    performed in celebration when
    King David brought the ark of the
    covenant to Jerusalem.
1 CHRONICLES 15:18; NEHEMIAH 12:9

UR
(*Flame*)
1 MAN/1 REFERENCE
1 CHRONICLES 11:35

URBANE
(*Of the city*)
1 MAN/1 REFERENCE
Christian acquaintance of the apostle
    Paul in Rome.
ROMANS 16:9

URI
(*Fiery*)
3 MEN/8 REFERENCES
EXODUS 31:2; 1 KINGS 4:19; EZRA 10:24

URIAH
(*Flame of God*)
3 MEN/28 REFERENCES
Most notably, called Uriah the Hittite,
    Bath-sheba's first husband and a
    warrior in King David's army. On
    King David's orders, he was killed
    in battle, to hide the king's sin of
    adultery. Same as Urias.
2 SAMUEL 11:3; EZRA 8:33; ISAIAH 8:2

URIAS
(*Flame of God*)
1 MAN/1 REFERENCE
Greek form of the name *Uriah*, used in
    the New Testament. Same as Uriah.
MATTHEW 1:6

URIEL
(*Flame of God*)
2 MEN/4 REFERENCES
One of a group of Levites appointed by
    King David to bring the ark of the
    covenant from the house of Obed-
    edom to Jerusalem.
1 CHRONICLES 6:24; 2 CHRONICLES 13:2

URIJAH
(*Flame of God*)
4 MEN/11 REFERENCES
Priest who followed King Ahaz's
    command to build a pagan altar as
    a place of worship. Also, priest who
    assisted Ezra in reading the book of
    the law to the people of Jerusalem.
    Also, faithful prophet executed by
    King Jehoiakim of Judah.
2 KINGS 16:10; NEHEMIAH 3:4;
    NEHEMIAH 8:4; JEREMIAH 26:20

UTHAI
(*Succoring*)
2 MEN/2 REFERENCES
1 CHRONICLES 9:4; EZRA 8:14

UZ
(*Consultation*)
2 MEN/4 REFERENCES
GENESIS 10:23; GENESIS 36:28

UZAI
(*Strong*)
1 MAN/1 REFERENCE
NEHEMIAH 3:25

UZAL
1 MAN/2 REFERENCES
GENESIS 10:27

UZZA

(*Strength*)

4 MEN/8 REFERENCES

Most notably, man who drove the cart in which the ark of the covenant was transported. The oxen stumbled, and Uzza reached out to steady the ark. God killed him for daring to touch the holy object. Same as Uzzah.

1 CHRONICLES 6:29; 1 CHRONICLES 8:7; 1 CHRONICLES 13:7; EZRA 2:49

UZZAH

(*Strength*)

1 MAN/4 REFERENCES

A variant spelling of the name *Uzza*. Same as Uzza.

2 SAMUEL 6:3

UZZI

(*Forceful*)

6 MEN/11 REFERENCES

Most notably, overseer of the Levites after their return from exile. Also, priest who helped to dedicate the rebuilt walls of Jerusalem by giving thanks.

1 CHRONICLES 6:5; 1 CHRONICLES 7:2; 1 CHRONICLES 7:7; 1 CHRONICLES 9:8; NEHEMIAH 11:22; NEHEMIAH 12:19

UZZIA

(*Strength of God*)

1 MAN/1 REFERENCE

One of King David's valiant warriors.

1 CHRONICLES 11:44

UZZIAH

(*Strength of God*)

5 MEN/27 REFERENCES

Son of Amaziah, king of Judah who obeyed God. In his power, he became proud and wrongly burned incense on the temple's incense altar, resulting in God striking him with leprosy. Same as Azariah.

2 KINGS 15:13; 1 CHRONICLES 6:24; 1 CHRONICLES 27:25; EZRA 10:21; NEHEMIAH 11:4

UZZIEL

(*Strength of God*)

6 MEN/16 REFERENCES

Most notably, army captain under King Hezekiah of Judah.

EXODUS 6:18; 1 CHRONICLES 4:42; 1 CHRONICLES 7:7; 1 CHRONICLES 25:4; 2 CHRONICLES 29:14; NEHEMIAH 3:8

—V—

VAJEZATHA

1 MAN/1 REFERENCE

ESTHER 9:9

VANIAH

(*God has answered*)

1 MAN/1 REFERENCE

EZRA 10:36

VASHNI

(*Weak*)

1 MAN/1 REFERENCE

Firstborn son of the prophet Samuel who served as a judge in Beersheba. His poor character caused Israel's leaders to ask Samuel for a king to rule over them. Same as Joel.

1 CHRONICLES 6:28

VASHTI

1 WOMAN/10 REFERENCES

Queen of the Persian king who refused to appear at his banquet. The king revoked her position and had no more to do with her.

ESTHER 1:9

VOPHSI

(*Additional*)

1 MAN/1 REFERENCE

NUMBERS 13:14

—Z—

ZAAVAN

(*Disquiet*)

1 MAN/1 REFERENCE

GENESIS 36:27

ZABAD

(*Giver*)

7 MEN/8 REFERENCES

Most notably, one of King David's valiant warriors. Also, one of two royal officials who conspired to kill Judah's king Joash.

1 CHRONICLES 2:36; 1 CHRONICLES 7:21; 1 CHRONICLES 11:41; 2 CHRONICLES 24:26; EZRA 10:27; EZRA 10:33; EZRA 10:43

ZABBAI

(*Pure*)

2 MEN/2 REFERENCES

EZRA 10:28; NEHEMIAH 3:20

ZABBUD

(*Given*)

1 MAN/1 REFERENCE

EZRA 8:14

ZABDI

(*Giving*)

4 MEN/6 REFERENCES

Most notably, man in charge of the grapes for King David's wine cellars.

JOSHUA 7:1; 1 CHRONICLES 8:19; 1 CHRONICLES 27:27; NEHEMIAH 11:17

ZABDIEL

(*Gift of God*)

2 MEN/2 REFERENCES

Notably, overseer of the priests who served following the exiles' return to Jerusalem.

1 CHRONICLES 27:2; NEHEMIAH 11:14

ZABUD

(*Given*)

1 MAN/1 REFERENCE

Principal officer of King Solomon's court and a friend of the king.

1 KINGS 4:5

ZACCAI

(*Pure*)

1 MAN/2 REFERENCES

EZRA 2:9

ZACCHAEUS

(*Pure*)

1 MAN/3 REFERENCES

Wealthy chief tax collector who climbed a tree so he could see Jesus, then repented and promised he would give half his goods to the poor and repay fourfold anyone he had wronged.

LUKE 19:2

ZACCHUR

(*Mindful*)

1 MAN/1 REFERENCE

1 CHRONICLES 4:26

ZACCUR

(*Mindful*)

6 MEN/8 REFERENCES

Most notably, rebuilder of the walls of Jerusalem under Nehemiah. Also, Levite who renewed the covenant under Nehemiah. Also, one of the temple treasurers appointed by Nehemiah.

NUMBERS 13:4; 1 CHRONICLES 24:27; 1 CHRONICLES 25:2; NEHEMIAH 3:2; NEHEMIAH 10:12; NEHEMIAH 13:13

ZACHARIAH

(*God has remembered*)

2 MEN/4 REFERENCES

Notably, son of King Jeroboam of Israel who reigned over Israel for six months before he was killed by the conspirator Shallum.

2 KINGS 14:29; 2 KINGS 18:2

ZACHARIAS

(*God has remembered*)

2 MEN/11 REFERENCES

Most notably, priest who received a vision that his barren wife would bear a child who would be great before the Lord—John the Baptist. When he doubted, he was struck dumb until the birth of the child. Also, a man, possibly a prophet, mentioned by Jesus. He was killed between the sanctuary and the altar.

MATTHEW 23:35; LUKE 1:5

ZACHER

(*Memento*)

1 MAN/1 REFERENCE

Chief of the tribe of Benjamin who
lived in Jerusalem.

1 CHRONICLES 8:31

ZADOK

(*Just*)

9 MEN/53 REFERENCES

Most notably, priest during King
David's reign who consecrated
Levites to bring the ark of the
covenant into Jerusalem, anointed
Solomon king and was later made
high priest. Also, young soldier
who helped to crown David king
of Judah in Hebron. Also, man
who repaired Jerusalem's walls
under Nehemiah. Also, Jewish
leader who renewed the covenant
under Nehemiah. Also, priest who
resettled Jerusalem following the
Babylonian Exile. Also, temple
treasurer appointed by Nehemiah.

2 SAMUEL 8:17; 2 KINGS 15:33;
1 CHRONICLES 6:12; 1 CHRONICLES
12:28; NEHEMIAH 3:4; NEHEMIAH
3:29; NEHEMIAH 10:21; NEHEMIAH
11:11; NEHEMIAH 13:13

ZAHAM

(*Loathing*)

1 MAN/1 REFERENCE

Son of Judah's king Rehoboam and a
grandson of Solomon.

2 CHRONICLES 11:19

ZALAPH

1 MAN/1 REFERENCE

NEHEMIAH 3:30

ZALMON

(*Shady*)

1 MAN/1 REFERENCE

One of King David's mightiest warriors
known as "the thirty."

2 SAMUEL 23:28

ZALMUNNA

(*Shade has been denied*)

1 MAN/12 REFERENCES

Midianite king whom Gideon pursued
and killed after Zalmunna killed
Gideon's brothers at Tabor.

JUDGES 8:5

ZANOAH

(*Rejected*)

1 MAN/1 REFERENCE

1 CHRONICLES 4:18

ZAPHNATH-PAANEAH

1 MAN/1 REFERENCE

Name the Egyptian pharaoh gave to
Joseph, the revealer of dreams.

GENESIS 41:45

ZARA

(*Rising*)

1 MAN/1 REFERENCE

Greek form of the name *Zarah*, used in
the New Testament.

MATTHEW 1:3

ZARAH

(*Rising*)

1 MAN/2 REFERENCES

Twin born to Jacob's son Judah and
Judah's daughter-in-law Tamar.

GENESIS 38:30

ZATTHU

1 MAN/1 REFERENCE

Jewish leader who renewed the
covenant under Nehemiah.

NEHEMIAH 10:14

ZATTU

1 MAN/3 REFERENCES

EZRA 2:8

ZAVAN

(*Disquiet*)

1 MAN/1 REFERENCE

1 CHRONICLES 1:42

ZAZA
(*Prominent*)

1 MAN/1 REFERENCE

1 Chronicles 2:33

ZEBADIAH
(*God has given*)

9 MEN/9 REFERENCES

Most notably, "mighty man" who supported the future king David during his conflict with Saul. Also, one of King David's captains of thousands. Also, Levite sent by King Jehoshaphat to teach the law of the Lord throughout the nation of Judah. Also, "ruler of the house of Judah" who was in charge of King Jehoshaphat's household. Also, Jewish exile who returned from Babylon to Judah under Ezra.

1 Chronicles 8:15; 1 Chronicles 8:17; 1 Chronicles 12:7; 1 Chronicles 26:2; 1 Chronicles 27:7; 2 Chronicles 17:8; 2 Chronicles 19:11; Ezra 8:8; Ezra 10:20

ZEBAH
(*Sacrifice*)

1 MAN/12 REFERENCES

Midianite king whom Gideon pursued—and killed—with three hundred men after Zebah killed Gideon's brothers at Tabor.

Judges 8:5

ZEBEDEE
(*Giving*)

1 MAN/12 REFERENCES

Father of Jesus' disciples James and John and a fisherman on the Sea of Galilee. His sons worked with him until they left to follow Jesus.

Matthew 4:21

ZEBINA
(*Gainfulness*)

1 MAN/1 REFERENCE

Ezra 10:43

ZEBUDAH
(*Gainfulness*)

1 WOMAN/1 REFERENCE

Mother of the evil Jehoiakim, the third-to-last king of Judah.

2 Kings 23:36

ZEBUL
(*Dwelling*)

1 MAN/6 REFERENCES

Ruler of the city of Shechem under King Abimelech.

Judges 9:28

ZEBULUN
(*Habitation*)

1 MAN/6 REFERENCES

Sixth and last son of Jacob and Leah.

Genesis 30:20

ZECHARIAH
(*God has remembered*)

27 MEN/39 REFERENCES

Most notably, Old Testament minor prophet who ministered in Jerusalem following the return from exile. Also, Levite who was chosen by lot to guard the west side of the house of the Lord. Also, prince of Judah sent by King Jehoshaphat to teach the law of the Lord throughout the nation. Also, prophet who influenced King Uzziah of Judah. Also, temple ruler during the reign of King Josiah of Judah. Also, Jewish exile charged with finding Levites and temple servants to travel to Jerusalem with Ezra.

1 Chronicles 5:7; 1 Chronicles 9:21; 1 Chronicles 9:37; 1 Chronicles 15:18; 1 Chronicles 15:24; 1 Chronicles 24:25; 1 Chronicles 26:11; 1 Chronicles 27:21; 2 Chronicles 17:7; 2 Chronicles 20:14; 2 Chronicles 21:2; 2 Chronicles 24:20; 2 Chronicles 26:5; 2 Chronicles 29:13; 2 Chronicles 34:12; 2 Chronicles 35:8; Ezra 5:1; Ezra 8:3; Ezra 8:11; Ezra 10:26; Nehemiah 8:4;

NEHEMIAH 11:4; NEHEMIAH 11:5;
NEHEMIAH 11:12; NEHEMIAH 12:16;
NEHEMIAH 12:35; ISAIAH 8:2

ZEDEKIAH
(*Right of God*)
5 MEN/62 REFERENCES
Most notably, originally named
   Mattaniah, he was a brother of King
   Jehoiachin of Judah. Nebuchadnezzar,
   king of Babylon, conquered Judah,
   deposed Jehoiachin, renamed Mattaniah as Zedekiah, and made him
   king. He rebelled against Babylon
   and did not heed the prophet
   Jeremiah. Also, false prophet who
   predicted that King Jehoshaphat of
   Judah would win over the Syrians.
   Also, false prophet aganist whom
   Jeremiah spoke after Judah went
   into captivity.
1 KINGS 22:11; 2 KINGS 24:17;
   1 CHRONICLES 3:16; JEREMIAH 29:21;
   JEREMIAH 36:12

ZEEB
(*Wolf*)
1 MAN/6 REFERENCES
Midianite prince captured and killed by
   the men of Ephraim under Gideon's
   command.
JUDGES 7:25

ZELEK
(*Fissure*)
1 MAN/2 REFERENCES
One of King David's valiant warriors.
2 SAMUEL 23:37

ZELOPHEHAD
(*United*)
1 MAN/11 REFERENCES
Descendant of Joseph through
   Manasseh who died during the
   wilderness wanderings. His five
   daughters asked Moses if they could
   inherit their father's property in the
   Promised Land, a right normally
   reserved for sons. God ruled that
   they should, since he had no sons.
NUMBERS 26:33

ZELOTES
(*Zealot*)
1 MAN/2 REFERENCES
Surname of Simon, one of Jesus' twelve
   disciples.
LUKE 6:15

ZEMIRA
(*Song*)
1 MAN/1 REFERENCE
1 CHRONICLES 7:8

ZENAS
(*Jove-given*)
1 MAN/1 REFERENCE
Lawyer whom the apostle Paul
   encouraged Titus to help on a
   journey.
TITUS 3:13

ZEPHANIAH
(*God has secreted*)
4 MEN/10 REFERENCES
Most notably, second priest in the
   temple whom King Zedekiah sent
   to the prophet Jeremiah, asking him
   to pray for Israel.
2 KINGS 25:18; 1 CHRONICLES 6:36;
   ZEPHANIAH 1:1; ZECHARIAH 6:10

ZEPHI
(*Observant*)
1 MAN/1 REFERENCE
1 CHRONICLES 1:36

ZEPHO
(*Observant*)
1 MAN/2 REFERENCES
GENESIS 36:11

ZEPHON
(*Watchtower*)
1 MAN/1 REFERENCE
NUMBERS 26:15

ZERAH

(*Rising*)

7 MEN/19 REFERENCES

Most notably, grandson of Jacob, born
to Jacob's son Judah and Judah's
daughter-in-law Tamar. Also,
Ethiopian commander whose army
fled before King Asa of Judah.

GENESIS 36:13; GENESIS 36:33;
NUMBERS 26:13; NUMBERS 26:20;
1 CHRONICLES 6:21; 1 CHRONICLES
6:41; 2 CHRONICLES 14:9

ZERAHIAH

(*God has risen*)

2 MEN/5 REFERENCES

Notably, priest through the line of
Aaron.

1 CHRONICLES 6:6; EZRA 8:4

ZERESH

1 WOMAN/4 REFERENCES

Wife of Haman, the villain of the
story of Esther. She and her friends
encouraged Haman to build a
gallows on which to hang Esther's
cousin Mordecai—the gallows that
Haman himself would later die on.

ESTHER 5:10

ZERETH

(*Splendor*)

1 MAN/1 REFERENCE

1 CHRONICLES 4:7

ZERI

(*Distillation*)

1 MAN/1 REFERENCE

1 CHRONICLES 25:3

ZEROR

(*Parcel*)

1 MAN/1 REFERENCE

1 SAMUEL 9:1

ZERUAH

1 WOMAN/1 REFERENCE

Widow and the mother of Jeroboam,
who became the first king of the
northern Jewish nation of Israel.

1 KINGS 11:26

ZERUBBABEL

(*Descended of Babylon*)

1 MAN/22 REFERENCES

Governor of Judah who returned from
the Babylonian Exile with many
Israelites in his train. He rebuilt an
altar so Judah could worship for the
Feast of Tabernacles and obeyed the
words God spoke through Haggai.

1 CHRONICLES 3:19

ZERUIAH

(*Wounded*)

1 WOMAN/26 REFERENCES

Sister of King David and mother of
David's battle commander, Joab, and
his brothers, Abishai and Asahel.

1 SAMUEL 26:6

ZETHAM

(*Olive*)

1 MAN/2 REFERENCES

Chief Levite during King David's reign,
in charge of the temple treasures.

1 CHRONICLES 23:8

ZETHAN

(*Olive*)

1 MAN/1 REFERENCE

1 CHRONICLES 7:10

ZETHAR

1 MAN/1 REFERENCE

Eunuch serving the Persian king
Ahasuerus in Esther's time.

ESTHER 1:10

ZIA

(*Agitation*)

1 MAN/1 REFERENCE

1 CHRONICLES 5:13

ZIBA

(*Station*)

1 MAN/16 REFERENCES

Servant of King Saul who told King
David where Mephibosheth lived
after David took the throne and also
brought food and the news that his
master sought to take David's throne.

2 SAMUEL 9:2

ZIBEON
(*Variegated*)
2 MEN/8 REFERENCES
GENESIS 36:2; GENESIS 36:20

ZIBIA
(*Gazelle*)
1 MAN/1 REFERENCE
1 CHRONICLES 8:9

ZIBIAH
(*Gazelle*)
1 WOMAN/2 REFERENCES
Mother of Joash, good king of Judah.
2 KINGS 12:1

ZICHRI
(*Memorable*)
12 MEN/12 REFERENCES
Most notably, brother of Korah, who
rebelled against Moses and was
killed by God. Also, chief of the
tribe of Benjamin who lived in
Jerusalem. Also, mighty man of
valor who served King Jehoshaphat
of Judah. Also, captain of hundreds
who made a covenant with the
priest Jehoiada. Also, "a mighty man
of Ephraim."
EXODUS 6:21; 1 CHRONICLES 8:19;
1 CHRONICLES 8:23; 1 CHRONICLES
8:27; 1 CHRONICLES 9:15;
1 CHRONICLES 26:25; 1 CHRONICLES
27:16; 2 CHRONICLES 17:16;
2 CHRONICLES 23:1; 2 CHRONICLES
28:7; NEHEMIAH 11:9;
NEHEMIAH 12:17

ZIDKIJAH
(*Right of God*)
1 MAN/1 REFERENCE
Israelite who renewed the covenant
under Nehemiah.
NEHEMIAH 10:1

ZIDON
(*Fishery*)
1 MAN/1 REFERENCE
1 CHRONICLES 1:13

ZIHA
(*Drought*)
2 MEN/3 REFERENCES
Notably, official over the temple
servants after the Babylonian Exile.
EZRA 2:43; NEHEMIAH 11:21

ZILLAH
(*Shade*)
1 WOMAN/3 REFERENCES
Second wife of Lamech, a descendant
of Cain. Her son was Tubal-cain.
GENESIS 4:19

ZILPAH
(*Trickle*)
1 WOMAN/7 REFERENCES
Servant of Leah whom Leah gave to
her husband, Jacob, as a wife because
she thought her own childbearing
days were ended. Bore two sons,
Gad and Asher.
GENESIS 29:24

ZILTHAI
(*Shady*)
2 MEN/2 REFERENCES
Notably, one of a group of "mighty
men of valour" who fought for King
David.
1 CHRONICLES 8:20; 1 CHRONICLES 12:20

ZIMMAH
(*Lewdness*)
3 MEN/3 REFERENCES
1 CHRONICLES 6:20; 1 CHRONICLES 6:42;
2 CHRONICLES 29:12

ZIMRAN
(*Musical*)
1 MAN/2 REFERENCES
Son of Abraham by his second wife,
Keturah.
GENESIS 25:2

ZIMRI
(*Musical*)

4 MEN/14 REFERENCES

Notably, king of Israel who conspired
against King Elah and killed him
and his relatives, fulfilling the
prophecy of Jehu. Zimri reigned
for seven days. Also, man killed by
Phinehas for blatant sexual sin.

NUMBERS 25:14; 1 KINGS 16:9;
1 CHRONICLES 2:6; 1 CHRONICLES 8:36

ZINA
(*Well fed*)

1 MAN/1 REFERENCE

Levite who was part of David's
reorganization of the Levites. Same
as Zizah.

1 CHRONICLES 23:10

ZIPH
(*Flowing*)

2 MEN/2 REFERENCES

1 CHRONICLES 2:42; 1 CHRONICLES 4:16

ZIPHAH
(*Flowing*)

1 MAN/1 REFERENCE

1 CHRONICLES 4:16

ZIPHION
(*Watchtower*)

1 MAN/1 REFERENCE

GENESIS 46:16

ZIPPOR
(*Little bird*)

1 MAN/7 REFERENCES

Father of the Moabite king Balak, who
consulted the false prophet Balaam.

NUMBERS 22:2

ZIPPORAH
(*Bird*)

1 WOMAN/3 REFERENCES

Daughter of the Midianite priest Reuel
(also known as Jethro) and wife of
Moses.

EXODUS 2:21

ZITHRI
(*Protective*)

1 MAN/1 REFERENCE

EXODUS 6:22

ZIZA
(*Prominence*)

2 MEN/2 REFERENCES

Notably, son of Judah's king Rehoboam
and a grandson of Solomon.

1 CHRONICLES 4:37; 2 CHRONICLES 11:20

ZIZAH
(*Prominence*)

1 MAN/1 REFERENCE

Levite who was part of David's
reorganization of the Levites. Same
as Zina.

1 CHRONICLES 23:11

ZOBEBAH
(*Canopy*)

1 WOMAN/1 REFERENCE

Daughter of Coz, a descendant of
Abraham through Jacob's son Judah.

1 CHRONICLES 4:8

ZOHAR
(*Whiteness*)

2 MEN/4 REFERENCES

Father of Ephron, who sold Abraham a
burial place. Also, grandson of Jacob
through his son Simeon.

GENESIS 23:8; GENESIS 46:10

ZOHETH

1 MAN/1 REFERENCE

1 CHRONICLES 4:20

ZOPHAH
(*Breadth*)

1 MAN/2 REFERENCES

1 CHRONICLES 7:35

ZOPHAI
(*Honeycomb*)

1 MAN/1 REFERENCE

1 CHRONICLES 6:26

ZOPHAR

(*Departing*)

1 MAN/4 REFERENCES

One of three friends of Job who
mourned his losses for a week and
then accused him of wrongdoing.
He was ultimately chastised by God
for criticizing Job.

JOB 2:11

ZOROBABEL

(*Descended of Babylon*)

1 MAN/3 REFERENCES

MATTHEW 1:12

ZUAR

(*Small*)

1 MAN/5 REFERENCES

NUMBERS 1:8

ZUPH

(*Honeycomb*)

1 MAN/2 REFERENCES

1 SAMUEL 1:1

ZUR

(*Rock*)

2 MEN/5 REFERENCES

Notably, Midianite king killed by the
Israelites at God's command.

NUMBERS 25:15; 1 CHRONICLES 8:30

ZURIEL

(*Rock of God*)

1 MAN/1 REFERENCE

Chief of the Levites under Eleazar.

NUMBERS 3:35

ZURISHADDAI

(*Rock of the Almighty*)

1 MAN/5 REFERENCES

NUMBERS 1:6

NOTES

Bible Reference for Everyday Use:

QuickNotes Simplified Bible Commentary Series

OLD TESTAMENT

*Volume 1: Genesis
thru Numbers*
978-1-59789-767-9

*Volume 2: Deuteronomy
thru Ruth*
978-1-59789-768-6

*Volume 3: 1 Samuel
thru 2 Kings*
978-1-59789-769-3

*Volume 4: 1 Chronicles
thru Job*
978-1-59789-770-9

*Volume 5: Psalms thru
Song of Solomon*
978-1-59789-771-6

Volume 6: Isaiah thru Ezekiel
978-1-59789-772-3

Volume 7: Daniel thru Malachi
978-1-59789-773-0

NEW TESTAMENT

Volume 8: Matthew thru Mark
978-1-59789-774-7

Volume 9: Luke thru John
978-1-59789-775-4

*Volume 10: Acts
thru 2 Corinthians*
978-1-59789-776-1

*Volume 11: Galatians
thru Philemon*
978-1-59789-777-8

*Volume 12: Hebrews
thru Revelation*
978-1-59789-778-5

Available wherever books are sold.